The Short Oxford History of Europe

The Later Middle Ages

T0355203

The Short Oxford History of Europe

General Editor: T. C. W. Blanning

NOW AVAILABLE

Classical Greece
edited by Robin Osborne

Roman Europe
edited by Edward Bispham

The Early Middle Ages
edited by Rosamond McKitterick

The Central Middle Ages
edited by Daniel Power

The Later Middle Ages
edited by Isabella Lazzarini

The Sixteenth Century
edited by Euan Cameron

The Seventeenth Century
edited by Joseph Bergin

The Eighteenth Century
edited by T. C. W. Blanning

The Nineteenth Century
edited by T. C. W. Blanning

Europe 1900–1945
edited by Julian Jackson

Europe since 1945
edited by Mary Fulbrook

The Short Oxford History of Europe

General Editor: T. C. W. Blanning

The Later Middle Ages

Edited by Isabella Lazzarini

OXFORD

UNIVERSITY PRESS

OXFORD
UNIVERSITY PRESS

Great Clarendon Street, Oxford, OX2 6DP,
United Kingdom

Oxford University Press is a department of the University of Oxford.
It furthers the University's objective of excellence in research, scholarship,
and education by publishing worldwide. Oxford is a registered trade mark of
Oxford University Press in the UK and in certain other countries

First Edition published in 2021

Impression: 1

Published in the United States of America by Oxford University Press
198 Madison Avenue, New York, NY 10016, United States of America

British Library Cataloguing in Publication Data

Data available

Library of Congress Control Number: 2020951693

ISBN 978–0–19–873164–1 (hbk.)
978–0–19–873163–4 (pbk.)

DOI: 10.1093/oso/9780198731641.001.0001

Printed and bound by
CPI Group (UK) Ltd, Croydon, CR0 4YY

General Editor's Preface

The problems of writing a satisfactory general history of Europe are many, but the most intractable is dearly the reconciliation of depth with breadth. The historian who can write with equal authority about every part of the continent in all its various aspects has not been born. Two main solutions have been tried in the past: either a single scholar has attempted to go it alone, presenting an unashamedly personal view of a period, or teams of specialists have been enlisted to write what are in effect anthologies. The first offers a coherent perspective but unequal coverage, the second sacrifices unity for the sake of expertise. This new series is underpinned by the belief that it is this second way that has the fewest disadvantages and that even those can be diminished if not neutralized by close cooperation between the individual contributors under the directing supervision of the volume editor. All the contributors to every volume in this series have read each other's chapters, have met to discuss problems of overlap and omission, and have then redrafted as part of a truly collective exercise. To strengthen coherence further, the editor has written an introduction and conclusion, weaving the separate strands together to form a single cord. In this the brevity promised by the adjective 'short' in the series' tide has been an asset. The need to be concise has concentrated minds on what mattered in the period. No attempt has been made to cover every angle of every topic in every country. What this volume does is a short but sharp and deep entry into the history of Europe in the period in all its most important aspects.

T. C. W. Blanning

Sidney Sussex College
Cambridge

Editor's Preface

To write about the history of Europe in the later Middle Ages is a challenge: well established grand narratives of decline or anticipated modernity weigh heavy on a period whose main feature seems to be the most transitional among all transitions, always in between among more solidly constructed images of past ages.

Moreover, this specific volume has a very distinctive story: it was designed in the early 2000s by Malcom Vale and it was inherited by me much later. As a consequence, its second life had to adjust to a previous, unfinished frame, and to the 'old' themes some new entries had inevitably to be added, partly modifying the traditional scheme of the series. The result—I hope—is at once coherent with the first project and with the research interests that followed.

As second and final editor, I wish to thank first of all the general editor, Tim Blanning, who trusted me to take the volume to completion: I sincerely hope that he will be satisfied by the result. My thanks go also to Malcolm Vale, who imagined the volume in the first place, and to the 'old' group of authors (John Watts, Robert Swanson, and Matthew Kempshall), who kindly agreed to rescue from their drawers the first, probably half-forgotten contributions, and patiently reread and reimagine them by adding new ideas and bibliographical updating. We all know how painful such a process can be. Among them, sadly, a long-time friend and colleague is no longer with us: Stephan (Lorenzo or Larry) Epstein, whose brilliant talent and warm personality are deeply missed by the many who knew him, died suddenly on 3 February 2007. His chapter has been masterfully reread and completed by Chris Dyer, to whom goes my heartfelt gratitude. My 'new' fellow authors have all my thanks as well: Catherine Holmes, Catherine Kovesi, and Alexander Lee have been a pleasure to work with, and their contributions fitted smoothly with the rest of the volume, adding to it a 2020s distinctive flavour. Finally, my work as editor has been greatly facilitated by the kindness, effectiveness, and support—through the good and the bad times—of Stephanie Ireland, Cathryn Steele, and the staff at OUP.

Isabella Lazzarini

Edinburgh, December 2019

Contents

List of Figures

List of Maps

List of Plates

Cover: Hieronymus Bosch, *The Garden of Earthly Delights* (1490–1510), detail, oil on panel, Prado Museum, Madrid. Wikimedia Commons

1. Paolo Uccello, *The Battle of San Romano* (1438–1440), detail, tempera on wood, National Gallery, London. Wikimedia Commons

2. Hartmann Schedel, *Liber Chronicarum* (the *Nuremberg Chronicle*), with woodcuts by Michael Wolgemut and Wilhelm Pleydenwurff (1493), incunabulum, Nuremberg. Wikimedia Commons

3. *A three-masted Mediterranean carrack* (fifteenth century), print, National Maritime Museum, Greenwich. Courtesy of the National Maritime Museum, Greenwich

4. Pinturicchio, *Pius II at the Congress of Mantua* (1502–1507), fresco, Piccolomini Library, Siena. Wikimedia Commons

5. Jan van Eyck, *The Arnolfini Portrait* (1434), oil on oak, National Gallery, London. Wikimedia Commons

6. Nicholas Oresme, *De Coelo et Mundo* (fourteenth century), BNF, French MS 565, c. 27r, Paris. Courtesy of the Bibliothèque Nationale de France

7. Bernardino Licinio, *Portrait of Arrigo Licinio and his Family*, (c.1530), oil on canvas, Galleria Borghese, Rome. Wikimedia Commons

8. Abraham Cresques (?), *Atlas of Maritime Maps said the Catalan Atlas* (c.1375), West Africa, BNF, Spanish MS 30, c. 11, Paris. Wikimedia Commons

9. Raffaello Sanzio, *Portrait of Baldassarre Castiglione* (1514–1515), oil on canvas, Louvre Museum, Paris. Wikimedia Commons

List of Contributors

Christopher C. Dyer is Emeritus Professor of History, University of Leicester, and held posts previously at the Universities of Edinburgh and Birmingham. He is the author of five books, has edited or co-edited eight others, and published numerous articles and book chapters, mainly on social, economic, and landscape history of the Middle Ages, and on medieval archaeology. He is a Fellow of the British Academy, and has served eight learned societies and journals as editor, secretary, chairman, or president.

Stephan R. Epstein (1960–2007) became Professor of Economic History in 2001 at the London School of Economics. Epstein's field of expertise was the economic history of medieval and early modern Europe. He is the author of dozens of articles in journals and books, and his books include *An Island for Itself: Economic Development and Social Transformation in Late Medieval Sicily Past and Present* (1992) and *Freedom and Growth. Markets and States in Europe, 1300–1750* (2000). He edited four volumes including *Town and Country in Europe, 1300–1800* (2001).

Catherine Holmes is Professor in Medieval History at the University of Oxford. Her research has focused principally on Byzantine political and cultural history between the tenth and fourteenth centuries, on relations between Byzantium and neighbouring societies, and on global history. She is the co-editor (with Naomi Standen) of a recent collection of essays in this field: *The Global Middle Ages, Past and Present* Supplement 13 (2018). She is also one of the editors of *The English Historical Review*.

Matthew S. Kempshall is the Cliff Davies Fellow and Clarendon Associate Professor in History at Wadham College, University of Oxford. He is the author of *The Common Good in Late Medieval Political Thought* (1999) and *Rhetoric and the Writing of History, 400–1500* (2011).

Catherine Kovesi is a historian at the University of Melbourne and Chair of the Australasian Centre for Italian Studies. She researches the discourses surrounding luxury consumption in early modern Italy; clothing, textiles, and gender; Florentine and Venetian family history; and the history of women religious in Australia. She is the author of *Sumptuary Legislation in Italy, 1200–1500* (2001), editor of *Luxury and the Ethics of Greed in Early Modern Italy* (2018), and co-General Editor of the forthcoming *A Cultural History of Luxury* (Bloomsbury).

Isabella Lazzarini is Professor of Medieval History at the University of Molise. Her research interests focus on the political, social, and cultural history of late medieval

Italy, with an emphasis on Renaissance diplomacy and the growth of different political languages in documentary sources. Her most recent works include *Communication and Conflict: Italian Diplomacy in the Early Renaissance (1350–1520)* (2015), and the edited volumes *The Italian Renaissance State* (with Andrea Gamberini, 2012) and *Social Mobility in Medieval Italy (1100–1500)* (with Sandro Carocci, 2018).

Alexander Lee is a fellow in the Centre for the Study of the Renaissance at the University of Warwick. His books include *Petrarch and St. Augustine: Classical Scholarship, Christian Theology, and the Origins of the Renaissance in Italy* (2012); *Humanism and Empire: The Imperial Ideal in Fourteenth-Century Italy* (2018); and *Machiavelli: His Life and Times* (2020).

Robert Swanson is currently a Research Fellow of the Institute for Advanced Study in Humanities and Social Science and Professor in the Research Center for Social History of Medicine in the School of History and Civilization at Shaanxi Normal University in China, and also Emeritus Professor of Medieval Ecclesiastical History of the University of Birmingham, UK. His books include *Religion and Devotion in Europe c.1215–c.1515* (1995), *Indulgences in Late Medieval England: Passports to Paradise?* (2007), and (as editor) *The Routledge History of Medieval Christianity, 1050–1500* (2015).

John Watts is Professor of Later Medieval History at the University of Oxford and Fellow and Tutor in History at Corpus Christi College, Oxford. He is the author of a number of books and articles on politics and political culture in later medieval Britain and Europe. He is currently working on a book for the New Oxford History of England series, provisionally titled *Renaissance England, 1461–1547*.

Plate 1. Paolo Uccello, *The Battle of San Romano* (1438–1440), detail

Introduction

Isabella Lazzarini

An end or a new beginning?

As soon as the Florentine Giovanni Villani died in 1348, his brother Matteo took over his *Cronica* and continued it until his own death, from a resurgence of plague, in 1363. Matteo's eleven books are not only even more moralistic than those of Giovanni but also—unsurprisingly—darker. Giovanni, according to his own words, had started writing in 1300 after his journey to Rome for the jubilee, inspired by what he had seen, in order to celebrate the glory of Florence, Rome's only and legitimate heir. Matteo opens his first book under the gloomy spell of the Black Death. Although very aware of the fallibility of human lives, he nevertheless glimpsed traces of renewal:

> Because in that plague died the author of the chronicle entitled *Cronica*, Giovanni Villani, citizen of Florence, and because I was strictly linked to him both by blood and by love, after many misfortunes, and with more knowledge of the calamity of the world than of its prosperity, I decided in my mind to begin our varied and calamitous subject at this time as a moment of renewal of time and the century.[1]

In the first decades of the sixteenth century, Francesco Guicciardini slowly but clearly realized that an era was coming to an end, and that unexpected

---

* I wish to thank Christine Shaw for polishing my English with her usual light touch, respectful at once of the English language and the author's writing style.

[1] G. Villani, *Cronica, con le continuazioni di Matteo e Filippo*, ed. Giovanni Aquilecchia (Turin, 1979), p. 294 ('Nella quale mortalità avendo renduta l'anima a Dio l'autore della cronica nominata la *Cronica* di Giovanni Villani cittadino di Firenze, al quale per sangue e per dilezione fui strettamente congiunto, dopo molte gravi fortune, con più conoscenza della calamità del mondo che la prosperità di quello non m'avea dimostrato, propuosi nell'animo mio fare alla nostra varia e calamitosa materia *cominciamento a questo tempo, come a uno rinnovellamento di tempo e secolo*': my translation).

The Later Middle Ages. Isabella Lazzarini, Oxford University Press (2021). © Isabella Lazzarini.
DOI: 10.1093/oso/9780198731641.003.0001

dangers and wonders, changes and challenges were transforming the world he used to know. Politics and warfare were no longer the same: with the French armies in 1494 'there entered into Italy a flame and a plague that not only changed the states, but also the ways of government, and the ways of war'.[2] Outside an old Europe bounded by the Mediterranean and the distant but familiar worlds of Africa and the East, the discovery of a new landmass, America, in Guicciardini's words was 'one of the most memorable things which happened in the world for many centuries', an unambiguous sign that humans, in the big scheme of things, were not infallible.

> These voyages have made it clear that the ancients were deceived in many
> ways in their knowledge of the earth [...] These voyages have not only
> refuted many things which had been affirmed by writers about terrestrial
> matters, but besides this, they have given some cause for alarm to the
> interpreters of the Holy Scriptures.[3]

A renewal and an end: or, more traditionally, an end and a renewal. Of all the sub-periods in which European medieval history has been divided over time, the later Middle Ages is possibly the one on which the burden of past and current grand narratives weighs the most. Its chronological and geo-political boundaries are in fact shaped by a heavy narrative of decline or transition, and consequently this period is often interpreted through the lenses of previous or following developments, becoming in turn the tail-end of the 'feudal', 'communal', 'imperial versus papal' era or the announcement of modernity. Chronological boundaries are blurred: when talking about the later Middle Ages, literature oscillates between wider or narrower frames (1300–1600, 1700 or even 1800; 1350–1550, and so on). Such an uncertainty derives from the opacity created by the many overlapping old grand narra-tives whose impact must be disassembled. To free this period from this burden, and from the influence of other ages, research must both recognize the artificiality of any chosen and rigid chronology and stick to a convenient time-span 'in which changes can be tracked in different ways in different places, without them having to lead teleologically to some major

---

[2] F. Guicciardini, *Storie fiorentine dal 1378 al 1509*, in *Opere*, ed. E. Scarano Lugnani (Turin, 1970), vol. 2, p. 117 ('era entrata in Italia una fiamma e una peste che non solo mutò gli stati, ma e' modi ancora del governargli ed e' modi delle guerre': my translation).

[3] F. Guicciardini, *The History of Italy*, trans. and ed., with notes and an introduction, by S. Alexander (Princeton, NJ, 1969), VI.9, pp. 177, 182.

event at the end'.[4] Geopolitical boundaries are not clearer. Europe is not a straightforward concept, apart from its geographical nature as a peninsula of Eurasia, even if this period saw a growing level of common development in practices and languages of politics and social life. The continent was still far from being a single unit. By adopting a conscious approach towards temporal and spatial variety, and by breaking the traditional and unitary narrative of decline and transition into one of many changes and continuities, the later medieval European experience can open up to different political cultures and societies, throw new light on older concepts, and reveal analogies and differences compared with other geopolitical contexts.

There is therefore an urgent need to revise and rewrite the story of the later Middle Ages and, in order to do so, to forge new critical and technical vocabularies not derived from the study of other periods. To quote from John Watts's *The Making of Polities*, this is an age for which 'reinterpretation is precisely what is needed'.[5]

Models and narratives

The later Middle Ages in Europe has long faced two grand narratives whose impact and weight still resurface here and there, having often undergone only a superficial restyling.

The first is decline: the Black Death of 1347–52 or even the Hundred Years War are events whose impact is difficult to underestimate as an indicator of change, and of change for the worse. As we will see in this volume, Larry Epstein summarizes the traditional narrative about economics by dividing the age between 1300 and 1500 into three distinct subperiods. From the early 1300s onwards, the tail of a secular wave of growth came to an end, followed by a century or more of demographic, economic, and social 'crisis', 'involution' or 'depression'. Such structural change ending in the early to mid-1400s gave way to the first stages of a new, more dynamic, market-oriented upswing that lasted to the early 1600s. John Watts emphasizes the impact of the theme of decline, crisis, and 'muddle' in the political history of the continent, which apparently was prey to 'a mass

---

[4] C. Wickham, *Medieval Europe: From the Breakup of the Western Roman Empire to the Reformation* (New Haven, CT, 2016), p. 5.
[5] J. Watts, *The Making of Polities: Europe 1300–1500* (Cambridge, 2009), p. 10.

of undignified petty conflicts'.[6] Catherine Holmes in turn, while analysing the global Middle Ages by focusing on the east, reconsiders the established idea of a common trajectory of integration, collapse, and recovery in the comparative history of the eastern and far eastern polities in the same period. Such an emphasis on decline—and its multiple applications to the various aspects of the history of the later Middle Ages—has of course been revised. Previous methods and assumptions have been reconsidered, and many case studies have been subjected to closer scrutiny, revealing significant inconsistencies within the general model. However, it is not easy—and probably not entirely useful—to get rid altogether of the idea of the existence of shared trajectories, provided that they are used in a non-teleological way (Wickham wisely reminds us that 'historical development does not go *to*, it goes from'),[7] and that the revision does not limit itself to substituting a pool of negative concepts by positive ones—such as, for instance, changing 'muddle' to 'complexity'[8]—without a thorough analysis.

The second main grand narrative preventing a better understanding of the European later Middle Ages is modernity. The ghost of this narrative, with its focus on outcomes, haunts the whole Middle Ages by working as 'the hidden heir of the old desire for history to provide moral lessons, periods to admire, heroes and villains',[9] but its impact on the later period is particularly heavy.

In a work that John Elliott twenty years later defined as a 'highly perceptive little book', *On the Medieval Origins of the Modern State*, Joseph Strayer wrote in 1970: 'by 1300, it was evident that the dominant political form in Western Europe was going to be the sovereign state.'[10] In 1974, in a valuable textbook aimed at American undergraduate students, William McNeill resumed the story by adding the Renaissance and the Reformation to the mix:

the Italian Renaissance contributed a sharpened consciousness of individuality in secular matters. This landmark in the liberation of humanity from

---

[6] G. Holmes, *Europe: Hierarchy and Revolt, 1320–1450* (London: Collins, 1975), , p. 2, quoted in Watts, *The Making of Polities*, p. 2.

[7] Wickham, *Medieval Europe*, p. 1.

[8] R. Starn, 'The Early Modern Muddle', *Journal of Early Modern History* 6 (2003), pp. 296–307.

[9] Wickham, *Medieval Europe*, pp. 2–3.

[10] J. Strayer, *On the Medieval Origins of the Modern State* (Princeton, NJ, 1970), p. 57; J. H. Elliott, 'A Europe of Composite Monarchies', *Past and Present* 137 (1992), pp. 48–71, at p. 48.

shackles imposed by medieval collectivities was swiftly followed north of the Alps by the Protestant assertion of individual autonomy and responsibility in relation to God. Taken together, therefore, all the noise and confusion of political and religious controversy, 1300–1650 betrayed a larger meaning: the twin movements of renaissance and reformation, by promoting the development of a population of responsible individual personalities in Europe prepared the way for the enlargement of Europe's political liberties in the 18th and 19th centuries.[11]

This double thread takes the theme of the later Middle Ages back to Sismondi and Constant—that is, to the problem of individual and political freedom—and to Burckhardt and his *Kultur der Renaissance*. The whole late medieval historical process is artificially oriented both towards intellectual, spiritual, and personal regeneration and towards political state-building in the form of the creation of a horizontal system of nation-states. At the heart of Europe, in France, England, and the Iberian kingdoms, such a process manifested itself in the building of a system driven from above, inevitably Eurocentric, and substantially monarchical. The path to modernity was opened by the emergence of territorial, sovereign, and princely or monarchical nation-states. Such a model survives even in very recent syntheses, such as an otherwise extremely rich book on international relations and diplomacy by Jean-Marie Moeglin and Stéphane Péquignot, in which the predominance of royal polities strongly resurfaces as the only basis of diplomatic interactions; 'à la fin du XVe siècle, la politique internationale s'identifie aux relations amicales ou hostiles entre les grandes maisons dynastiques qui dominent le jeu politique.'[12] As for Italy, the birthplace of humanism and the Renaissance, the ostensible paradox between great creativity and innovation in economic practices, political thought, and the arts on the one hand and, on the other, an almost embarrassing weakness in state-building on a national scale blocked the peninsula from the very road towards modernity that its 'inventions' had so massively contributed to establish. Alternative solutions—in such a conceptual framework—have mostly been considered irrelevant.

The wide-ranging impact of this grand narrative has influenced the research on politics for quite a long time, and its outcomes cover a very

---

[11] W. McNeill, *The Shape of European History* (Oxford, 1974), pp. 8–9.

[12] J.-M. Moeglin and S. Péquignot, *Diplomatie et 'relations internationales' au Moyen Âge (IXe–XVe siècle)* (Paris, 2017), p. 96.

long chronology. In the 1950s and 1960s, during the decolonization process in Africa and the Far East, the idea of the primacy of the nation-state form—springing from the premises established in the later Middle Ages—spread on a global scale. Even in contexts like Nigeria, in which the coexistence of different religions, cultures, and ethnic groups made a nation-state object-ively difficult to build, the whole process was still labelled as 'nation-building effort'. Nation-state and rationalism—the two main facets of western modernity—not only still shape our view on modern times but have heavily projected their retrospective shadow on the blurred, transitional age between the 1300s and the 1500s.

Evidence

Records played a substantial role in the later medieval political, social, and economic dynamics; on a continental scale their impact on the lives of people was significant, although of course in different ways at different places and times. While the so-called *révolution scripturaire* is a thirteenth-century phenomenon, the quality and quantity of public and personal or familiar written records, and the general literacy of lay Europeans, grew at an unparalleled pace between 1300 and 1500. Such a process represents a shared and distinctive feature of the period, and at the same time provides scholars with an unprecedented amount of information.

Governmental and public records multiplied and differentiated them-selves in order to guarantee both the regular management of various public and patrimonial functions and the implementation of an effective system of communication and information-gathering within and outside the many active and increasingly interacting polities of a region, or on a broader stage. Records increasingly filled the halls, rooms, and corridors of the imperial, papal, royal, princely, and urban chanceries, which in turn became more articulated. Chancellors, notaries, and secretaries developed a distinctive competence in written and spoken communication by adopting and fluently using different, and sometimes competing, political languages (the last one was humanism) in order to disseminate, impose, and promote their masters' will. The languages of records multiplied as well: Latin was no longer the only written language of power, and multilingual chanceries—such as the English chancery, in which records were written in English, French, Welsh, and Latin—became the norm. The use of written records became regular in every office whose duty was to manage individuals or resources. Registers of *litterae clausae* (letters) and *patentes* (appointments to offices, graces, exemptions, decrees), loose correspondences, account books, and administrative records (the so-called *écritures grises*) increasingly filled chests and cupboards, boxes and cabinets.

The use of written records, however, was not monopolized by central authorities or royal officials: every community, lord, or village consistently recurred to the written word in order to define, preserve, and defend its identity. Chris Wickham rightly argues that one of the most crucial features of the late Middle Ages was the widening of the public sphere: such a process was also fostered by the increasing literacy and familiarity with written records of ever-wider groups of people. Not only communities, but also individuals—women, merchants, artisans, peasants—started to read, and often to write. Personal, familiar, economic, or community records increased, and were regularly preserved: the archive of the merchant Francesco Datini of Prato contains more than 150,000 loose papers and about 600 registers for the years 1348–1430.

Archival order and an increasing attention to records preservation are an integral part of the process. The daily use of records pushed chanceries and the various central and territorial offices, as well as local lords and communities, to preserve in an orderly and functional way the written texts that were fundamental for government and administration; and the growing amount of records fed the need for archival order. Inventories were made and remade, and shaped not only the practical profile of the archives but also the political memory and sovereign identity of rulers, governments, and communities.

Printing was the last element to erupt onto the scene of written communication: even if its effects would only later begin to emerge in a significant way, the invention of movable type added a new layer to an unprecedentedly complex and multifaceted relationship between people and literacy.

Events

The fourteenth and fifteenth centuries were characterized by some crucial events, by expansion and contraction, by change and discovery. A period notorious for wars and disorder, conflicts, and plagues cannot be summarized in a few sentences: however, some among the seemingly chaotic succession of events can be outlined as major fractures in the fabric of this age.

The Black Death is one of them. First documented in the Crimea in 1346–7, from there it spread around all the coasts of the Mediterranean, reaching the far north in 1349–50, coming back at last through Russia. The death rate, although estimates are still controversial, included at least a third of the population, and was made even worse by the fact that the plague became endemic, with minor outbreaks occurring less and less regularly and dramatically for centuries.

A network of wars spread over the continent and the Mediterranean: among them, the defining war was the conflict between the two intertwined kingdoms of England and France later known as the Hundred Years War. It began because of a dynastic problem (the succession to Charles IV of France, d. 1328), but it was grounded in an almost irresolvable tangle of ancient layers of dynastic, political, and economic interests. After the battle of Poitiers in 1356 and the capture of the French king John II (1319–64), the open war slowed down, leaving room in France for a crisis of the kingdom as a whole, and the endless conflicts among the brothers of the increasingly unreliable Charles VI (1338–80). Open war resumed at the beginning of the fifteenth century: after the battle of Agincourt (1415) Henry V of England (1386–1422) launched a full-scale campaign in northern France which, despite his untimely death in 1422, brought the country under English control by 1429. Such a development triggered a response from the French also thanks to the intervention of Joan of Arc, and Charles VII of France (1403–61) fought back to the point of freeing the kingdom from the English by 1453, except for the sole outpost of Calais. The war not only shaped the internal structure of the two kingdoms, and the nature and forms of monarchical and aristocratic power, but also influenced a wider part of Europe that in one way or another was involved in it or suffered some consequences of it.

A third crucial event was the Great Schism: after the transfer of the papal curia to Avignon, in southern France, thanks to a sequence of French popes that followed the death of Boniface VIII (pope from 1294 to 1303), in 1377 the return to Rome promoted by Gregory XI (pope from 1370 to 1378) was jeopardized by his death in 1378. A series of popes and anti-popes, starting with the Italian Urban VI (1378–89) in Rome and the French Clement VII (1378–94) in Avignon, then opened the long-lasting and unsettling period of the so-called Great Schism, which came to an end after two universal councils of the church (Pisa, 1409, and Constance, 1414–18) with the election of Martin V (1417–31). The Schism not only undermined the moral authority and the constitutional legitimacy of the church but also opened up an international arena in which lay and ecclesiastical powers could fight for local benefices, authority, and control. Moreover, the councils (the first two were followed by the Council of Basle, 1431–49, and the partly contemporary Council of Ferrara and Florence, 1438–9), also offered the European polities and the various members of the church a long-lasting example of great assemblies in which voting mechanisms, systems of representation, and collective decisions were tried out for the first time on this large scale.

Events were complemented by slower but crucial processes. While the influence of the Mongols was reducing, the Ottoman Turks were relentlessly expanding, to the point of conquering Byzantium in 1453. Mehmet the Conqueror put a dramatic end to the Byzantine empire, and the Ottomans became a permanent and very problematic feature in Mediterranean and eastern Europe. They reached Friuli, menacing Venice and the Habsburg and Hungarian influence in the Adriatic and the Balkans, and in 1517 subjugated the Mamluk sultanate of Egypt. The last years of the 1400s also saw the end of the Islamic presence in the West: in 1492 Ferdinand of Aragon and Isabella of Castile annexed the Arab emirate of Granada, concluding the *Reconquista* of the whole Iberian peninsula.

A last phenomenon must be remembered: in the 1420s the Portuguese prince Henry the Navigator (1394–1460) promoted a wave of maritime journeys towards Madeira (1419–21), the Azores (1427–32), and Cape Verde and the African coast as far as Cape Bojador (1422–33) that would take European ships towards new horizons. The journey would culminate at the end of the century with the travels of Columbus (1492–3) and Vasco da Gama (1497–8). As Guicciardini pointed out, the novelty of such a broadening of the ancient geographic boundaries did not go unnoticed: letters and travel diaries brought to the European chanceries news of a whole new world. These texts were copied and printed and circulated to a wider audience; the economic, political, and cultural consequences of these discoveries—a significant element for change in the new century—were rooted in the 1400s.

Features

If the need for a rewriting and reinterpreting of the later Middle Ages is deeply felt, it could be useful to conclude the brief introduction to this volume by summarizing some of the newest lines of research that are questioning and renewing the general framework.

Political power and agency are at the heart of some of the most interesting efforts at a revision of the old idea of the later Middle Ages as a transition from something distinctively medieval (universal, imperial, feudal, communal) to something else more modern (more functional and rational, closer to what looks familiar to us). The confluence of cultural and social anthropology, geography, gender studies, and an attentive and critical global history—that is, all the recent efforts to bring the ideas of 'authority', 'sovereignty', and 'legitimacy' into the broader field of 'power' and to detach it from its deep western roots—has provided the grand narrative of the building of the 'modern' nation-state—always resurfacing in its pristine form of a centralized, bounded, sovereign kingdom—with a wealth of alternatives.

Wim Blockmans has listed twelve possible late medieval political units, ranging from the free peasant or urban communities and their federations or leagues, to princely unions, integrated kingdoms, empires. The term 'unit' (unit of politics) to indicate any polity is increasingly used in analysing the medieval world, and in particular the building blocks of the German and imperial system. Blockmans' list shows with his characteristic clarity how much a unitary model of authority and power is anachronistic, and how badly a more critically focused attention to concrete variety is needed. The public forms of power were indeed multiple, and their existence should not be dismissed as an endless sequence of 'exceptions'.

If multiplicity was the norm, then the dynamics between the many political units within or outside a bigger frame becomes crucial. The notion of 'associative' or 'composite' polities tries to provide a framework in which what has been defined by André Holenstein as 'state-building from below' could have a significant impact in defining the nature and functioning of authority. Analysis is being increasingly directed to the connecting mechanisms that kept together leagues and federations (such as the Swiss *confoederatio*) and the web of parallel, complementary, or conflicting agreements, pacts, leagues, and treaties that constituted the daily fabric of political interaction in the later Middle Ages.

In this direction, great emphasis has been put on the local political level—i.e. the community (rural, seigneurial, urban, etc.)—and on the oscillation between consent and dissent among the many components of a composite domain. The notion of territory is scrutinized more closely in order to redefine the complementary notion of a political, social, and economic space. Boundaries and frontiers are read as spaces in which disparate jurisdictions were locally negotiated and constructed as much through performance as through authoritative projection.

The idea of power as multiple and divided among many different agencies has led also to what Manuel Hespanha defined in 1982 as the analysis of the molecular and omnipresent nature of power mechanisms. Such interpretation of the polyphonic workings of power has in turn prompted a renewal of the vocabulary with which current historiography describes the functioning of late medieval polities. Concepts like negotiation, brokerage, segmentation, integration, incorporation, shifting are more frequent, and an idea of conflict as a structural principle of political life—for instance in the cities—rather than a disruption of ordinary government has gained ground.

Again, in such a context, political agency (so to speak) 'thickened'. Interactions at all levels and among an increasingly wide range of actors multiplied and, by defining different, conflicting (or converging) projects and languages of politics, increased participation in the public sphere. People started thinking about how governments should be run, and different discourses around the concrete content of authority, or justice, or fiscality arose and confronted each other at a local or a central level, or at both.

Such a broadening of the concept of power of course carries with it its own risks. It can dissolve any visible or operative patterns into a fragmented world in which the only principle is the here and now, carrying us back to the old 'muddle' via the new 'complexity'. However, it is worth taking the risk, provided that we are aware of the need for both distinctiveness and shared trajectories. As Catherine Holmes argues in the opening of her chapter in this volume, 'this was not necessarily a period of chaos, but one in which the balance of power between those who claimed authoritative positions and those who provided the resources and political support on which those claims rested was delicate and constantly shifting.'

Political multiplicity was reflected by social variety. The broader documentary evidence available reveals the cultural assumptions and social impact of different components of society that passed unnoticed before. Of course, more records mean more information, and not necessarily more action: but the two phenomena are indeed strictly related if you consider reading, writing, and preserving texts as a social practice—what Armando Petrucci has often defined as the social function of writing. Social complexity and growing literacy had the effect of multiplying the ways through which groups and individuals could have a voice, and could make it heard by their contemporaries and by us.

Such a trend towards a broader spectrum of social actors includes both gender diversity and social variety. Society was predominantly male: women were constrained by male power, and even when they had some agency, it was mainly circumscribed to certain roles and certain moments (such as female rulers acting as regents, or exercising soft power by influencing male choices). Professional expertise was gendered, families and dynasties were increasingly male-lined, behaviour control was exerted particularly strongly on women. However, some signs of an increasing complexity are visible. The growth of male-line lineages increased the relevance of queens and princesses as regents—that is, as preservers of the main male line when it was most vulnerable and fewer options than before were available. The Angevin queens of Naples (Joanna I (1326–82) and Joanna II (1371–1435)), the eastern sister queens (or, as they were called, kings) Mary of Hungary (1371–95) and Jadwiga of Poland (1373–99), Margaret I of Denmark (1353–1412), Isabella of Portugal, duchess of Burgundy (1396–1471), and Isabella of Castile (1451–1504) all had the opportunity of exercising some power as regents. They also continued to do this even when a male line was re-established, or by themselves, maybe over a region or in a function that was distinctively theirs (such as over dynastic kingdoms, or in inter-dynastic relations prompted by marriage). Power-sharing among the ruling couple increasingly emerged. In Italy, urban lordships and principalities showed since the 1350s a trend towards a routine sharing of governmental and administrative tasks between the prince and the princess (such as in fourteenth-century Milan, with Bernabò Visconti and Regina della Scala, or in Mantua in the golden age of Isabella d'Este and Francesco Gonzaga), but also in wider and more complex polities, such as the Iberian kingdoms of Aragon and Castile, even before the wedding between Ferdinand and Isabella unified them. Royal and princely power, however, was far from representative. As Chris Wickham rightly points out, 'every time power was exercised by collectivities, it also moved away from being available to women',[13] even though some craft guilds admitted female members, and some crafts—such as spinning—could sometimes be all-female.

That said, literacy, economic complexity, and social variety allowed ambiguity: and in ambiguity, some space was found for female distinctive trajectories, whether spiritual, such as Catherine of Siena, or military, such as Joan of Arc, or intellectual, such as Christine de Pizan. More broadly, and maybe more significantly, literacy and complexity allowed some women to exercise a more ordinary but crucial role in the economic and social daily life of their families. The lifes of Margherita Datini of Prato, the wife of the merchant Francesco, who learned at an adult age how to write in order to

---

[13] Wickham, *Medieval Europe*, p. 193.

control the many correspondences of her husband's company when he was not at home, or Alessandra Macinghi Strozzi, the widowed mother of Filippo Strozzi who spent her whole life in trying by any means to have her sons' sentences of exile revoked, and to see them return to their native city, show that even in a merchant, male-dominated city like Florence some sort of female agency was possible. As Catherine Kovesi argues in her chapter, 'the later Middle Ages saw an increasing audibility if not yet visibility of the voices of women'.

Spirituality, rural and urban political participation, and the spread of vernacular literature (both religious and secular) were also signs of the growing participation of different social groups in collective life. The cultural assumptions and practices of an ever-wider spectrum of individuals and groups reveal increasing involvement in what can be defined the 'public sphere'.

On the other side, the contradictions and conflicts generated by the growing complexity and multiplicity of power at both central and local level prompted the slow but undeniable sharpening and defining of social and collective boundaries. Even though recent research on social mobility emphasizes its persistent vigour, in many cases mobility became more and more an affair internal to social groups rather than a process allowing people to cross social and professional boundaries. This sharper defining of roles also caused a growing hostility towards minorities (in particular, religious minorities such as the Jews).

Multiplicity therefore meant contradictions: if the late medieval world made space for more players than before, it also generated fractures and conflicting forms of public and personal participation in social life.

Underlying the vigour of political participation and social variety was a complex transformation of the economic system. As Larry Epstein argues in his chapter, a series of badly needed reassessments have put later medieval economic dynamics in a broader geographic and chronological context. Decline has been relativized: the later Middle Ages is increasingly seen as 'the era when the European economy began to take on the technological and institutional features that would allow it first to catch up with, and then forge ahead of, the most advanced regions elsewhere in Eurasia'.

Instead of a narrative of crisis and decline, more recent research emphasizes a story of adjustment and change: many economic processes were taking place at different paces in different places to adapt to new situations. Recent research on economic change and social mobility in Italy shows how the network of small-to-medium urban centres (for instance in the Marche region, or in Piedmont) readjusted to the changed conditions of the aftermath of the Black Death by taking advantage of their geopolitical position and networks. In turn the major cities—such as Florence—modified their productive and mercantile features to accommodate new industries (such as silk manufacturing) or different working solutions (i.e. by substituting the composite mercantile, financial, and productive powerhouses so successful in the thirteenth century by smaller, more specialized, stronger companies).

Technical innovations and adaptability fostered a more general political and economic integration of regions and countries with different economic backgrounds—such as the economic convergence between semi-peripheral countries like England and more advanced regions such as Flanders and Italy—while the growth of more complex public and institutional frameworks probably created new regional differences. Such multi-layered processes of political and economic integration provided the late medieval economy with its unusually innovative dynamic, despite different regional trajectories and results.

Richness of interpretations and adaptability towards emergence and change are also clearly visible if we turn to ideas and languages. The later Middle Ages—we are told by another powerful grand narrative, the one linked to humanism and the Renaissance—was an age of profound change in intellectual thinking and political language. Politics and law became a mine of innovative ideas about authority and political power in order to suit the emergence of new, multiple political agencies. Bartolus of Saxoferrato, Baldus degli Ubaldi, Marsilius of Padua, William Ockham, the humanists from Salutati to Pontano, Machiavelli and Guicciardini, Erasmus of Rotterdam, and Thomas More changed the way in which people and rulers looked at politics, authority, and political participation.

Ideas and practices of collective representation were also enhanced by the development of representative bodies—parliaments, assemblies, councils. Their nature and features differed according to context (from the church to the smaller alpine communities), but they introduced an approach at once collective and outspoken to expressing needs and defending rights, experimenting in the process with new practices such as developing voting systems or recording debates.

If radically new ways of discussing questions of power were developed in this period, however, the prime motivation of fourteenth- and fifteenth-century writers and thinkers was to provide solutions to problems presented by the realities of political life, and especially questions of power. Recent research emphasizes that the supposed fracture between scholastic culture and its humanistic counterpart was actually more a questioning—sometimes radical—of inherited fundamental presuppositions (such as the Augustinian theory about authority) than a revolutionary overturning of them. Jurists and political thinkers faced a changing reality, and coped with it by creatively using and modifying an existing intellectual armoury. The 'new' juridical and humanist tools and vocabulary were in practice also used outside the classic dichotomies of freedom and republicanism against peace and princely sovereignty. They were applied, modified, and adapted every time a new form of authority or a newly assembled territory was in need of legitimacy. That was true even in intellectual fields other than politics and law: as Matthew Kempshall argues in his chapter on scientific thought, if conceptions of space and time did change, what was discovered was not the result of a brave new vision of the world—it was a *re*-connection with what had already been known.

In this sense, the more substantial, widespread, and long-lasting change was in the pragmatic languages and practices of politics, justice, diplomacy, and government. Authority and sovereignty were daily affirmed and maintained by adjusting old concepts to the flow of single cases generated by the extension of royal, princely, or collective authority over broader territories, and by the parallel emergence of contrasting interests—provided with an unprecedented ability to express them—from below. The intensifying and thickening of political interaction among different actors on a different territorial scale induced rulers and subjects to resort to written communication in order to set out conflicts, problems, or even ordinary issues. The unprecedented multiplying of public records was a consequence and a cause for the elaboration and maintenance of many shared languages of interaction, which in turn provided common ground for political confrontation. In this direction, diplomacy (i.e. political interaction between the many late medieval composite polities) and politics (i.e. political interaction within them) during the 1400s elaborated a number of communicative languages to express the complex dynamics in place.

In particular, and during a long Quattrocento that spanned the 1350s to the 1520s, people active in both politics and diplomacy developed a way of dealing with reality that was based on a reciprocal and uninterrupted confrontation of hypotheses and projects, ideas, and options. Inherited traditions of public debate and rhetorical arts merged in order to shape a new political language made of a creative combination of discursive strategies, linguistic and lexical techniques, an argumentative attitude towards political analysis, and intense narrativity. Even though this language developed simultaneously in diplomatic negotiations and internal political debates, it was translated and diffused in writing mostly through diplomacy because of the urgent need to transmit information on political interactions to distant interlocutors. To cut a long story short, diplomacy offered to politics an ideal workshop in which new communicative and analytical strategies for dealing with reality could be shaped. In the process, diplomatic correspondence used, adapted, and diffused the many pragmatic, literary, juridical, political, and theological foundations of what we are used to calling 'the Renaissance'. If the roots of such a distinctive process were mainly Italian, its diffusion was much broader, and resulted from the many structural changes described above.

The last element worthy of mention is the need to adopt a global approach to the period. Of course, it is not an easy task. From the disparity in documentation to a legitimate scepticism about the adoption of common frameworks in periodization or conceptualization, there are many methodological caveats regarding a global history of the European world before the 1500s. However, a view of European developments through global lenses seems intriguing for at least two reasons. First, the enlargement of the geopolitics of Europe allows the consideration of important questions about European history in this period for which a more globalized perspective seems essential. Among them are the impact of climate change and disease, and the influence and nature of changing long-distance trade on the process of re-adapting the medieval economy to a different world. To them, the impact of the ongoing expansion and consolidation of religious beliefs across broad regions and finally the parallel process of political thickening and public growth, and the diffusion of brokerage systems in regions that were ancient friends or foes of Europeans, such as in the Christian and Muslim Mediterranean can be added. All these questions can only benefit by a deeper knowledge of trajectories and practices across the later medieval world and not purely of those of western Europe.

A second advantage of introducing a global perspective in the analysis of the later medieval period is more methodological, and aims at breaking the old unitary and 'European' or 'western' mould for models of development or change. Recognizing and restoring the original variety of political, economic, and cultural patterns in action in Europe during such a complex age means also disconnecting them from a rigid path of regularity and exception, and opening up both the definition of general patterns and the analysis of single case studies to the impact of crossings and contacts with a broader world. Such a methodological approach would allow comparisons of the functioning of the many systems that were coexisting and interacting, at different levels of intensity, in a shared space, or of the various functions across them. It will also foster a better understanding of their nature by revealing, and taking into account, unexpected similarities or differences.

Plate 2. Hartmann Schedel, *Liber Chronicarum* (the *Nuremberg Chronicle*, 1493)

1

Power, government, and political life

John Watts

On 23 November 1407, Louis, duke of Orléans, uncle of the king of France and effective ruler of his kingdom, was set upon in the streets of Paris and murdered, his head cut in two by a halberd, so that his brains spilled on the pavement. The murderers, it emerged a few days later, had been hired by the duke's nephew, John 'the Fearless', duke of Burgundy, who went on to justify his crime in an open letter to the court and the crowned heads of Europe as a form of tyrannicide, committed 'for the safety of the king's person' and 'thesh general good of the realm'.[1] Burgundy was soon pardoned, and then—just as soon—his pardon was rescinded, as Orléans' heirs and allies regained control of the French court. There followed a lengthy civil war, lasting at least into the 1430s, if not the 1470s or later, in which the so-called 'Burgundians' were opposed by a group of western and southern lords, who came to be known as 'Armagnacs'. This war was, in the first place, a division of factions within France, jostling for control of a mad king, Charles VI, whose government raised huge sums in taxation, dispensed favours and pardons, and managed an extensive network of officers; these factions reached deeply into every province and every city, merging into the local squabbles of knightly landowners, urban oligarchs, and workers. But it was also a public and political conflict, involving the assertion and defence of policies, principles, and values—positions on the duties of the subject and the ruler; on the importance of defending the kingdom; on the proper level of taxation; on the appropriate liberties of towns and nobles. To bid for the support of lords, citizens, and commons, both sides used the available technologies of preaching and demonstration, letter-writing, and the circulation of pamphlets. At the same time, this was a conflict which spread out across Europe. Orléans had been allied to the recently deposed Holy Roman Emperor, Wenceslas IV; in the long-running papal schism, he supported the

---

[1] R. Vaughan, *John the Fearless: the Growth of Burgundian Power* (London, 1966), pp. 45, 70ff.

The Later Middle Ages. Isabella Lazzarini, Oxford University Press (2021). © Isabella Lazzarini.
DOI: 10.1093/oso/9780198731641.003.0002

Avignon pope against his Roman counterpart; and he sponsored French royal interests in Italy—in Genoa, Milan, and Naples. Burgundy, on the other hand, was linked to the new emperor, Rupert of the Palatinate; he supported the moves to establish a general council of the church that could remove the contending popes; he was not interested in Italian adventures, but was instead building an assemblage of territories across the Low Countries, extending the dominance of his family to the north and east. These two princes thus represented extensive connections that reached deeply into France and well beyond, but that was not the limit of the impact of their conflict. Charles VI was not the only claimant to the French crown: his cousin, Henry V of England, exploited the troubles in France to conquer Normandy, seize Paris, and, in the 1420 Treaty of Troyes, obtain recognition as heir to the kingdom. Charles and his heirs, Charles VII and Louis XI, countered by supporting enemies of the English crown in Scotland and Ireland, and intervened in the Wars of the Roses to support rebels and pretenders. The conflict of Burgundians and Armagnacs thus merged into the later stages of the Hundred Years War, as well as the struggles of popes and councils and the domestic affairs of France and its neighbours.

This highly specific act of violence and its multiple ramifications capture some of the central features of later medieval political life. It was often bloody and personal, but the resort to bloodshed was politically purposeful, and the focus on individuals reflected the parts they played in larger frameworks of power. Those frameworks were both 'private' and 'public'—they were followings of men and women, linked together in relationships of marriage, service, or friendship for mutual advantage; but they also involved the performance of official roles, the negotiation of public business, the management of institutions. The frameworks of power were national, inter-national and 'transnational'. Europe was divided into self-conscious political spaces, each with a measure of sovereignty and identity, but these spaces also overlapped and any significant power-holder was likely to be able to operate across them, as well as within them. And, within virtually any political setting, authority was contestable, so politics were lively, convulsive, prone to sudden swings of fortune: they involved a complicated mixture of rela-tionships among elites and much wider movements, voiced and promoted by representative assemblies and popular revolts. There were numerous wars between states (and between cities, provinces, principalities, and churches), but those wars also arose from, and fed into, the internal politics of all these units: war is always 'the continuation of politics', as Clausewitz famously observed, but in this period the continuity was closer than ever.

These features of contemporary political life have made the later Middle Ages a peculiarly challenging period to study. For a long time dismissed as 'a mass of undignified petty conflicts', repellently complicated and impossible to disentangle without oversimplifying, the politics of the later Middle Ages have recently come to be seen in a more positive light.[2] As we shall see, this is partly because we have reached new understandings of the relationship between political discord and the growth of government, but it may also reflect the changed perspectives of historians, as we enter an era of deep political uncertainty, both nationally and internationally. In this short essay, my aim is to survey the main patterns of later medieval politics, and to consider whether or not—and in what ways—there is a trajectory to be traced across the fourteenth and fifteenth centuries. But first, it will be helpful to look at the historiography.

Political history—past and present

For the great French historian of the late Middle Ages, Bernard Guenée, the murder of the duke of Orléans exposed a yawning gap between the ideology of French government, as orderly, protective, authoritative, and the messy reality of its dependence on individual relationships.[3] This irony had not been lost on the historians of the nineteenth and early twentieth centuries, who had seen the later Middle Ages as a period of declining political morality. In their eyes, the achievements of medieval civilization were destroyed over the course of the fourteenth and fifteenth centuries by a mixture of social crisis, caused by famine, plague and war, and cultural change, in which commercialization, individualism, and a rising penchant for violence seemed to be the main drivers. But Guenée himself saw positive developments in the later Middle Ages, as did some contemporaries of his between the 1960s and the 1980s—among others, Philippe Contamine in France; K. B. McFarlane, Peter Lewis, and G. L. Harriss in England; Carlo Cipolla and Giorgio Chittolini in Italy; Peter Blickle and Peter Moraw in Germany. To these historians, the period was one of political advancement, in which governments reached more deeply and effectively into society, and

---

[2] Quotations from G. Holmes, *Europe: Hierarchy and Revolt, 1320–1450* (London, 1975), p. 12; J. Heers, *Parties and Political Life in the Medieval West*, trans. D. Nicholas (Amsterdam, 1977), pp. 1–2.

[3] B. Guenée, *Un meurtre, une société. L'assassinat du duc d'Orléans, 23 novembre 1407* (Paris, 1992), back cover.

the intersection of the 'private' power of aristocrats and oligarchs with the 'public' power of governmental institutions was not inherently disorderly, but potentially integrative.

Later generations have built on these foundations. For Jean-Philippe Genet, Wim Blockmans, and their collaborators in the 1990s and beyond, this period saw the 'genesis of the modern state', especially between about 1280 and 1360, when new institutions of military service, taxation, and representation were developed across Europe.[4] More recently, there has been a turn away from 'the state', to acknowledge the full range of political activity—not only the formal operations of institutions, but the less formal workings of influence, debate, networking, and the like. This has led some historians to prefer the term 'polity' to 'state', incidentally acknowledging the political and governmental qualities of bodies other than kingdoms (principalities, leagues, cities, churches, rural communes, and so on) and linking together the story of constitutional development with the practice of politics.[5] Others have focused on 'empowering interactions', emphasizing the ways in which political communities were built from below as well as from above, or on 'logics of political conflict', accepting what the historical sociologist Charles Tilly called 'contentious politics' as normal, rather than pathological.[6] Against this background, there has been a renewed interest in popular political activity and in its political (as distinct from economic) causes and consequences.[7] Equally, as part of a larger concern with 'political culture'—in part a legacy of the so-called 'linguistic turn'—later medieval historians have paid increasing attention to the sphere of political communication—the exploitation of spreading technologies, such as preaching, written vernaculars, and rising literacy, to address and shape an emerging public opinion, or public sphere.[8]

---

[4] J.-P. Genet, 'L'État moderne. Un modèle opératoire', in J.-P. Genet (ed.), L'État moderne. Genèse, bilan, perspectives (Paris, 1990), pp. 261–81; C. Tilly and W. Blockmans (eds), Cities and the Rise of States in Europe, AD 1000–1800 (Boulder, CO, 1994). For the European Science Foundation volumes on the 'birth of the modern state', see 'Further Reading' at the end of this volume.

[5] J. Watts, The Making of Polities: Europe, 1300–1500 (Cambridge, 2009).

[6] W. Blockmans, A. Holenstein, and J. Mathieu (eds), Empowering Interactions: Political Cultures and the Emergence of the State in Europe, 1300–1900 (Aldershot, 2009); P. Lantschner, The Logic of Political Conflict in Medieval Cities (Oxford, 2015); C. Tilly, Regimes and Repertoires (Chicago, 2006).

[7] S. K. Cohn, Lust for Liberty: the Politics of Social Revolt in Medieval Europe, 1200–1425 (Cambridge, MA, 2006); J. Firnhaber-Baker (ed.), The Routledge History Handbook of Medieval Revolt (London, 2017).

[8] J. Dumolyn, 'Political Communication and Political Power in the Middle Ages: A Conceptual Journey', La Edad Media 13 (2012), pp. 33–55; P. Boucheron and

Taking all these developments together, it is clear that today's historians regard the political life of the Middle Ages from a much less jaundiced perspective than their predecessors before the Second World War (or even the 1980s). The period has shed its reputation as an era of decline, crisis, and chaos, and is now seen as a time of growing governmental and political exuberance—one in which authorities were obliged to negotiate with those they wished to subject, and one in which representation was a key facet of political assertion (i.e. representation in the dual sense of standing for others and seeking to create a public impression, through ritual, propaganda, debate, and so on). The sphere of the political, and the ways of understanding that sphere, have significantly increased, and the kinds of confrontations that were characteristic of the period—popular revolts, wars and civil wars, coups and magnate rebellions—are recognized not as mindless violence, but as rational products of political and governmental dynamics. Equally, the scope of the Europe under discussion has broadened. As recently as the 1970s, it was common for the 'European history' of this period—at least in Britain—to confine itself to the west and centre of the continent, drawing a line more or less along the Cold War 'iron curtain', and excluding the British Isles and Scandinavia into the bargain. Now we are able to access a much richer literature in English covering the Baltic and central Europe, Lithuania and the Russian polities, the eastern Mediterranean, and the Ottoman world. There is still surprisingly little work that sets the kingdoms of Sweden, Poland, and Hungary, for example, alongside those of France or Castile, or that considers the city-dominated polities of Italy and the Low Countries alongside Lübeck, Novgorod, or Constantinople (the history of Byzantium in its late days is only now coming to be incorporated with the history of the west, with which it was so substantially intertwined). So there is still much to be done—but a rich, broad, comparatively minded picture of the later medieval political world is beginning to emerge, and we shall aim to trace its contours in the next few pages. One of the central questions someone encountering this period for the first time will want to know is, 'what is the storyline?' *Is* there one, in fact, or have the scholars of this period simply replaced 'muddle' with the more pretentious term 'complexity'? Like any students of politics, we shall also want to explore the causes of conflict and the causes of consensus, or at least of cooperation. But there are two obvious starting points for our enquiry: one is to understand the background to our

N. Offenstadt (eds), *L'Espace public au Moyen Âge* (Paris, 2015); I. Lazzarini, *Communication and Conflict: Italian Diplomacy in the Early Renaissance, 1350–1520* (Oxford, 2015).

period—the legacy of the high Middle Ages, and specifically of the thirteenth century, 'greatest of centuries' in the view of the early twentieth-century historian James J. Walsh; the other is to examine the major political forms of the period, and their distribution across Europe.[9] Let us take these in turn.

The inheritance from the thirteenth century

The central Middle Ages were the scene of what might be called a 'legal-bureaucratic revolution', in which many characteristic forms of state power were devised and implemented. There were perhaps four overlapping elements to this revolution. The first was in the sphere of law and jurisdiction. During the eleventh and twelfth centuries, a common body of Roman and Canon (church) law was recovered and codified by scholars working in cathedral schools, the papal curia, and the first universities. It came to form part of the training of clerks in church and state, and so to influence the identity and activity of governments, who began to legislate for themselves and their subjects and dependants, on the model of Roman emperors. Custom—agreed principles relying on memory and face-to-face negotiation—came to be reshaped as law: fixed, written, authoritative, and publicly known (so the conventions governing the relations between lords of land and their followers came to be recast as a kind of 'feudal law' by the end of the twelfth century). Courts came to be arranged in hierarchies, with top-level rulers—popes, emperors, kings—asserting control over the highest crimes and claiming for themselves the right to examine and overturn the judgements of lower courts; 'jurisdiction' became a common word to describe authority, as the holder of high justice and the person with the power to legislate (usually in some form of assembly, or at least on the basis of petition or complaint) was readily recognized as sovereign. Roman and canon law also bestowed a series of axioms and principles which could be used to define and redefine the rights of rulers and subjects—a process which involved a series of innovations. The idea that a given king or lord was *imperator in regno suo* (emperor in his realm), for instance, made him the sole source of rule, entitled in a state of *necessitas*, or emergency, to military and financial aid from his subjects. So it was that Romano-canonical ideas underpinned the development of new forms of military

---

[9] J.J. Walsh, *The Thirteenth: Greatest of Centuries* (New York, 1907).

service and public taxation in the course of the thirteenth century. These ideas did not only benefit rulers—the notions of the *digna vox* (what was appropriate for a ruler) and the *lex regia* (the law that made rulers) confined them to what was in the common interest of their subjects; the canonical tag *quod omnes tangit* bound the ruler to the consent of his subjects, or at least their representatives, in matters of law and tax—but it is not hard to see how they created the raw materials of modern states, both in the central notion of a common authority, and in many of the lineaments of state power: jurisdiction, legislation, taxation, representation, 'national' service. The Latin church, and most of the kingdoms, principalities, and cities of Europe, had developed this kind of authority, and the governmental machinery to assert it, by the end of the thirteenth century.

A second element lay in the sphere of political ideas, where the key notions of Roman and canon law were afforced by concepts drawn from the classical tradition—particularly the works of Aristotle, translated into Latin in the mid-thirteenth century, but also those of Cicero, and those of Augustine, and other Christian interpreters of Greek and Roman culture. A cluster of jurists, theologians, and litterateurs—men such as Thomas Aquinas, Giles of Rome, Marsilius of Padua, Ramon Lull, and Dante Alighieri—wrote glosses, handbooks, novels, and poems which fleshed out the idea of the political community and explained how it should operate. The content of these writings varied in all sorts of ways. Some texts presented authority in 'republican' terms, as collective and law-bound, others as monarchical; some presented the ruler as a kind of priest, others as a kind of knight; they differed in the relationship they prescribed between the ruler's grace or will and the dictates of law, or between hierarchy and collectivity; they might depict the natural setting for politics as a kingdom, or an empire, or a city, or a church. But these texts tended to agree on the naturalness of an association between ruler and people: the former ought to protect the latter; the latter ought to feel a common obligation, and a common identity, under the former. In other words, these works of theory—again widely circulated among clerks and influential in governing circles—advanced the concept of the state or political community, even if they differed on how it should be configured.

A third element in this 'legal-bureaucratic revolution' was the instrumentalizing of writing as a technique of government. We now realize that this was not new in the twelfth and thirteenth centuries, but it is clear that it grew dramatically in that period. Rulers began to keep systematic records of their judicial, legislative, and fiscal rights and activities on a large scale from around the second half of the twelfth century. This was an important part of the hardening of custom into law, as record-keeping authorities tied those below and around them to particular duties. And a fourth element went alongside it: the development of notions, ideals, and structures of office in which agents of the powerful accepted that they had defined roles and functions to perform on behalf of those they represented—whether kings and popes, as in the case of judges delegate, or towns, as in the case of urban leaders and councillors, aldermen, *échevins*, jurats, or *podestà*. Instead of extracting intermittent submissions from the more or less autonomous lords within and around their domains, rulers tried to pin them down by defining their status and hemming them in with loyal officers.

It is clear that, together, these ideas and practices created templates for the rule of large collectivities, whether these were concentrated in cities or spread out across kingdoms (or, in the case of the Latin church, across much of Europe itself). During the thirteenth century, individual rulers were able to realize a remarkably complete and well-defined jurisdiction over large terrains—we think of the ecclesiastical empire of Pope Innocent III, for example, able to impose a universal crusading tax and to legislate for the whole of Christendom in the Lateran Council of 1215; or we think of the France of Philip II, Louis IX, and Philip IV, in which much of the territory of today's republic was subordinated to the rule of Paris, most of the great vassals and much of the church were placed under the jurisdiction of the king's court of *Parlement*, and—by the 1290s—taxes were levied across this great space; or we think of the governments of Venice or Florence, ruling populations of more than 150,000 people each, defining the terms of participation in the rule of the city, gaining control of surrounding territory and creating frameworks of taxation and service, whether military or naval. It is these examples, and others like them, that once underlay the reputation of the thirteenth century as 'greatest', and as witnessing 'the medieval origins of the modern state', as the American constitutional historian J. R. Strayer put it.[10] Set alongside these achievements, the wars and broils of the later Middle Ages seemed degenerate by comparison. And yet twelfth- and thirteenth-century regimes were equally marked by conflict, and the periods of 'success', in which large-scale governments seemed to have traction, need to be set alongside the periods of disarray, in which would-be authorities were challenged, subverted, or—like the German empire of the Hohenstaufen, the

---

[10] J. R. Strayer, *On the Medieval Origins of the Modern State* (Princeton, NJ, 1970).

Sicily of the house of Anjou, or the hegemony of Wenceslas II across Bohemia, Silesia and southern Poland—destroyed. Indeed, the thirteenth century ended in a series of confrontations that look very 'late medieval' in form—the revolt of the Sicilian Vespers and the long war that followed between Angevin and Aragonese interests in Sicily and Naples; the conflict between Pope Boniface VIII and King Philip IV of France, in which the supreme pontiff was roundly defeated, died in custody, and was soon threatened with posthumous charges of heresy and sodomy; the struggles of town leagues, lords and short-lived kings in the Castile of the 1280s and 1290s; the long-drawn-out failures of the French intervention in Flanders and the English intervention in Scotland; or the deposition of Emperor Adolf of Nassau in 1297. In all, it is clear that the constitutional developments of the thirteenth century could have disintegrative results. But why?

Some of the answers are insignificant, because they could apply to any political regime—exogenous disasters, interpersonal and dynastic rivalries, the personal idiosyncrasies and shortcomings of key politicians. But three answers are more important, both because they pertain to our period in particular and because they are pitched at a more structural level. The first is that the attempts of authorities to define relationships inevitably provoked conflict: matters which had been negotiable came to be fixed, and there was certain to be disagreement on the terms of fixing. Lords, churches, and towns threatened with new forms of subordination reacted sharply; kings and others who were forced to concede too much returned to the charge when circumstances changed. The growth of government that was part and parcel of the 'legal-bureaucratic revolution' was thus inherently conflictual, and conflicts were not necessarily won by top-level authorities. Two further answers are connected to this. One is that the same process that created new aspirations and devices for rulers created aspirations and devices for those they were trying to make subjects—charters of rights and liberties, leagues of sworn allies, representative assemblies, plaints, petitions, and manifestos— these could all be exploited by opponents of the ruler, and so they were, time and again, with a tendency to limit or even to neutralize assertions from above. Apparently 'constitutional' challenges—such as the movements of barons that extracted Magna Carta from King John of England, or the Golden Bull from Andrew II of Hungary, or the charters of liberties from King Louis X of France—could have the temper of rebellions or feed through into civil wars or foreign invasions, such as those that beset England in the later 1210s, or the troubles in Flanders and northern France in the 1320s, 1330s, and after. Kings and peoples could be brought into harmony, certainly, but that harmony could be overturned, and we should take care before concluding that the former pattern is the natural one. A third and final important point is that thirteenth-century constitutional developments were not limited to empires and kingdoms: the same facilities deployed by popes and kings were exploited by princes and lords, towns and churches—government grew everywhere, at the same time, generating copious conflict as different authorities attempted to annexe and manage the same resources. Since, as we have seen, government provokes resistance as well as compliance—and since it creates the means of resistance too—it is not surprising that the thirteenth century ended in a world so full of conflict. The forms of political life that we associate with the later Middle Ages were up and running well before 1300; they were forged in the developments of the central Middle Ages.

Political geography

Before we consider the political dynamics of the two centuries after 1300, it would be helpful to gain a sense of the distribution of power across the continent. We have seen that by 1300, there existed a basic template of polity, found practically everywhere. It featured five main elements. First of all, there was a ruler, possessing some kind of domain which belonged to him and his family, as well as various ancient rights, some ritualized authority, and normally some elements of romano canonical *imperium*—claims or rights to legislate and do justice, to tax, to coordinate the defence of the realm, to direct relations with other countries, and to summon assemblies. Second, there was a nobility, with some measure of control over land and men, and often over other local assets—royal offices, churches, towns, provinces. Third, there was usually some form of representative assembly, organized by class ('estates') or locality, meeting rarely or frequently, sometimes a single gathering for the whole polity, sometimes multiple gatherings for constituent regions. Fourth, there were churches, partly coordinated under bishops, archbishops, and the pope, and partly—in the case of monasteries and other religious orders—under a mixture of papal headship, royal, noble and urban patronage, and practical independence. And fifth, there were towns, typically with some autonomy, and the larger ones subdivided into rulers and bodies representing the oligarchs and the mass of the citizens (so that towns, themselves, were like small polities).

This five-part model varied greatly in reality. Sometimes, the ruler was remote and his powers and estates vestigial—effectively colonized by others, such as nobles or towns; in other cases, he was rich and powerful, ruling on the basis of extensive domains controlled by loyal officers, and also (and increasingly) on the basis of public authority—jurisdiction, taxation, rights to military service, and so on—an authority which was maintained by a mixture of top-down force and bottom-up acceptance of its utility to subjects. Taxation existed more or less everywhere by 1300, but its scale and its format varied, and so did the extent to which it was controlled by the centre, rather than absorbed by lords, or towns, military contractors, or networks of tax collectors. Representation might be centralized and formal—in parliamentary assemblies—or it might be maintained by groups of subjects themselves, in the form of leagues, like the *hermandades* of thirteenth-century Spain or the *Bünde* and *Landfrieden* of Germany; or it might take the form of adventitious assemblages of subjects claiming to represent the collectivity, as in the Burgundian example I began with, or when the towns and lords of Aragon established a *Unión de Aragón* in 1283, or the rebellious peasants of 1381 claimed to be 'the loyal commons of England'.[11] Towns could be large, more or less independent, and able to dominate the territories around them—sometimes, like Venice, Barcelona, or Genoa, they headed huge networks of trading posts and colonies—or they might be generally under the thumb of effective lordship, as the rich cities of Paris and London typically deferred to the kings of France and England respectively, and realized commercial and political opportunities under their aegis. Nobles might be poor and numerous and divided into clans—as in the Basque country, or in Scotland, Ireland, and parts of France and Poland—or they might be stratified, into a class of magnates, benefiting from inheritance rules that preserved large estates, and the lesser nobles, who may or may not be linked to them by ties of service or protection. In all, then, the basic forms of polity might be realized in different ways, but it should be clear from this discussion that there were also other patterns and formats—leagues, assemblies, different types of jurisdiction, tax, inheritance, or association—that were recognized and widely copied or adapted across Europe. It is helpful to think in this way, because it reminds us that national histories favour only one subset of available political forms, and not necessarily the ones that were most dominant or permanent: we think of England, France, Hungary,

---

[11] R. B. Dobson, *The Peasants' Revolt of 1381* (London, 1970), p. 127.

Castile, rather than the components of these realms: components which could easily be in conflict, or come to be recomposed in different ways.

So the map of Europe was still fluid in the fourteenth and fifteenth centuries, and much of it—Italy, the Low Countries, the east and the south-east—would change very significantly over the period. The international empire of the Roman church underwent four major changes of format—the 'Avignon papacy' of 1309–78; the Schism of 1378–1417; the era of councils, 1409–49; and the time of 'Renaissance papacy' and 'national churches' which followed. France was twice dismembered and twice recomposed; the king of England lost, and partly regained, his controlling position in the British Isles; the Iberian kingdoms struggled against each other, but Aragon and Castile were finally united; the centre of gravity in the empire shifted several times before the gradual emergence of a lasting Habsburg hegemony, based in Austria and the Low Countries. We shall discuss these developments, and others like them, in the sections that follow, but it may be more helpful to take a different tack here and identify broad continuities. Latin Europe can be roughly divided into three zones, each characterized by particular forms of polity.

The first zone is sometimes called the 'Carolingian core', reflecting the empire of Charlemagne, which covered most of the area between the Pyrenees and the Rivers Elbe and Danube, including much of northern Italy.[12] In the later Middle Ages, the centre and east of this area were covered by the Holy Roman Empire, though the power of the emperor was in practice restricted to parts of Germany, while most of the huge imperial space was governed by cities, princes, and lords, often in leagues and alliances (especially in the German lands). This core of Europe was rich and populous, the scene of an 'urban belt' or 'urban axis' of large cities, running down from Bruges and Ghent in Flanders (with outliers in London and Paris), through the Rhineland and into the Mediterranean littoral and northern Italy, where Barcelona, Genoa, Milan, Florence, Rome, Naples, and Venice were dominant, and back up through Vienna and Prague to Kraków and the Baltic network of trading cities, managed since the thirteenth century by the German Hansa or Hanseatic League. The size of the cities, the importance of trade, the traditions of Roman rule across much of this area help to explain why the centre of Europe was dominated by city-states

---

[12] For the concept of a 'core' and an 'urban axis', see R. Bartlett, 'Heartland and Border: The Mental and Physical Geography of Medieval Europe', in H. Pryce and J. Watts (eds), *Power and Identity in the Middle Ages* (Oxford, 2007), pp. 23–36.

or (mostly small) city-based principalities, the largest of which were: first, the crown of Aragon, comprising the more or less autonomous principalities of Catalonia, Valencia, Majorca, and Aragon proper; and, second, the Valois duchy of Burgundy, which grew between the 1380s and the 1470s to cover much of north-eastern France and the Low Countries. The area also featured two other big players. One was the papacy, based mainly at Rome, and controlling a cluster of territories in central Italy and southern France, while exercising regional influence in southern Italy and a more general authority, derived from its headship of the church, across all of Latin Europe (i.e. the north, west, and south of the continent, and as far east as Poland and Hungary). The other was the crown of France, ruler of a large kingdom in the second zone, but conscious of imperial traditions and deeply invested (often as papal ally) in the affairs of Italy and the Rhône region, the Low Countries and Spain.

Around this core was a less populous area of mostly larger polities, typically monarchies, which might (rather crudely) be divided into two zones—one western, and one northern and eastern. The western, or second, zone was dominated by the kingdoms of England, France, and Castile, each an expansionist power, typically ruling a large space (England itself was small and underpopulated, but its king exercised a fluctuating power over the British Isles and western France). The rulers of these kingdoms saw themselves in imperial terms, and meant to exercise jurisdiction over the people and territories beneath them; while all three dealt with powerful princes, and—in Castile particularly—large and powerful cities, they were consistently able to project authority at a local level, so the politics of their realms always involved some kind of dialogue between centre and locality. These realms were themselves quite highly developed, with historic identities and growing structures of jurisdiction and represen- tation; frequently, there were tensions between the expansionist aims of the ruling dynasties and the more localized interests of smaller powers which came together to assert a kind of domestic opinion. Similar kingdoms existed at times in Sicily, Naples, and Hungary, but the political coordination of southern Italy was disrupted by warfare for much of the period between the 1280s and the 1440s. The kingdom of Hungary, on the other hand, centralized first by its Árpád rulers, and then by the Angevins after 1301, was rather like France or Castile in featuring an assertive monarchy operating in tension with powerful magnates, through royal officers, supervision of property, and direct dialogue with local communities.

The kingdoms of northern and eastern Europe make a third zone, characterized by low population, strong provincial solidarities, and relatively weak monarchies with limited capacity to penetrate the regions. To be sure, some of these monarchies were stronger than others—the rulers of Poland and Denmark could often be very effective, and so, from time to time, could the kings of Bohemia—but in all of these places, and in Scotland, Sweden, and Norway, there were powerful bulwarks against royal power: 'land-courts' protecting aristocratic liberties and strong provincial assemblies; regnal councils or regional officers ruling in place of the monarch; castle lordships and allods (independent property) which the ruler could not easily access or confiscate. While institutions like these could also be part of the repertoire of western kingdoms too, they typically had less permanence and efficacy in that region. So it is that we might characterize these northern and eastern kingdoms as 'cellular'—assemblages of provinces under loose royal headship. It is not insignificant that most of them were lumped into unions for much of the fifteenth century, nor that Poland came to be seen as a 'noble republic', a format more or less shared for a time by Sweden, Bohemia, Hungary, and Scotland.

Beyond these three zones lay the steppe empires of Lithuania and Moscow, both of them expanding to cover very large spaces during our period, and—further south—the sphere of the Byzantine empire, discussed in Chapter 7, which was gradually overrun (or reconstituted) by the Ottoman Turks from the 1320s onwards. Most of these vast territories were ruled in different ways from the areas on which this chapter focuses, though the trading cities of northern Russia and the eastern Mediterranean, such as Novgorod, Tver, Thessalonica, and the Levant, the polities of the Aegean, and the Balkan kingdoms of Serbia and Wallachia would certainly merit comparison with their western counterparts.

Patterns of conflict

We have seen that the political and governmental developments of the central Middle Ages both encouraged and enabled rulers to coordinate power and resources across large or populous spaces, and that these spaces possessed some historical, institutional, and cultural solidity. In other words, a series of polities—empires, kingdoms, principalities, leagues, city-states, and so on—existed across Europe even at the beginning of our period. At the same time, it is clear that these polities were highly contestable, both internally and externally, and that few of their features—even their boundaries—were fixed. Like the thirteenth century, the later Middle Ages were absolutely full of political conflict, and the aim of this section is to characterize, explore, and explain its patterns.

The fourteenth century is famous for international wars—perhaps, above all, the so-called Hundred Years War between England and France (1337–1453)—while the fifteenth century is better known for civil wars, coups, and plots. There is a rough and ready truth in these perceptions: the major conflicts of the period before about 1450 were more likely to involve the transformation of political geography and institutional organization than their equivalents in the last 50 years of our period. If we turn back to the decades around 1300, for instance, we can immediately identify a series of long-running and far-reaching confrontations. Between the 1290s and about the 1310s, the papacy was in conflict with the leading western rulers over the power to tax the church and to make major appointments; in 1302 it made a last-ditch attempt to assert its universal jurisdiction, with the claim in *Unam sanctam* that 'every human creature [must] be subject to the Roman pontiff'.[13] Up to the 1330s, the papacy was still trying to control affairs in the German lands of the empire, and was engaged in wars throughout northern Italy to advance its own power and that of its Angevin and Valois allies: it was possible that the whole peninsula would fall under Franco-papal rule, and that a French prince would become Holy Roman Emperor. At the same time, the English king, who had already conquered Wales, was trying to reduce Scotland and Ireland to obedience, while the king of France attempted to annexe Flanders and Gascony. Out of these confrontations came the Hundred Years War, the first phase of which ended in 1360 with the transfer of a third of the French kingdom to Edward III of England in the Treaty of Brétigny. Meanwhile, in the same 1280–1330 period, the kings of Aragon attempted to gain control of Sicily and Naples, the kings of Bohemia attempted to conquer Austria, Hungary, Silesia, Sandomierz, and Małopolska, while Władisław Lokietek and his successor, Casimir III, reunited the warring duchies of Poland and re-established the Polish kingdom. Some of these ventures succeeded, others failed, but their potential to override customary boundaries should not be missed. Many of them also gave rise to significant internal changes—a turn towards what has been called 'princely polyarchy' in France, for instance, as the crown

---

[13] B. Tierney, *The Crisis of Church and State, 1050–1300* (Toronto, 1988), p. 189.

suspended its hard-nosed pursuit of jurisdiction in favour of endowing its cadets with huge domains in the interests of defence (or expansion). In war-ravaged Sicily and Naples, meanwhile, there was the near-abandonment of centralized governance; and the papacy of the 'Avignon' era (1309–78) shifted towards accommodation with lay rulers, following the conflicts of Boniface VIII's reign, and intensified its management of ecclesiastical resources. Almost everywhere there was experimentation with new taxes and new modes of representation, as rulers rose and fell and populations were mobilized for attack or defence.

From about the middle of the fourteenth century, however, international conflicts gradually became more localized. The papacy stopped trying to control northern Italy and the German lands; the English were driven out of France, Scotland and most of Ireland; Holy Roman Emperors stopped invading Italy; the borders of kingdoms began to stabilize. It would certainly not do to overstate this trend—many of these conflicts were renewed between 1350 and 1450, and new ones broke out; much of Italy was overrun by Ladislas of Durazzo in 1413–14 and northern France by Henry V between 1415 and 1420; south-eastern Europe was conquered by the Ottomans in the later fourteenth century, and again from the 1420s onwards; the Latin church, which was itself a kind of polity, experienced revolutionary changes in the era of the Schism (1378–1417) and Councils (1409–49); Moravia, Silesia, and most of Austria were briefly conquered by the adventurer king of Hungary, Matthias Corvinus, in the 1470s and 1480s, and between 1482 and 1492, the newly united kingdoms of Castile and Aragon took over the Muslim realm of Granada. So there was plenty of change after 1350 or even 1450; but, dramatic as these episodes were, they did more to confirm existing trends in the development of European polities than to alter them. This was even more the case with the civil wars that struck almost every kingdom in the course of the fifteenth century. Although they were often bitter and lengthy—perhaps especially in the heretical kingdom of Bohemia from the 1410s to the 1450s, or in France between the 1400s and 1470s—civil wars affirmed the identities of the polities in which they occurred, and tended over the longer term to strengthen and consolidate them.

It is important to remember that these major conflicts on which the history books focus were just the tip of an iceberg of confrontation that marked every part of the continent and every political level; but there was, even so, a trend towards the stabilization of the political order, both within individual polities and (to some extent) between them. We need to consider why this was, but first of all it may be helpful to discuss the types of conflict experienced in Europe during the period. In the literature, there is an emphasis on natural competition for resources—and this is fine, as far as it goes, though we need to remember that, while it may be normal for individuals to compete for resources, the dynamics of group conflict are not the same, and there are always pressures for compliance with authority and adherence to principle. There is also a tendency among historians to emphasize succession disputes among the causes of conflict, but these can occur at any time and in any society, and they are typically associated with—even dependent upon—other kinds of conflict. By and large, the political conflicts of the later Middle Ages can be divided into two groups: conflicts of jurisdiction and conflicts of political community. The key difference between them is that the first kind of conflict was between parties that refused to accept each other's authority or right, whereas the second kind of conflict occurred when one party accepted a general subjection to the authority of the other, but challenged the way in which that authority was exercised. Clearly there was some overlap—the actions of an authority might seem all the more obnoxious to its subjects if they involved challenges to existing rights and customs—but the distinction is helpful because it captures something about the way in which political life was developing.

Jurisdictional conflicts were very common in the first half of our period, because every kind of power, ecclesiastical and secular, royal, provincial, and municipal, was developing its legal and administrative apparatus. Sometimes these were literally conflicts over the power to do justice—as, for example, when the French king asserted the jurisdiction of his court against the judicial claims of the duke of Gascony (i.e. the king of England) and the count of Flanders: these were the major causes of the Hundred Years War, alongside the similar assertions of the English king in Scotland, his acceptance of a vicariate (lieutenancy) from the Holy Roman Emperor over the Low Countries, and his advancement of a legal claim to the French throne itself in 1340 (which would rescue him from the justice of the Valois ruler). More widely, jurisdictional conflicts arose over other kinds of governmental assertion—over the right to tax, for instance, or to raise troops, or to control disputed territory. A good example of this kind of confrontation is the conflict between Boniface VIII, Philip IV, and Edward I over the right to tax the clergy in 1296–7. In this conflict, all parties could feel that right was on their side: the kings were defending their realms, of which the clergy formed part; they had been receiving ecclesiastical taxation on a regular basis for a long time beforehand; but the papacy had previously authorized such taxes, and now it wished to withdraw that authorization. These jurisdictional conflicts involved high-level players, but they were common at lower levels too, as lords and towns disputed rights to judge peasants and tax passing trade, or as oligarchs and citizens contested the organization of offices in towns. Quite often, different levels of conflict intersected, as the struggles of the towns of southern Germany to protect themselves from local nobles in the 1380s and 1390s became interwoven with the tussles between Emperor Wenceslas IV and the Electors, or as the struggles of lords and towns in early fourteenth-century Castile exploited, and were exploited by, the contenders in a disputed succession to the throne. It is not surprising, then, that the tendency of jurisdictional disputes was to ramify, pulling in potential allies from neighbouring conflicts, spreading uncertainty and violence ever wider. They reflected a first stage of institutional growth, and were shaped by the strongly legalistic and juridical emphasis of thirteenth-century political thought. This means that the root cause of thirteenth- and fourteenth-century wars was the 'legal-bureaucratic revolution' of the 'greatest of centuries'.

Conflicts of political community, on the other hand, reflected the development of more complex polities, in which smaller powers—towns, lords, churches, citizens, peasants—might be willing to accept a common authority, but were determined to negotiate or adjust the terms of that acceptance; these conflicts became more common as the period went on. Fuelled by powers of justice, taxation, and/or troop-raising, top-level authorities could be hard to resist, but the smaller powers around and beneath them could league together to protect customary rights or agree—through charters, laws, treaties, and assemblies—tolerable terms of engagement. Over time, the pressures of contingency—incompetent rulers, unaffordable wars, natural disasters—and the continuing elaboration of government (again, at every level) produced tensions and confrontations which the coordinating mechanisms of fourteenth- and fifteenth-century polities were unable to contain. The commonest kinds of conflicts of political community were popular revolts, magnate rebellions, and civil wars. Typically, indeed, these overlapped or combined—dissenting magnates, even when they were claimants to the throne (or to headship of a city or a church), usually tapped into grievances expressed by estates assemblies or common people—and while historians typically regard this kind of action as cynical, it is better understood as representative: whatever the motives or ambitions of individuals, they were obliged to raise public support, and their actions reflected public grievances. We can see examples of this kind of conflict in every political space. The fifteenth-century civil war in France, with which this chapter opened, reflected the inability of the regime of an enfeebled king to manage its leading subjects, or to contain tensions over taxation, foreign policy, and the distribution of power in towns and provinces. Other civil wars were similar—including the Hussite revolution in Bohemia (c.1415–c.1448), which followed several decades of conflict between the king and the nobility, and articulated tensions between Czechs and Germans and between towns, peasants, and lords, as well as a controversial process of religious reform. The mass uprising in the county of Flanders in the 1320s is another example—against the background of French invasion, the peasants of this prosperous region rose up against tax increases, while workers and manufacturers jostled with the owners of capital for control of the towns. Even the international church manifested this same kind of politics: the Schism of 1378 was partly caused by the crude reformism of Pope Urban VI, but his actions—and those of the conciliarists over the next seven decades—were driven by widespread (and conflicting) tensions among the clergy about the forms of papal government. Conflicts of political community could eddy out of control, crossing borders and becoming embroiled with other conflicts— as the fourteenth-century phase of the Hundred Years War, for instance, was at once a French civil war, a war between England and France, and an additional source of fuel to conflagrations in the Low Countries, Spain, and the Empire. To some extent, the same tendency to cross borders is apparent in fifteenth-century civil wars—certainly the war of Burgundians and Armagnacs, discussed above; also the civil wars in Castile (1438–45, c.1464–76), which pulled in Navarre in the 1440s and Portugal in the 1470s; or the Wars of the Roses in England (c.1450–c.1500), which intersected with conflicts in France, Scotland, Ireland, and the Burgundian lands. Even so, these wars were understood by contemporaries in highly nationalistic and constitutional terms: they arose in domestic protests and stimulated campaigns of domestic reform. As we shall see in the next section, their net effect was to confirm the development of more sophisticated and robust polities.

Consolidation

Governmental growth was not restricted to the thirteenth century, but persisted, and expanded, throughout our period. Early experiments with taxation, for example, could raise significant sums, but only occasionally:

regular taxation only became possible in large polities like kingdoms in the middle decades of the fourteenth century, and by the end of that century, their revenues had outstripped those of the richest cities. In the fifteenth century, the revenues of high-tax polities like the kingdom of France grew still higher, and were able to support both an elaborate infrastructure of princely pensions and—from the 1440s—a standing army, two resources which strengthened the king's hand in managing his massive realm. Similarly, if the thirteenth century was the starting point for most national and provincial assemblies, it was in the fourteenth century that these really flourished, meeting regularly and (in most places) enabling the growth in taxation just discussed, and also a significant expansion in regulation, through laws, ordinances, and statutes. Besides assemblies, the fourteenth and fifteenth centuries also witnessed the growth of councils and secretariats, to manage an increased volume of business and facilitate the influence of leading interests at the centre of government. At the same time, the courts and households of rulers, whether popes or kings, princes or urban leaders, became more substantial and permanent, providing a setting where ministers, magnates, and foreign visitors could mingle and offer informal advice to one another and the ruler. Beyond all this, there were developments in the raising of armies—made much more effective and manageable by developments in taxation—and in networks of office, which tended to proliferate, potentially increasing the number of local agents with an interest in the projects of the political centre.

In older literature, these instances of 'state growth' are assumed to have had a positive effect, leading naturally from the experiments of the central Middle Ages to the mature nation-states of the sixteenth century and beyond. But this approach has now been discarded. For one thing, it makes it very hard to explain the copious conflict of the later Middle Ages without recourse to external explanations, most of which have been shown to be unconvincing. Rather, it should be clear from everything discussed above that the growth of government itself was the major cause of political conflict. As every political unit developed legal, administrative, and constitutional resources, conflict between them was inevitable. Equally, the development of government raised political expectations and provided mechanisms which even groups with fewer resources to their name—such as peasants and workers—could exploit to press their concerns. It is true that the new resources of high-level authorities enabled them to assert themselves, and altered the stakes of any confrontation with lesser authorities, and this is why, in many parts of Europe, towns, churches, and lords accepted the rule of kings. But it is also important to acknowledge that there were areas where rulers could not create this competitive edge, where the political landscape remained variegated, and smaller powers could league together to protect their freedoms. The German lands are the classic example of this kind of region, and a number of historians have shown how an 'associative political culture', based on alliances, local assemblies, and feuding, tended to prevent the formation of larger political blocs which could compel or negotiate obedience.[14] In northern Italy and the Low Countries, powerful cities could resist the relatively distant authority of popes, emperors, and neighbouring kings, but here a number of effective principalities did develop—the 'territorial states' of Milan, Venice, and Florence, for example, which conquered the smaller cities and countryside surrounding them in the first half of the fifteenth century, or the counties of Flanders, Hainault, and Holland, and the duchy of Brabant, moulded into a large and state-like principality by the Valois dukes of Burgundy in mid-century. These principalities may be better understood as '*bricolages*'—loose assemblies of smaller units—than as mini-kingdoms; but, as we have seen, kingdoms themselves were often weakly coordinated, especially in the thirteenth and fourteenth centuries. Overall, then, the picture is quite equivocal, particularly before the fifteenth century. Even where kings could prevail, they could not necessarily prevail for long. Wars to suppress opponents could go badly wrong, and more emollient devices—representative assemblies which addressed complaints, endowments of land or money to loyal subjects—could be turned against the ruler, hemming him in with charters or councils, challenging his handling of the fisc, or using his gifts to raise the regions in opposition. No king could live forever, and every change of regime brought in new uncertainties and opportunities for challenge; and collective regimes, such as the governments of Italian city republics, were no better—changes of personnel were more normal, but they often involved factional strife and constitutional innovation. These were the pressures that pushed Florence, for example, into allowing the informal hegemony of the Albizzi and then the Medici, but such developments faced the city with all the problems of monarchy, as well as those of corporate rule.

And yet, behind the ebb and flow of individual political regimes, there is a discernible trajectory towards political consolidation at a regional or national level. We have already seen that outright clashes of jurisdiction

[14] D. Hardy, *Associative Political Culture in the Holy Roman Empire: Upper Germany, 1346–1521* (Oxford, 2018).

became less common and conflicts of political community more common as the fourteenth century gave way to the fifteenth. We have seen that more countries acquired stable boundaries, and that larger formations of more or less contiguous territory were able to develop in the fifteenth century, even in the apparently unpropitious setting of the imperial core (even in the German lands a number of quite sizeable and durable principalities grew up during the course of the period—Bavaria, Brandenburg, the Palatinate of the Rhine, the lands of the 'house of Austria' are examples—while the Empire itself acquired more stable and convincing leadership, from the well-endowed Habsburgs and the regular meetings of reform-minded *Reichstage*). Single-town city states became a thing of the past, and even town leagues—notably the Hansa—tended to subside and be absorbed into surrounding polities. The reasons for these developments are multiple. One, long noted, is the growing fiscal and military capacity of the larger centres— a capacity which is now understood to be more than a matter of tax and standing armies, and to include control of credit and the enlisting of major commercial interests. A second factor lies in the practice of politics: the repeated experience of confrontation and negotiation between rulers and communities created a kind of constitutional fabric in each polity, which— especially from the later fourteenth century onwards—came to be celebrated in national literatures, works of history, and (by the fifteenth century) constitutional treatises. Arguably, too, the mechanisms of incorporation deployed by states became more sophisticated and less liable to provoke explosions—better-targeted taxation, better means for influencing policy, modes of local government that struck more manageable compromises between central direction and local interest, forms of social regulation that enlisted hierarchies against less controllable solidarities. The later fifteenth century has often been seen as an era of 'new monarchy' or rising 'princes', and there is something in this hackneyed image; but we need to remember that the more stable polities of the period were more collaborative than older accounts suggest, and that they were built by the multiple actions of political societies, not by rulers alone.

Europe in 1500

By 1500, most of the inhabitants of Europe lived in relatively fixed and stable polities, with fairly complex institutions of government, at least regional in scope, and often covering large areas. The seeds of this dispensation had been laid in the central Middle Ages, but the effervescent politics of our period had played a crucial part in the growth and development of these regimes. The historians of the early modern period are now rather hostile to the older picture of a Europe of nation states in which the present narrative may appear to culminate. They tend to emphasize the power of dynasties— Valois, Habsburg, Jagiellon—rather than the solidity of kingdoms and principalities; they identify 'composite monarchies' and 'unions' as the key players on the sixteenth-century stage.[15] Of course, it matters a great deal that Sicily, Naples, and Aragon were lastingly joined together with Castile and its Atlantic holdings in the fifteenth century, and that this agglomeration—joined by American colonies—was attached to the Netherlands and Austria in the sixteenth century (though it matters some-what less that Denmark and Norway had the same kings, and so did Bohemia and what was left of Hungary, and that they were closely related to the kings of Poland-Lithuania). It is also true that new solvents to the hardening structures of later medieval polities emerged in the later fifteenth and sixteenth centuries—the intensifying world of Renaissance diplomacy, for one, the Reformations and the rise of transnational confessions, for another. But this more nuanced picture of early modern politics does not contradict the developments we have been exploring: the polities of our period were the components of the 'composite states' of the following century, and they were a great deal more coherent and developed than the political forms of the thirteenth century and before. The later Middle Ages, so long seen as an era of chaos, deserves to be understood rather differently—as a time of growing government and lively politics, a combin-ation which thickened the constitutional texture in every European polity.

[15] J. H. Elliott, 'A Europe of Composite Monarchies?', *Past and Present* 137 (1992), pp. 48–71; R. I. Frost, 'Unions, States and Nations: a Historical Perspective', *British Academy Review* 31 (2017), pp. 36–41.

Plate 3. *A three-masted Mediterranean carrack* (fifteenth century)

2

The economy

*Stephan R. Epstein (with Christopher Dyer)**

The economic history of the late Middle Ages is substantially better documented than that of earlier ages, thanks to thirteenth-century improvements
in private and public law and administration and commercial organization,
and to the growth in urban literacy and numeracy and the increased
availability of writing paper. It is also substantially more complex, in that
it includes no fewer than three distinct sub-periods: the tail of a secular wave
of demographic and urban growth, economic expansion, and growing
international trade associated with the late twelfth and thirteenth-century
'commercial revolution', that came to an end in the early 1300s; a century or
more of demographic, economic, and social 'crisis', 'involution', 'depression', and 'structural change' ending in the mid- to late 1400s; and the first
stages of a new, more dynamic, market-oriented, early capitalist upswing
that lasted to the early 1600s. Consequently, interpretations of such a
complex era have been intensely controversial.

Recently, these controversies have lost some of their edge as economic
historians have reconsidered previous methods and assumptions. This revi-
sionism can be subsumed under four headings. First, the fundamental issues
of agricultural production have been reformulated more precisely in terms
of 'five long-enduring dilemmas': the 'ecological dilemma' of avoiding
overcropping and overgrazing and maintaining an adequate balance of
nutrients in the soil; the 'Ricardian dilemma' of diminishing returns on
land and labour; the 'Malthusian dilemma' of controlling the balance
between population and agricultural output; the 'tenurial dilemma' of how
to deliver the best returns to land, labour, and capital under prevailing
property rights to land; and the 'entitlements dilemma' of how and to
whom to transfer the fruits of production. Second, more attention is being
paid to trade and exchange, to services and manufacturing, to urban

* Stephan Epstein wrote the chapter and prepared the tables and figures; Christopher Dyer
added the last paragraph and the section in 'Further Reading'.

economies, and to economic institutions defined more broadly than simply who owned or controlled the land; there is a stronger focus on economic incentives for production, and a less pessimistic opinion of medieval peasants' productive capacities. Third, there is greater interest in comparison. On the one hand, the comparative method is essential for testing alternative causal claims; on the other, historians now assume that the answer to the old question of whether there was a single 'European' economy or a set of disarticulated local and regional economies can only be found by comparing regional patterns. Fourth, there has been an important change in chronological perspective. The late medieval economy is now situated squarely within broader debates on the performance of 'premodern' economies in Europe and the rest of Eurasia between the years 1000 and 1800. In this context, the late Middle Ages are increasingly viewed as the era when the European economy began to take on the technological and institutional features that would allow it first to catch up with, and then forge ahead of, the most advanced regions elsewhere in Eurasia. Between 1250 and 1550 the economy of Europe changed fundamentally, and this chapter will show how.

Population

Towards the end of the thirteenth century, after over three centuries of growth and a more than doubling in population size, the first signs of demographic fatigue became apparent. One century or so later, the continent's population was one third to one half smaller—evidence, for many historians, of a fundamental inability of the medieval society and economy to feed and clothe its people without incurring a 'Malthusian' crisis. Yet, if we move forward another century, many countries had recovered all their intervening losses, and the population in Brabant, the future Dutch Republic, and Poland was even larger. Although France and parts of Scandinavia had to wait to the 1550s to recover fully, and England substantially longer (see Table 2.1), a comparison of population numbers in 1300 and 1550 might suggest that little had happened, demographically, in the intervening years, and that talk of a systemic crisis two centuries earlier is overblown.

Population size in our period experienced three very different phases: an initial *inflection*, lasting from the 1280s to the early 1340s, marked by increasing economic hardship and by a slowing or inversion of growth in numbers; a long-drawn-out *collapse*, beginning with the Black Death of

Table 2.1. Population of European lands, 1300–1550

	1300	1400	1500	1550
Scandinavia	1.8	1.2	1.5	1.7
England and Wales, Scotland, Ireland	5.0	3.0	3.5	5.2
Netherlands	0.8	0.6	1.0	1.3
Belgium	1.3	1.0	1.3	1.7
Germany	14.0	9.0	9.5	13.5
France	19.0	7.0	10.0	19.0
Switzerland	0.8	0.4	0.6	0.8
Italy	12.5	8.0	9.0	11.5
Spain	4.0	3.0	4.7	5.2
Portugal	1.3	0.9	1.2	1.2
Western Europe	60.5	34.1	42.31	61.1
Austria, Bohemia, Hungary	6.7	5.4	6.6	7.1
Poland	3.5	2.8	4.0	3.0
Balkans	6.0	4.5	6.0	6.0
Romania	2.5	2.0	2.5	2.5
Russia (European)	13.0	10.0	13.5	15.5
East-central Europe	31.7	24.7	32.6	34.1
TOTAL	96.2	61.8	77.7	97.4

1347–52 and reaching its nadir some time in the early or mid-fifteenth century; followed by a long phase of sustained *recovery* and *expansion* lasting to the late 1580s or 1590s.

Most short-term crises during the first period were caused by poor weather and military instability, which caused diseases to surge in the wake of food shortages and drove poorly immunized rural immigrants to the better-supplied towns. Neither set of factors followed a uniform pattern. Between 1315 and 1317 a series of wet springs and summers rotted harvests and spread murrain in Germany, the Low Countries, and the northern half of France. The great Flemish towns of Bruges and Ypres lost a tenth of their population; in England, the resulting catastrophic Great Famine (whose effects were felt until 1322) caused the death of perhaps 10–15 per cent of the rural population, and has been described as the true turning point in the medieval economy. By contrast, southern and Mediterranean Europe experienced neither climatic deterioration nor famine in those years; the structural crisis of the medieval economy seemingly passed it by. Famines did occur in the western Mediterranean—Italy experienced major subsistence crises in 1328, 1339–40, and 1346–7—but were apparently more localized, possibly because more efficient urban markets helped transfer food supplies more effectively between surplus and deficient areas.

Long-run trends in population are the outcome of short-term mortality, in- and out-migration, and regulation of birth rates. Whatever the incidence of each individual factor, their aggregate result varied substantially across late medieval regions. Demographic decline before the Black Death is reasonably well attested for parts of central and southern Italy (Tuscany may have hit its demographic peak in the 1290s), Navarre, northern France, and parts of England, but was matched by continued population growth elsewhere in England and in Lombardy, parts of Catalonia, lower Provence, and Flanders. In central and southern Castile the thirteenth-century *reconquista* opened up unsettled lands for which the number of immigrants was too small and, not surprisingly, symptoms of a Malthusian crisis (stagnant or declining population, volatile and rising prices, land fragmentation) were muted. The size of the losses is anyhow hard to define, because we only have snapshots of conditions that could change quickly. In pre-Black Death Navarre and Provence, for example, the sizes of rural and urban communities varied substantially from year to year as a result of strong migratory flows caused by pestilence, warfare, and other factors. Attributing every individual loss to death rather than out-migration, therefore, can cause losses from the Black Death to be overestimated; high rates of mobility, for example, might help explain the substantial discrepancies in population estimates for early fourteenth-century England, which range from a peak of 6 million (based on top-down comparisons of tax data before and after the Black Death) to 4.5–5 million (based on more plausible bottom-up estimates of agricultural output).

Differences in the chronology and intensity of decline may have been even greater in the century after the Black Death. Florence lost up to half its population between March and September 1348; the area around Milan was spared. Some more peripheral regions like Bohemia, parts of Poland and European Russia, Finland, northern Sweden, Iceland, and Greenland escaped the Black Death entirely; others like northern England and Scotland, Ireland, and Hungary did not—in Norway population losses are estimated at 60–65 per cent. Most core European regions in the triangle between southern England, Germany, and Portugal experienced losses between 30 and 40 per cent (but the proportion was closer to 50 per cent in England); Castile, by contrast, was mostly spared. There was a 'second plague' in 1361–3 in the west and Mediterranean regions, followed by renewed, scattered outbreaks until the late 1390s; between 1399 and 1401 a major crisis hit above all France, Italy, and the Low Countries, while other regions were apparently passed by.

Over time, however, the incidence of these attacks slowly declined, possibly because of increased immunity among the population. Recovery in most regions began in the 1460s and 1470s, but still there was great variation: there are signs of population growth already in the 1430s in the Lyonnais and Sicily, and perhaps earlier in Castile, whereas the demographic upturn in Norway, Normandy, and England only began well into the sixteenth century. Once started, however, recovery was swift; by about 1550, population in most countries was at least as large as in 1300. The only major exception was England, which—for as yet unexplained reasons— fully regained its pre-Black Death size only by 1700, by which date its economy was fundamentally transformed.

Explaining the crisis

To understand why demographic decline and recovery varied so extensively over time and space, we must examine how late medieval societies produced and distributed basic food supplies in the face of climatic and epidemic shocks they could not control. The demographic crises of the fourteenth and early fifteenth centuries were long believed to be the unavoidable outcome of the Ricardian, ecological, and Malthusian 'dilemmas' recalled above. In this view, the period between the 1280s and the 1340s marked a watershed for the agrarian economy. Due to primitive technology and low rates of investment, the only way to feed the growing population was to extend cultivation to new lands—but by the late thirteenth century European societies had run out of fertile land and were pushing increasingly onto agriculturally unsuitable territories, subject to rapidly diminishing returns. At the same time, lords responded to rising military costs by imposing ever harsher demands on the peasantry, who reduced capital investments and agricultural output even further. Increased famine pushed peasants and urban wage-earners to their physiological limits. Food deprivation raised mortality and prepared the ground for the Black Death. The feudal economy entered a period of involution, and the Black Death brought the crisis of an entire society to a head.

Attention has turned to the opportunities and incentives related to local, regional, and international patterns of trade; to the factors—war, purveyance, taxation—that increased transaction costs or interrupted trade flows altogether. Other, more positive influences included agricultural stimulation of urban demand, and the urban and rural manufactures that peasants bought in exchange. Markets in land, labour, and credit also could raise labour productivity and mitigate economic shocks.

Earlier discussions focussed overwhelmingly, and misleadingly, on grain production. It is now understood that already by 1300 the cereal share of GNP of even a comparatively underdeveloped economy like England's was less than 40 per cent, and that the proportion must have been significantly lower in more advanced economies like those of Italy and Flanders. Clearly, rural dwellers faced a substantial range of occupational alternatives to simple grain production, including pastoral activities for wool (which accounted for up to a third of rural output in early fourteenth-century England), meat, dairy and leather, tree crops, and various kinds of by-employment in manufactures and services. The increased fragmentation of peasant holdings observed during the period, which is often interpreted as a sign of growing poverty, can just as plausibly be taken as evidence of growing opportunities for non-agrarian employment.

Older generalizations about the low levels of medieval agricultural prod-uctivity have also been questioned. By the 1320s Norfolk and Kentish peasants had achieved levels of land productivity that were only regained during the eighteenth century. In thirteenth-century Tuscany, land prod-uctivity increased steadily thanks to investments in drainage, reorganization of plots, the planting of higher-value crops, and improvements in transport and distribution that required no major technical change. Such gains led to a rough doubling of the total population and a tripling of the proportion of urban residents, levels that Tuscany would only recover after 1800. Similar performances are recorded for northern France, Flanders, the lower Rhineland, and Valencia's irrigated *huerta*. Although the number of agri-culturally advanced regions was still rather small, their existence—and the fact that agricultural output was still rising before the Black Death in several regions including Norfolk, Kent, southern Germany, Castile, and Lombardy—challenge the view that the economic 'crisis' was unavoidable.

This brief survey also suggests that levels of economic development before the Black Death must have varied substantially across western Europe. A crude but simple way of establishing this is to estimate different countries' 'carrying rate' by measuring the number of inhabitants per unit of agricul-tural land, including pasture (Table 2.2); this carrying rate reflects agricul-tural productivity in a predominantly agricultural economy, or the capacity to trade manufactures and services for food in a predominantly industrial or

Table 2.2. Inhabitants/km^2 of agricultural land in Europe, 1300–1550

	1300	1500	1550
Scandinavia	24.3	24.3	23.0
England	115.0	61.4	63.9
Wales, Scotland, Ireland	50.2	47.8	55.0
Netherlands	107.4	127.5	167.8
Belgium	138.9	138.9	183.3
Germany	90.7	90.7	120.9
France	86.9	92.4	103.2
Switzerland	190.3	149.7	203.0
Italy	141.6	128.8	146.8
Spain	29.5	34.6	38.3
Portugal	78.6	75.5	75.5
Poland	28.6	32.6	24.5
Western Europe	77.5	75.3	87.7
Western Europe and Poland	70.2	68.9	78.2

service-driven economy. Thus, mountainous Switzerland's high carrying rate expresses its capacity to compensate for a relative lack of arable by exporting livestock and animal produce (and increasingly, from the fifteenth century, labourers, skilled workers, and mercenaries who generated substantial remittances); the high carrying rates of late medieval Italy and 'Belgium' (mainly Flanders and Brabant) express, instead, more industrial and service-oriented economies.

Although national aggregates are composed of many, diverse regional profiles, this rough and ready estimation suggests, plausibly, that Europe in 1300 had three sorts of economy. The economic vanguard, occupied by geographically semi-peripheral but trade-intensive countries, included the Low Countries, Switzerland, and north-central Italy. The intermediate rank was occupied by a feudal core including Portugal, Catalonia and Aragon, southern Italy, France, and much of Germany and England. The least developed regions were geographically peripheral, underpopulated and partly feudalised, and included Eastern Europe, Spain, Scandinavia, and the Celtic fringe.

The most plausible reason for these substantial differences in carrying capacity was a country's degree of commercial development, which was strongly shaped by its degree of feudalization. The economic vanguard, with well-developed overland and maritime transport routes, strong concentrated demand in politically powerful towns, and comparatively low tariffs and stable political conditions, was generally under-feudalized. The

20–40 per cent lower carrying rates of the more heavily feudalized societies suggests that they were commercially less developed than the core regions, possibly because feudalized societies found it harder to organize and coordinate markets than strong towns. Regions lacking both powerful towns and powerful lords had the lowest carrying rates—presumably because their powers of market organization and coordination were even weaker— although they also had abundant natural resources to expand into.

Interestingly, the most serious symptoms of an economic crisis before the Black Death were felt in the areas where feudal power was most entrenched and where the risks and consequences of warfare for trade and investment were felt most severely. The growing incidence of feudal and royal taxation and purveyance in Europe's feudal core, especially in France and England, caused by intensified warfare from the 1280s and 1290s reduced the agricultural surplus for peasants to reinvest, and caused commercial disruption. Increased market instability was reflected in the growing volatility of grain prices. Price instability is the effect of poor short-term supplies, and poor short-term supplies can be due to both bad harvests and interrupted transport systems. However, since the climate got worse after 1350 yet grain prices were more quiescent, it seems likely that the main source of price volatility from the 1280s onwards was political and institutional rather than agricultural. Indeed, except under extreme conditions, price volatility is less a reflection of absolute levels of supply than a measure of the efficiency with which a society distributes and allocates available food. One of the more striking features of the crisis of 1315–17 is the fact that north-west Europe did not import any grain from the Mediterranean where it was available— not, it would seem, for lack of adequate shipping, but because of heightened maritime insecurity.

What is more, supply irregularities mattered more to late medieval people than absolute shortages, because individuals seldom die of starvation and persistently low levels of food intake do not generally raise susceptibility to crisis mortality; by contrast, sharp fluctuations in food intake associated with high price variation *do* increase susceptibility to infectious disease. But the absence of effective mechanisms to mitigate unexpected falls in income was also problematic. Some historians suggest that the catastrophe of 1315–17 could have been averted if the peasantry had been able to call on their main store of movable wealth, livestock, to raise cash for food—or, lacking that, if they had had access to effective credit markets that could tide them over hardship. Others point to the absence of effective welfare systems that could help the most needy—the small peasants, the crofters, the less skilled wage labourers and their families. Most rural and urban poor obtained support from family, confraternity, or guild, and from occasional small distributions by religious institutions; but these largely ad hoc, small-scale networks could easily collapse in the face of a major, unexpected crisis. In England, for example, a more extensive support system for the rural poor based on local parishes began to be mooted in some parts of the country only after the Black Death.

However, even well-developed welfare systems could be counterproductive if they relied on unbalanced entitlements. In the most advanced and urbanized regions of late medieval Europe, the larger towns had developed systems for collecting and storing cereals against the threat of famine, underpinned by political and legal powers over their hinterlands. Townspeople received the grain at subsidized prices, while rural populations received nothing. When dearth struck, hungry peasants moved to nearby towns in search of bread, raising prices, disrupting the social fabric, putting their hosts' food and labour markets and sanitation under stress, and exposing themselves to virulent pathogens they were unused to—thus bringing about the very conditions they had fled the countryside to avoid. In sum, the 'general' or 'demographic' crisis that stalked parts of western Europe from the 1280s onwards, and the huge volatility in the price of basic food that is synonymous with it, reflects those societies' poor organizational and commercial structures rather than their technical inability to produce enough food.

After the Black Death

Much of the debate on the late medieval economy has concentrated on the extent to which—despite significant regional differences—the fall in population changed the bargaining power between lords, peasants, and labourers, leading to lower rents and improved living standards for the poor. These improvements are well attested. Personal consumption of more expensive food such as meat, fruit, and vegetables, of dairy products and beer (in central and northern Europe), and of wine and olive oil (in the Mediterranean south) rose sharply, while probate inventories, dowry lists, and archaeological excavations show marked increases in the use of cheap cloth, crockery, wooden utensils, and suchlike. The changes are rarely quantifiable, but several aggregate measures—such as individuals' heights based on excavated skeletons—support the view that food intake improved substantially for a large proportion of the population. For example, between 1341 and 1398 Genoa's population fell from 60,000–65,000 to 36,000–40,000 (a loss of 40 per cent), and tolls on foreign cloth imports collapsed by 61 per cent (probably as a result of the Genoese defeat by Venice at the battle of Chioggia in 1381, which badly hit Genoa's foreign trade); but tolls on local cloth consumption rose by 3 per cent and those on wine consumption fell by only 25 per cent. Another, 'rough and ready' measure of changing living standards is based on the difference between rates of growth of the urban sector (which reflects an economy's degree of specialization and productivity) and of the total population. This estimate suggests, consistently with the narrative literature, that living standards in Italy improved by about 30 per cent between 1300 and 1500, although most of the gains were in the south. In England, consistently with recent estimates that average English incomes nearly doubled between 1300 and 1470, the method suggests that average living standards improved by 60–70 per cent between the 1330s and the 1520s. As we shall see, late medieval England's considerably larger gains over Italy are not just evidence that poor countries can grow faster than wealthy ones if they are merely catching up—but are very much a harbinger of the future.

The oft-quoted description of the late Middle Ages as the 'golden age of the peasant and labourer' is, therefore by and large correct. But those gains were substantially reversed during the subsequent demographic upswing as rents rose and wage labour became cheaper; and to concentrate exclusively on them—important as they are—would be to lose sight of perhaps more significant changes in fundamental economic structure. Uneven development and the variety of responses to hardship before the Black Death suggest that the economic dynamic of feudalism was driven by two forces, production for trade and political centralization that lowered the costs of trade. Since the late eleventh century, increasingly powerful political and economic forces had been pressing for territorial and jurisdictional integration. Those pressures were coming to a head towards the end of the thirteenth century, as two Hundred Years Wars broke out in the feudal core between England and France, and Catalonia–Aragon, Sicily, and Naples and spilled over into their economically more developed neighbours. The fourteenth-century Black Death turned this process into a wave of economic, technological, and organizational 'creative destruction'. Over and above the periodic setbacks in production and trade, three features stand out from comparing the early fourteenth and the early sixteenth centuries: first, an undeniable deepening and broadening of the market, with an attendant increase in the complexity of trade; second, a deepening, broadening, and (arguably) quickening of technological change; and third, a shift of Europe's economic dynamo northwards from Italy towards central and northern Europe.

Market integration

Tariffs, tolls, and measures

The political, jurisdictional, and territorial consolidation of late medieval states, discussed elsewhere in this volume, also helped lower the costs of trade. At its simplest, jurisdictional integration into a larger territory had the same effect as joining a customs union—it lowered feudal and urban tariffs, raised domestic competition, and intensified deflationary pressures, especially on cheaper commodities on which transport costs weighed heavily. Political integration also provided opportunities for monetary integration and for standardizing measures. Monetary agreements between independent lords and towns had been common during the twelfth and thirteenth centuries, but the pace quickened after the mid-fourteenth century. Monetary unions flourished after the Black Death in Alsace, Swabia, Franconia, in the Upper Rhineland and the Netherlands, and elsewhere in south-western and western Germany. In Italy, coinage by individual city-states was supplanted by that of territorially dominant cities like Milan, Florence and Venice. In France, the royal silver *blanc* began to compete for hegemony over monetary regions that had themselves only recently emerged from feudal fragmentation. Inasmuch as political fragmentation was more likely to lead to competitive devaluation, political integration may also have reduced the incidence of monetary debasement. The growing use of gold coinage for large internal and international payments also made trade less susceptible to local abuse. In the course of the fourteenth century the Florentine florin and the Venetian ducat became benchmarks for national gold currencies elsewhere; only England, the fifteenth-century Rhineland principalities, and briefly France produced gold coins to a different standard. In the north European Hansa trading area, gold coins account for one fifth of all hoards in the fourteenth century, but the proportion rises to four fifths in the fifteenth.

The proliferation of local measurements that typified post-Carolingian Europe was a constant source of commercial friction and a major source of fraud. But measures were also one of the most visible attributes of sovereignty, and their regulation and simplification was an important sign of state power. Thus, even though extreme localism made unification little more than a dream, efforts to establish common 'regional' or 'national' measurements intensified after 1350. Even in England, where the monarchy had been acting to unify the country's measures for centuries, the enforcement of common national standards became a matter of growing concern during the fourteenth century.

A well-established though more circuitous way to lower tariffs and the associated customs formalities that was very popular among towns and large trading companies like the Ravensburger Gesellschaft and the Augsburg Walser was to seek toll exemptions with their main foreign and domestic counterparts. These agreements, which intensified during the late fourteenth and fifteenth centuries as patterns of trade between towns became more settled and predictable, differed from standard merchant franchises by being restricted to specific communities rather than applying indiscriminately to an entire country. Finally, the ancient law of reprisal, which made a debtor's countrymen collectively liable for his misdeeds, disappeared during the fifteenth and early sixteenth centuries. As legal systems became more formalized, commercial laws more sophisticated, and state jurisdictions less contested, individual responsibility replaced collective liability and the costs and benefits of trade were more clearly apportioned.

Grain markets

Some of the clearest evidence that late medieval markets were becoming safer, more predictable, and more competitive comes from the price of a staple food, wheat, sold on urban markets. Between the 1280s and the 1340s, prices had been extraordinarily volatile, with average changes from one year to the next of 50 per cent or more. From the late 1370s, after the end of a great pan-European famine, volatility slowly fell. Prices stabilized and converged mainly because producers stopped growing cereals on less productive land, military security increased, and customs dues fell inside territorial states. More stable and predictable prices improved consumer welfare because wages were 'sticky' and did not respond quickly to sharp rises in the cost of food, and because they made it less risky for peasants and farmers to specialize, which reduced average costs. Importantly, these improvements occurred when the *total* size of the grain trade was falling due to population losses, and were not reversed when the population recovered.

Although agricultural markets became more integrated *within* most regions, integration *between* regions was less clear-cut. Between the thirteenth and sixteenth centuries, political authorities introduced a range of price and trade controls over bread grains to dampen price volatility and ensure regular supplies. Urban regulation included a variety of public storage systems, price controls, and subsidies that aimed to stabilize bread prices for urban consumers; these measures were probably trade-neutral. Territorial regulation by states, on the other hand, aimed to maintain low average prices through export bans and import bounties; it was generally defensive and protectionist and quite probably reduced trade. Whereas domestic controls varied substantially in extent and effectiveness, controls over the export trade were more similar across Europe and were also largely successful.

Regional fairs

The growing capacity of late medieval states to enforce contracts through their territories contributed to a sharp rise in the number of seasonal and annual fairs after 1350. These fairs, often benefiting from toll exemptions and other tax privileges, were mostly held in small towns and villages engaged in pastoral and proto-industrial activities, and they supplied the organizational backbone to an emerging continental trading system connecting local, regional, and continental markets.

Animal husbandry was strongly seasonal and was usually situated far from urban markets; it therefore suffered particularly from poor trade networks. As demand for animal products increased after the mid-fourteenth century and depopulated uplands converted to pasture, those problems became more acute. Fairs set up where uplands and lowlands joined up helped minimize travel distance. In northern Lombardy, for example, a circuit of half a dozen new fairs at the foot of the Alps attracted livestock and horse merchants from the inner Swiss cantons, Piedmont, the Veneto, and the southern Lombard plain. Outside Italy a complex system of rural and urban fairs governed the cattle trade in the Low Countries and in west-central Germany; in the region of Sologne, in the duchy of Orléans, the expanding pastoral economy was served by at least five distinct fairs. Between 1470 and 1520 many of these events linked up into transcontinental networks that moved thousands of cattle from Scandinavia and east-central Europe to metropolitan markets in the Low Countries, west Germany, and northern Italy. Other regional fairs, like those of Mons in Hainaut, of Romorantin, Courmesmin, Châlons in France, of Petronell in Austria, and of Colchester and Coventry in England, were better known for medium-quality wool or linen cloth. But no fair ever specialized entirely in one commodity. Large quantities of wool and hemp cloth, metal ore, and salt were traded at the livestock fairs of Briançon; the two fairs of Reims dealt extensively in both cattle and wine; the cattle fair in the Sicilian town of Randazzo was known for cheap linen and fustian cloth; and the fairs of Lanciano in the Abruzzo dealt in saffron, cloth, leather, metalwork, and luxury goods imported by Venetians in addition to cattle and pigs.

Fair networks, which emerged through a slow process of trial and error, reduced the costs of search and coordination, improved information about commodity and credit markets, and made it easier to monitor contracts. Traders could buy up commodities wholesale at one fair for shipment elsewhere, dispose of manufactures to local intermediaries, and settle accounts at a neighbouring fair later on in the season. Since fairs offered scale economies in carriage and handling, membership of a network increased each individual fair's profitability and success. Thus, fairs bred more fairs. Castile had four distinct systems of connected fairs: in Galicia and the Cantabrian mountains, Castile and Léon, New Castile and Estremadura, and Andalusia and Murcia. Southern Italian regions—Sicily, the Abruzzi-Molise, Puglia, Calabria, and Lucania, and the Tyrrhenian coast north of Calabria—had their own fair system. In Lombardy, most of the 14 fairs strung across the northern lowlands were established after 1400 to serve the growing Alpine trade. In France, regional fairs are recorded for the Forez after the 1330s, Languedoc after 1350, and Brittany and Burgundy after 1400. In Flanders, new fairs were established in the 1360s under count Louis of Male and then again during the fifteenth century; in the northern Low Countries they proliferated in the late fourteenth and early fifteenth centuries under the counts of Holland. Similar developments took place in fifteenth-century Switzerland, Germany, and Poland.

England differed from this broadly similar continental experience on two counts. First, before the Black Death both markets and fairs were much more numerous than anywhere else in Europe, with English kings granting over 1,500 fairs between 1200 and 1349. The difference is even more remarkable in the light of England's small population of 4.5 to 5 million, compared to 11–13 million in Italy and perhaps 20 million in France, around 1300. Second, after the mid-fourteenth century dozens of English fairs disappeared without trace. In contrast with continental Europe, new fairs were seldom granted and a large proportion of the new concessions went to established marketplaces, the larger towns and boroughs. Despite this, regional and interregional trade, particularly in livestock but also in grain, wool, cloth, fuel, and building materials, appear to have increased.

The origin of these differences was institutional and political. Whereas the English monarchy had established its prerogatives over markets by the late twelfth century or before, most continental states only did so during the fourteenth and early fifteenth. In England, the combination of early political centralization, strong manorialism, and rather weak powers of towns (which elsewhere opposed new markets and fairs) made it possible for feudal lords to negotiate directly with the king—such that by the late thirteenth century the supply of markets and fairs in England exceeded strictly commercial needs. On the continent, regional fairs faced more powerful opposition by towns and more fragmented princely authority, and so were costlier to establish. Before the Black Death, England's peculiar institutional arrangements gave rise to an unusually dense network of rural markets and fairs. Compared to the regional fairs established in continental Europe after 1350, however, most English fairs before the Black Death were little more than glorified local markets. After 1350, as the more recently established and commercially fragile events disappeared, the remaining fairs in England began to resemble their continental counterparts in terms of size and specialisation.

Proto-industry

The growth of village and small town manufactures selling to regional and supraregional markets—frequently at the fairs just outlined—is a well-documented feature across much of late medieval Europe, including Flanders, Brabant, and Holland, Essex, Suffolk, Wiltshire, the West Country, and Yorkshire, east Switzerland, the German Rhineland, Silesia and Bohemia, Normandy, the Forez, Provence and Languedoc, Catalonia, Aragon and parts of New Castile, Sicily, Umbria, Lombardy, the Veneto, and Piedmont. As usual, total numbers are hard to come by, but a recent survey of English milling finds that the proportion of industrial mills used for cloth- or leather-making or the beating of metals as opposed to grinding grain rose from 6–7.5 per cent in 1300–1348 to 12.2 per cent c.1400, to 15.9 per cent c.1500–1510 and 23.3 per cent in 1530–40, despite a surprisingly small decline in the total number over the same period.

Like the better known proto-industry of the late seventeenth and eighteenth century, its late medieval predecessor was mostly situated in small to medium-sized settlements and in dispersed farms and homesteads, and employed mainly low-skilled and unskilled labour. Although late medieval proto-industry was smaller in scale and more concentrated in the textile sector than its early modern version, its expansion was seldom the cause of straightforward decline in urban competitors. Rather than destroying regulated manufacture in the towns, both late medieval and early modern proto-industrial competition forced urban, guild-based industries to convert to higher-quality products that used town workers' greater technical skills.

Proto-industrial opportunities after the Black Death were generally good. Capital requirements for cheap cloth-making were low, many peasants had basic spinning and weaving skills, cheap wool, flax, and water to power fulling mills were easily accessible, and popular demand for clothing was high and rising. However, late medieval proto-industry was not just a reaction to low production costs and growing consumer demand, or even the natural outcome of earlier patterns of urban putting-out. It was a fundamental component of the institutional, economic, and technological 'creative destruction' referred to above.

First, the rise of new textile industries forced a new division of labour between 'town' and 'country'. Initially, urban producer guilds in the Low Countries, France, parts of Iberia, and north-central Italy responded to proto-industrial upstarts by outlawing competitors in their hinterland. These measures could be successful—in Tuscany, the Florentine woollen makers stopped non-urban production in its tracks—but over time most guild controls were circumvented. The crafts' more effective response was to diversify into new fabrics, fashions, and industries like silk or high-quality linen, and to offer technically sophisticated finishing services to the proto-industries themselves. Indeed, proto-industries wishing to capture some of the urban crafts' added value frequently took up the latter's organizational trappings, including long periods of compulsory apprenticeship. Although urban industrial conversion was not always successful, the growing number of urban craft guilds and craftsmen after the mid-fourteenth century, discussed below, suggests a generally positive response to proto-industrial competition.

Second, late medieval proto-industries generated fledgling industrial districts with shared industrial and commercial features. Some were upland areas unsuited to cereal production, but manufacturing clusters also developed around the larger towns in the plains. The most successful clusters developed nearby a strong guild-based urban industry, whose technical and commercial skills and supply networks they could utilize. Clustering, which reduced transactions costs, created a larger pool of skilled labour, and raised the speed of technical innovation, explains why many late medieval industrial districts persisted for centuries and in some cases even to the present day.

A third important and novel feature of late medieval proto-industry was the growing role of the state. As a highly capitalized, labour- and skills-intensive industry that could also be easily taxed, the urban cloth industry and the trade in raw materials had begun to attract rulers' attention from the late thirteenth century, the introduction of a wool tax by England's Edward I in 1294–7 being a notorious case in point. During the late Middle Ages, conflict between urban and proto-industrial producers led to demands for arbitration, and territorial rulers found the opportunity to broaden their political support and strike a blow against urban privilege irresistible. In southern Germany, the Low Countries, and northern Italy the legal privileges and 'freedoms' from urban controls granted to proto-industrial communities acted as a sort of 'infant industry protection' that could permanently change a region's industrial profile. Even where the state did not actively support proto-industries, political integration that helped establish more competitive markets made it easier for smaller towns and villages to pursue industrial activities.

Labour markets

Demographic shortages after the Black Death resulted in a sharp increase in the mobility of skilled and unskilled workers, with rural hiring fairs coordinating seasonal migrants between uplands and lowlands and across lowland regions with different specializations. But the most far-reaching changes occurred in the world of skilled urban workers associated with craft guilds, whose total numbers increased markedly. In the context of a sharply falling population, this fact substantially raised the number of trained workers in relative and absolute terms (Figure 2.1). An important factor driving this expansion seems to have been the sharp fall in the cost of credit, discussed below, which lowered the cost of training and increased capital investment and demand for skilled labour.

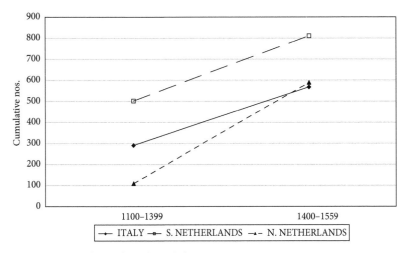

Figure 2.1. Craft guilds, Italy and the Low Countries

Craft guilds also responded to the growing demand for skilled labour by introducing more rigorous standards of training and craftsmanship and by improving the movement of skilled workers, by means of technical entry tests for guild masters who were not locally trained, of regional and inter-regional agreements between towns and specialized master artisans, and of the development of journeymen associations that supplied their members with information and support.

Informal or kin-based networks of skilled workers had existed since at least the thirteenth century in the highly specialized and seasonal building, shipping, and mining industries. More formal arrangements probably developed first in the building and woollen industries, which concentrated large numbers of workers in one place. Building journeymen in some early fourteenth-century French towns had their own leaders and 'ordinances'; in England in the same years, the masons had their own 'lodges' and attended regional or even national gatherings; and in northern Italy, the religious movement of the *Umiliati* was associated in the thirteenth and early fourteenth centuries with highly mobile, technically skilled woollen weavers. These cases were still unusual, however, partly because the number of young, unattached journeymen was still small. Journeymen weavers in German and Swiss towns seem to have been the only ones to adopt systematic tramping before the Black Death. Thus, in 1336 the journeymen weavers of Zürich asked to set up their own independent organization along the lines of those in the Rhineland, which they had probably observed in the course of their travels; a few years later, in 1343, the council of Speyer complained about the damage caused by a large outflow from the town of foreign workers 'from many lands'. However, the first indisputable evidence of organized tramping in German-speaking central Europe comes from a time, the 1370s, of growing political instability and of increased imbalances in skilled labour markets. Although the geographical scope of these early organizations was generally quite small, German-speaking workers (sometimes including craft masters) were sufficiently well organized to engage in large-scale migrations as far as Riga, Reval, and Bergen in the north and Venice, Florence, and Rome (where German bakers were particularly popular) in the south. Between 1430 and 1455, 55 per cent of weavers in Florence came from an area including Holland, Flanders, Brabant, northern France, and northern and southern Germany. This pattern of migration took in other Tuscan cities in addition to Venice, Milan, Vicenza, and Rome.

Outside German-speaking Europe, journeyman tramping is recorded in the fifteenth century as far west as the Burgundian lands and northern France—most notably in a 'league of 42 cities' organized in 1453 by the journeymen fullers of Brussels that included Lille, Lyon, Saint-Omer, and Paris—and as far east as Bohemia, but references are few and ephemeral. Tramping seems to have been mostly done informally, and during the late fourteenth and fifteenth century this kind of 'un-organized' migration became accepted as a normal way of life. Individual journeymen were employed on production of indentures or of certificates of service; if incoming journeymen could not find work locally, they were offered a small cash allowance and temporary lodgings to help them on their way. In Germany, France, and Flanders the practice became gradually more elaborate, including secret signs of recognition and specialized hostels or inns for putting up itinerant journeymen that were later incorporated more formally. Although after about 1550 tramping became a compulsory feature of apprenticeship in German-speaking lands, not all German craft guilds participated and not every craft was organized as a guild; organised French *compagnonnages* and a regular *tour de France* only appear in the late sixteenth or early seventeenth centuries. By contrast, journeyman organizations were weak or nonexistent in the peripheral economies of late medieval Castile, Scandinavia, and Ireland, and in the advanced economies of northern and southern Italy and Holland. In both cases they were not needed: in the first instance, demand for skilled labour was too low; in the second, skilled labour markets were well developed and information between the densely packed towns flowed easily.

Technological progress

The late Middle Ages were remarkably innovative by earlier standards, and the fourteenth and fifteenth centuries seems to have marked a sharp increase in the rate and scope of European technological progress. Economists are tempted to explain this as a reaction to the rising cost of labour, which caused investors to switch to more capital-intensive activities. But although labour scarcity may have played a part, it does not explain why the rate of innovation did not slow down again once population recovered and the relative price of labour fell again. Three factors probably had a more lasting impact. First, most technical knowledge before the nineteenth century was transferred by migrant experts, rather than through texts. Hence, the rate of diffusion and 'recombination' of technical knowledge—which underlie the rates of innovation and invention—were mostly the result of the ease and speed with which skilled technicians were trained and could migrate. The substantial rise in the number of craft guilds greatly improved the support for training young skilled workers and for integrating skilled migrants, and therefore made it easier for technology to diffuse. Second, higher rates of mobility spurred workers and engineers to make their technical knowledge more readily available through alphanumerical, visual, and three-dimensional codification. Codification allowed technicians to build on past knowledge and made it easier to transfer. Third, technical transfer was aided by the rise of consolidated territorial states and monarchies, which fed a growing competition for technologies that were militarily effective, econom-ically relevant, or culturally prestigious.

Technological transfer

Over and above the transfer of technical knowledge between individual towns and regions, the late Middle Ages stands out for marking the begin-ning of a long-drawn-out process, culminating in the Industrial Revolution, whereby the ancient technological and economic leadership of the Mediterranean shifted to north-western Europe—moving over a period of centuries from Italy (leader to *c*.1450), to the southern Rhineland and southern Netherlands (c.1450–1570), to the Dutch Republic (1570–1675), and finally to Britain after c.1675. This occurred principally thanks to skilled individuals trained by guilds or by other communities of specialized technicians (miners, builders, shipbuilders, etc.) that responded, increasingly from the fifteenth century, to concerted international demand by migrating.

The main source of innovation in the late Middle Ages was Italy, and the major initial recipient was southern and central Germany. Cotton-weaving, for example, was transferred to Germany from northern Italy in 1363, and already by 1383 German fustian was sold in large quantities on north European markets. Although 'Milan' and its declensions are frequent among the earliest weavers' names, the transfer was also facilitated by German merchants or by returning German weavers who had learned the craft in Genoa, Venice, and Lombardy. Following the craft's speedy diffusion in upper Germany, regional industries established the central European standards in cloth types and qualities. Following the large-scale migration of upper German weavers to Leipzig between 1471 and 1550, many east German towns adopted the Augsburg ordinances on cotton, and guilds in the region are said to have flourished from the time 'the Swabians came flocking'.

Public clocks began to spread from Italy in 1370–80. By 1400 all major European towns had their clock, and by 1500 the innovation had spread across the whole of the continent entirely due to migrant technicians. The diffusion of papermaking in central Europe relied on help from Fabriano artisans in the late fourteenth century; the first German paper came from Nuremberg, where a mill was converted to this purpose in 1390 by Ulman Stromer, at the time managing director of an established import–export firm that had been shipping paper, among other commodities, from Italy. The exceptionally rapid diffusion of book printing—which had been a purely German affair until 1465—occurred thanks to wandering printers and craft experts, who already by 1472 were returning with Italian book characters to their country.

Bans on migration offer the best evidence that itinerant journeymen transmitted valuable knowledge. Fifteenth- and sixteenth-century Nuremberg tried to protect its leadership in the metal industries by banning all emigration: apprentices had to swear not to practise their craft anywhere else, journeyman tramping was forbidden, and to avoid the poaching of workers, masters and employers had to ply them with work and 'not allow them any holidays'—or, if necessary, provide them with holiday pay. Every so often Nuremberg's town council proceeded against crafts like the wire pullers, which allowed journeymen to be lured by outsiders to whom they divulged manufacturing secrets. Over time, however, the lockout may have hindered the local industry, for Nuremberg craftsmen were unable to travel and acquire new ideas elsewhere. By contrast, truculent craft and government policies were unable to stop Venetian glassmakers from maintaining close relations with the outside world. On the one hand, as a statute of 1271 noted, it was impossible to stop 'foreigners' from practising glassmaking in the city. On the other hand, production had to be shut down every year for three to four months, during which workers were free to find work elsewhere. Worker migration eventually led to the diffusion of Venetian technologies to other European courts and cities; the reason competitive industries took so long to develop in Antwerp, Amsterdam, Paris, and London was due to the difficulties with transferring context-bound chemical knowledge and the lack of adequate raw materials elsewhere, rather than to the Venetians' capacity to enforce secrecy.

Testing and modelling

Technical codification in its broadest sense was certainly not a late medieval discovery, but it seems to have become more intensive and widespread. Some of the earliest evidence of individual testing and experimentation comes from the Venetian glass industry. According to local tradition, Angelo Barovier was a Venetian glass-worker who during the 1450s invented new kinds of glass that consolidated the popularity of the Venetian product across European and Levantine markets. In fact, Barovier's successes were the result of a series of small-scale innovations stretching over the preceding century that included, most crucially, the purification of the ash that increased the amount of sodium, and the discovery of a material that reduced the problem of *cristallo* glass corrosion. These early experiments may not have been recorded in writing, but the first known reference to a recipe book dates from the same years, and by the sixteenth century it was normal practice for family-based glass-making firms to keep their own books of recipes or 'secrets'.

During the late Middle Ages it also became more common for technicians to use three-dimensional models in wood, clay, and gypsum to convey information about machines (including buildings), and to test their performance. Like drawn plans, three-dimensional models are meant to store information and to help communicate it from one person to another (e.g. designer to client, builder, or supplier), and to help produce in the engineer and client the necessary level of confidence that the proposed structure will work and can be built. Although the use of three-dimensional building models is attested even in Babylonian Mesopotamia, it became a more regularly documented practice only in fourteenth-century Tuscany; a century later, the use of models for building purposes was mentioned as a matter of fact in architectural treatises by Leon Battista Alberti, Antonio Averlino, and Francesco di Giorgio Martini. Soon after 1500 the usage of building models spread to southern Germany and France, with the English following about a century later.

Far less is known about the related practice of making scaled-down models of working machines. The earliest reference to a mechanical model is found in a late fifteenth century description of a new wire-drawing machine invented in late fourteenth century Nuremberg. A few years later, in May 1402, the master masons at Milan cathedral were asked to inspect sketches submitted in a contest to find the best mechanical device for sawing stone blocks 'without manpower'; the most promising design was then to be realized in the form of a wooden model in reduced size, suggesting a well-established combination of sketch-based and three-dimensional mechanical planning, experimentation, and expert demonstration. By the early 1500s scaled-down models were being used both in engineering competitions and in applications for technical privileges or patents. Models were commonest until the mid-sixteenth century in the two most advanced industrial regions of the time, north-central Italy and southern Germany, but thereafter they began to be used also in Spain and France. In the early decades of the sixteenth century a Nuremberg craftsman made a 'nice wooden design for the king of England, about one *Ellen* long, in which one water wheel drove mechanisms for grinding, sharpening, polishing and fulling', but this may have been an article for the king's private collection; three-dimensional models are first recorded in English shipbuilding in the early seventeenth century.

The use of modules and templates was particularly common in building construction and shipbuilding. Medieval Venetian shipwrights based their dimensions on a module that was normally the beam of the proposed galley, multiplied in a fixed proportion to give the deck length; a fraction of this gave the length of the keel. Between the late fifteenth and the early sixteenth century north Atlantic ships, previously clinker-built, began to be built according to the Mediterranean carvel-built system. As the technology migrated to Portugal and Spain and then to England and the Baltic, it changed from a purely tacit and demonstrative form that employed no graphic support to a system that relied increasingly on graphic design (the Venetians had written up their shipbuilding schema already in the fifteenth century, followed by the Portuguese in the mid- to late sixteenth, but these drawings were purely descriptive and were not used for planning purposes).

Invention and innovation

There is no doubt that the list of inventions and improvements during the fourteenth and fifteenth centuries is far longer than for any equivalent previous period—and the difference does not seem purely due to better documentation. Listed randomly, improvements to consumer and inter-mediate goods include the mass diffusion of linen underwear (which raised standards of cleanliness with unquantifiable benefits for public health and created a source of cheap linen rags for the kind of higher-quality, more durable paper needed for movable type printing); the diffusion of four- and five-needle knitting, which created a new stocking and cap industry from scratch; the creation of transportable hard cheese (*caciocavallo* and parme-san) and of *maccheroni* pasta in Italy, which generated a new specialized demand for agricultural produce; the increased use of barrels for transport-ing wine, olive oil, and other perishable products, which made it possible to produce quality wines identified by their place of origin; the development through selective cross-breeding of the Castilian *merino* sheep, which laid the base for the Spanish woollen industry's success in the fifteenth and sixteenth centuries; the invention in the Low Countries and south-western England of ways of processing and preserving herring and pilchard (sar-dines) directly on board fishing boats; the transformation of flat pane glass into an accessible middle-class commodity (glass panes became a common sight in the homes of the wealthier bourgeois, and the first plantsman's glass-house made its appearance in the Low Countries during the fifteenth century).

Other better-known inventions and innovations include, in the financial and commercial sectors, the development of an international market for state loans in Nuremberg; the creation of the first chartered public banks in Barcelona (1401) and Genoa (1407); the diffusion of maritime insurance contracts and of bills of exchange, and the late fourteenth-century invention of double-entry book-keeping and of the 'multinational' merchant com-pany; and the introduction of the compass, the invention by the Portuguese of nautical astronomy, and the rediscovery of the astrolabe. Among the better-known industrial innovations can be found the invention of the wire-drawing mill in southern Germany, which tripled labour productivity; increases in the size and efficiency of traditional furnaces, which turned ceramics from a luxury good into a commodity; the invention of pure crystal glass in early fifteenth-century Venice; the diffusion of the 'indirect method' of smelting, the invention of the blast furnace in the fifteenth century, and the improvements in underground drainage that made deep-shaft mining possible; technical improvements to water locks for inland navigation in Lombardy and the introduction in 1407–8 of windmills for land drainage in Holland; and the industrial production of gunpowder, portable guns and movable cannon.

Increased artisan mobility accelerated cross-fertilization between industrial sectors and economic regions. Examples include the sectorial (from the Italian cotton fustian industry to the woollen industry) and geographical diffusion and improvement of the great or Saxon spinning wheel, which hastened the replacement of combed by carded wool and allowed for productivity gains of up to 80 per cent; the transmission via the Venetian and Florentine fleets of Mediterranean shipping technology to northern Europe, including the galley and, more significantly, the two- and three-masted carrack and caravel; the invention of the north Atlantic barge; the 'cartographic revolution' that brought together the distinct traditions of portulan charts, 'imaginary' world maps, and 'empirical' local and regional maps to radically transform Europeans' knowledge and perceptions of their space; the technical cross-fertilization between metallurgy, goldsmithing, and engraving that produced spring-driven clocks and watches and movable type; the increased application of water power for metalworking, for spinning wool (in fifteenth-century Cologne) and silk (particularly in Bologna, where it would make the fortunes of the city's early modern industry), and for grinding Toulouse woad and Sicilian sugarcane; and the combination of European and Arab dyeing techniques, including the increased use of alum mordant. Last but far from least, the fifteenth century witnessed the invention by the Florentines and Venetians of the technological privilege or 'patent', which gave recipients a temporary monopoly over any new or imported innovation.

Although technical diffusion was harder in agriculture, where local knowledge was essential for successful adaptation, agricultural 'best practice' spread notably in the Rhineland, the County of Flanders, and the Low Countries, England (which introduced Flemish hops in the fifteenth century), and Lombardy and Tuscany. Peripheral regions like Zeeland, Poland,

and Russia introduced high medieval innovations like the heavy plough. In many cases innovation was instigated by the peasantry, perhaps because of the lower cost of capital. Plants of Islamic origin like indigo, rice, spinach, sugarcane, artichokes, and probably eggplant, which had been little more than garden curiosities before the Black Death, became more widely accepted and spread across the western Mediterranean.

The quickening pace of innovation in production and trade was reflected in the development of written and spoken languages. This was the time when dominant 'national' or regional dialects began to emerge, with London English and Parisian *langue d'oil* leading the way. The creation of regional *linguae francae* in place of Latin marked the triumph of secular commercial, administrative, and popular forces and brought the languages of elites and masses closer together. The gradual standardization of regional languages made communication easier and more effective for trade, for the settling of disputes (in 1362 English became the official language of legal proceedings), for the enforcement of legislation, or simply for travel.

Capital markets

International financial markets underwent substantial change, building on the development in thirteenth and early fourteenth-century Italy of the bill of exchange—whose functions as a transfer medium for cash and for credit have changed little since the Middle Ages. During the fifteenth century, after the Italian invention of endorsement had made the bill of exchange nego-tiable and discountable, specialized 'exchange fairs' emerged in France (Besançon, Geneva), Castile (Medina del Campo), Germany (Frankfurt), and the Low Countries (Bruges, later Antwerp) to service growing north–south and east–west trade. These periodic fairs, which adopted Italian commercial techniques and displayed a high degree of integration, rested on a far broader network of commercial centres where monetary exchange rates were quoted and whose Mediterranean epicentre was well established by the early fourteenth century.

Among the forces driving these developments was the growth in financial borrowing by states facing escalating military costs. Heightened demand for military expenditure coincided with a compensating growth in the sophis-tication of financial markets and by the growing credibility of state policy and administration. Lenders were more willing to advance capital to gov-ernments because debts were more likely to be honoured; governments were less likely to default because they could raise taxes more effectively—alternatively, they faced the threat of being unable to pay for war. Growing political credibility explains the remarkable fall in interest rates paid by larger monarchies, which dropped from 20–30 per cent before the Black Death to 8–10 per cent (on long-term credit) in the early sixteenth century; the corresponding drop in the financially more developed Italian, German, and Netherlands cities was from 15 to 4 per cent. These improvements occurred in the face of sharply rising financial requirements—in Italy, for example, the official interest rates in Florence, Venice, and Genoa fell at the same time as their combined consolidated debts soared from 2 to 9.5 million florins over just two generations (c.1340–80).

As to private credit markets, by the late thirteenth century, lending and borrowing was frequent even among the poor. Short-term consumer credit was commonest; extended to capital-poor, landless or near-landless labourers and peasants who lacked collateral, it was often associated with 'usurious' rates above 15–20 per cent a year. Transactions of this kind were ubiquitous, and much of the time left no written record. Investment credit was rather different. Raised by the middle-ranking and wealthy stratum of peasant landholders and by landlords who could use their land as collateral, it was motivated by economic opportunity, was long-term, and could obtain substantially lower rates of interest. Long-term credit markets of this kind relied critically on three factors: clear title to land, making land an easily tradable commodity in case of borrower default; clear modes of dispute settlement and contract enforcement; and accurate information-gathering about the contractual counterparts. Land markets—and therefore credit markets—probably developed earlier in the more urbanized and commercialized Mediterranean area than north of the Alps, but the more advanced regions of north-western Europe caught up quickly after the Black Death. In England, the economic hardship experienced by peasant smallholders during the late 1280s and 1290s, which forced them to sell their holdings to better-off villagers, probably spurred the development of active, not purely crisis-driven land and credit markets. Contract brokering and enforcement also differed substantially across Europe. In late medieval southern Europe, the main credit brokers were the town and village notaries, and contracts were enforced through urban courts and their rural appendages. In central and northern Europe, where notaries did not exist, village communities and their elites and a combination of manor, feudal, and royal seem to have played the same role.

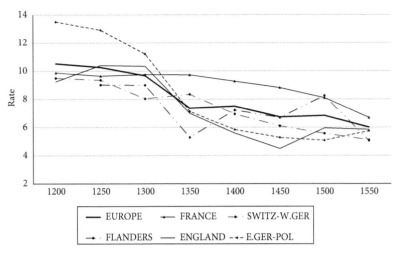

Figure 2.2. Private cost of capital in Europe, 1200–1500

Despite these regional differences, long-run rates of interest on private capital fell across most of late medieval Europe at an unprecedented scale. In England, for example, the real cost of long-term mortgaged loans fell from 9.5–11 per cent—a rate of interest that had prevailed for two centuries before the Black Death—to 7 per cent in the half-century after 1350 and to just 4.5 per cent by the late fifteenth century; proportionally similar gains occurred elsewhere in western Europe. To put these gains in context, it took England another 300 years to achieve a real rate of 3 per cent, which has remained in essence unchanged until the early twenty first century. By the second half of the fifteenth century, Europeans were enjoying a huge financial 'free lunch', as it became substantially cheaper to substitute capital for labour just at a time when labour had become unprecedentedly scarce (Figure 2.2).

Four factors help explain the change: commercial and institutional risk fell sharply, as state authorities became more reliable and contract enforcement improved; lower barriers to trade increased opportunities for investment; a growing range of consumer goods raised individuals' propensity to save; and most importantly, it became easier to use land as collateral, as feudal hindrances to the land market were relaxed and legal innovations to property transfer were introduced. Viewed comparatively, no other pre-industrial society appears to have developed a free market in land to the same extent and with the same effects on capital markets. Viewed retrospectively, the late medieval emergence of relatively competitive, open capital markets based on land must count as one of the period's most important contributions to the development of a capitalist economy some centuries later.

Urbanization and specialization

The effects of growing investment and specialization are best traced through changing patterns of urbanization, which reflect both the division of labour between 'town' (where the industrial and service sectors were concentrated) and 'country' (dominated by the primary sector) and the degree of specialization among towns.

In terms of absolute size, number, and distribution of towns, the urban profile of Europe in 1500 was not very different from that of 1300. The metropolises with over 100,000 inhabitants included Venice, Milan, Paris, and possibly Constantinople, but no longer Florence; London, which had perhaps 80,000 residents in 1300, had only 50,000 inhabitants two centuries later. In 1300 most townspeople had lived in a crescent-shaped area stretching from Sicily through northern Italy, south Germany, Flanders, and Brabant up to south-eastern England to the north, and to Catalonia, Valencia, the Rhône valley, and Paris to the west. In 1500, they were still concentrated in the same regions. The most highly urbanized country was still Italy, followed closely by Spain, which had begun to benefit from transatlantic trade; Bruges had lost its leadership to Antwerp in the Low Countries, but Ghent was still strong; in France, Rouen and Toulouse were still major commercial centres, but Lyon was beginning to outpace them thanks to its successful international trade fairs. The most striking change had occurred in south Germany, where Augsburg and Nuremberg had taken advantage of the nearby mining and trading booms in copper, silver, and iron to turn themselves into industrial and commercial leaders. Urban life at the Celtic and Scandinavian fringes was still largely an oxymoron, however, and everywhere the average size of towns was smaller than before the Black Death.

Viewed in relative terms, on the other hand, European towns around 1500 or 1550 looked substantially different compared to 1300. First, they were generally better off. Second, their share of the total population had risen in most countries because they could be supplied more easily with food. However, most of those gains occurred in the less advanced regions of southern and north-western Italy, and in other relatively backward economies like Castile, Portugal, Holland, northern and southern Germany, Bohemia, Poland, and possibly England. By contrast, after 1350 urbanization in the more developed economies of Flanders, Tuscany, Sicily, and Catalonia fell or stagnated, indicating an inability for further economic growth. Patterns of urbanization became more similar, as previously lagging regions began to catch up with the leaders.

The most important difference between 1300 and 1500 was the increasing division of labour and specialization between a region's towns. Political centralization increased economic competition and concentrated a growing share of administrative, military and tax resources within newly designated regional and national capitals. Indeed, among the most striking feature of this process was the 'invention' during the later Middle Ages of the capital city as the state's political and administrative centre, although the full effects would take centuries to fully work themselves out (late medieval London's dominance was quite unusual for a large-scale European country). Stronger competition and larger markets also gave rise to a clearer division of labour between craft guilds and 'proto-industrial' clusters, and to greater concentration in towns of specialized textile, metallurgical and luxury crafts and trades. Not all towns benefited from these developments, of course; the worst-affected by the economic and administrative changes were small market centres that saw their industrial and trading base eroded by the sharp fall in population and the rise of rural competition. But towns that could capitalize as commercial gateways to international trade routes, like Cologne, or Frankfurt, or Ravensburg, or as administrative capitals, like Rome or Naples—or ideally as both, like Lisbon and Antwerp—did especially well.

Trade

Were the late Middle Ages a period of commercial contraction, depression, or expansion? Did the economically most significant changes occur in the trade of high-value luxuries (spices, silks and luxury woollen cloth, gold- and silverware) over long distances, or in the exchange of lower-value agricultural and industrial products (grain, timber, wine, leather, salt, and so forth) over shorter distances? In general, historians of the luxury trades are more pessimistic than those who focus on trade in lower-value goods. The difference is easily explained. On the one hand, luxury trade was more susceptible to disruption—it travelled longer distances, crossed more political and geographical barriers, and was more likely to attract the attentions of stationary and roving bandits than bulk trade—and would therefore have suffered more from late medieval instability. On the other hand, the two kinds of trade supplied markets that reacted differently to the demographic crisis. Luxury trades supplied a relatively narrow group of wealthy consumers, whose demand was constrained by their income from the land. Since demographic decline caused demand for land and thus land rents to drop, demand for luxuries is likely to have fallen too. Trade in bulky, relatively cheap essentials also supplied a market heavily influenced by levels of population. However, whereas overall demand for grain probably fell, lower rents and higher wages raised the peasants' and labourers' real disposable income. This pushed up demand for new foods, manufactures and services; at the margin, it may have even increased demand for some luxuries previously restricted to the elites, although it is unlikely to have fully made up for the fall in upper-class demand.

In brief, during the century and a half after the Black Death both the total and the per capita volume of luxury trades probably contracted. The total volume of trade in staple foods quite certainly fell too, although the volume of staple trade per person may have increased, as some people ate more and others switched from grain growing to manufacturing, animal raising, or growing fruit and vegetables, and bought their food on the market. By contrast, trade per person—and probably total trade volume also—in non-staple foods, raw materials, and manufactures certainly rose. We know this because a growing proportion of the population lived in towns, where they required trade to make a living, and because trading networks were becoming increasingly complex. It is the case, of course, that neither of these trends—falling long-distance trade, especially by sea; expanding short- and medium range trade, especially overland—was strictly linear and unbroken. Warfare disrupted all kinds of trade, and local traders probably found it harder to escape conflict in their area than international merchants. Yet the latter could also evade or minimize their risks by bundling their goods together with less valuable products and sending them with pack animals overland, a pattern that became quite common from the 1340s and 1350s onwards and which, by 1500, had quite transformed European patterns of overland trade.

The answer to the question which of these developments 'mattered' most for overall economic activities depends not only on the time frame and the region under consideration, but also on the relative size of the two kinds of trade. To estimate the relative size of maritime trade (including trade in both luxury and non-luxury goods), we can combine a 'wild and risky' (Peter Spufford) estimation of the total value of Mediterranean trade in the 1370s

(7.5 million gold florins) with the average net value of declared possessions of the $c.264{,}000$ inhabitants of Tuscany in 1424–7 (56.8 gold florins), and the estimated western Mediterranean population in 1400 (20 million). Taking a 7 per cent rate of capitalization (the mean rate of return to capital at the time), the upper-bound share of western Mediterranean GNP traded by sea $c.1370–1430$ was 9 per cent (it is upper-bound because the Tuscan economy at the time was more commercialized than most). Interestingly, this tallies roughly with a similar estimate for late medieval Sicily, which puts the value of international trade of this unusually 'open' economy—which exchanged grain, sugar, and livestock for wool cloth—at 10–15 per cent of GNP. This trade, of course, was largely composed of bulk agricultural products—indicating that the share of luxuries in the total maritime trade must have been very substantially less.

In the long-term view taken in this chapter, however, two facts stand out above the undeniable destruction, setbacks, and instability of the later Middle Ages. In the first place, the extent and complexity of trade undeniably increased. The patterns of trade established during the long, expansive thirteenth century, based around a few very large 'gateway' cities and a galaxy of smaller towns each with its separate, fragile links to a narrow hinterland, were replaced by the early sixteenth century with a patchwork of increasingly integrated economic regions, with well-defined internal hierarchies of towns, linked to their neighbours by networks of fairs, improved roads and stone bridges, causeways, and tunnels.

Regional integration spurred growing specialization between regions. The development after 1400 of a pan-European cattle trade and of less far-flung interregional trade networks for metals (copper, iron, tin, and silver), salt, and grain are instances of the process. The astonishing growth of the fifteenth-century Dutch economy, based largely on its role as commercial intermediary between the North and Baltic seas, is another. An underpopulated economic backwater in the early fourteenth century, by the late fifteenth century the province of Holland was on its way to being one of the wealthiest and developed regions in western Europe. Taken together with the rapid growth of the southern German economy, these were the first signs of a move northwards of the economic epicentre of Europe. A third example of the growing international division of labour was the emergence and consolidation of highly specialized agricultural regions in east-central Europe (Hungary, Greater Poland, Bohemia) and the Mediterranean (Sicily and Puglia in south Italy, Andalusia in Spain) that exported foodstuffs and raw materials to neighbouring regions or abroad in exchange for foreign cloth and other luxuries. Although the exchange has often been described as exploitative, in fact the exporting regions benefited substantially; they did, however, suffer greatly when those trade links were irreparably damaged during the seventeenth-century political and economic crises. Other, less intensive examples of regional specialization include west Lombardy and northern Languedoc for woad, Biscay and southern Sweden for iron, the Rhine and Rhône valleys for wine, central Castile and the south-eastern Italian seaboard for transhumant sheep, and—as we saw—a scattering of cloth-making proto-industrial districts in most countries.

The economic consequences of the late medieval crisis were not felt everywhere to the same extent, and its effects within individual regions were to some degree contradictory. On the one hand, the crisis set off a process of economic convergence between semi-peripheral countries like England and more advanced regions such as Flanders and Italy. On the other hand, state formation probably created new regional differences. The processes of political and economic integration, which provided the late medieval economy with its unusually innovative dynamic, followed different trajectories. They generated different opportunities and constraints for investment, specialization, and trade, and set regional economies on different growth paths. The regions that led the thirteenth-century 'commercial revolution', Tuscany and Flanders, entered long periods of relative stagnation, while the baton of innovation and growth passed to Lombardy, south and central Germany, and to Brabant and Holland.

New developments on the late medieval economy

Stephan Epstein who wrote this chapter ten years ago was at the forefront of the subject, so that to some extent subsequent trends in the subject have served to extend and continue approaches that he highlighted. For example, he was a great advocate of the role of institutions not just in providing a framework within which the economy functioned but also in moulding the shape and direction of the economy. Contributions by van Bavel have highlighted the importance of institutions in fostering economic growth in the Low Countries, though Ogilvie has shown that some institutions, notably the merchant guilds, could be obstacles to economic development. The emergence of techniques for insuring ships and their cargoes emerged from self-help measures among Italian merchants, and state intervention came at a late stage, as documented by Leonard. In the rural world the institution of the commons has attracted growing attention, and the management of commons, once seen as an inefficient archaism, is now appreciated by de Moor and others as a well-organized and balanced approach to the efficient use of resources. In the field of institutions, and in other areas of enquiry, it has become increasingly common for historians to link the later Middle Ages with the early modern period—the decades around 1500 are no longer seen as a dividing line.

A trend to make large-scale calculations, and not to be timid about estimating the size of the whole economy, was already well developed when Epstein was writing, but has attained a new height with the publication of the book by Broadberry (and others). This confidently quantifies the GDP for Britain over seven centuries, including figures for production in different sectors, divisions between occupations, and fluctuations in GDP per head. British documents enable such a comprehensive picture to be painted, but similar methods have been used for other European countries, such as Italy, notably by Malanima. Mathematical sophistication is also being applied to more specialized fields of enquiry, such as changes in inequality—a subject at the forefront of current economic debates, as in a study of Florence by Alfani and Ammannati. Welfare policy and remedies for poverty, again the subject of increased public interest in social security and deprivation in our own day, have also been quantified by van Bavel and Rijmpa in terms of trends in spending on poor relief.

Not all of the tendencies in the subject have been dominated by economic models and complex calculations. The onward march of cultural history among historians, coinciding with the growing awareness of demand among economic historians, has extended the attention given to the consumer. Work has included a study of the spice trade approached from the appreciation of those luxury commodities by Freedman, and lower down the social scale To Figueras has demonstrated the appreciation by Catalan peasants of textiles from north-west Europe. A revived awareness of credit has been partly stimulated by anthropological approaches to economic behaviour, as shown in Lange's work.

Another interaction between economic history and other disciplines is apparent in the growing sub-discipline of environmental history. Campbell's book about the calamities of the fourteenth century has already been mentioned, but a more comprehensive overview has been provided by Hoffman. One of a four-volume agrarian history of north-west Europe, edited by Thoen and Soens, contains evidence for the responses that enabled vulnerable communities to escape from the hazards of nature.

Plate 4. Pinturicchio, *Pius II at the Congress of Mantua* (1502–1507)

3

The church and religious life

Robert Swanson

Late medieval Europe identified itself as explicitly Christian and specifically catholic. Christianity provided moral and ethical guidelines for organizing and structuring human society; it also presented moral and ethical challenges to contemporary social structures and practices. It accordingly provoked constant debate on issues like the violence of warfare, the validity of lending money at interest, social differentiation (especially serfdom's persistence), and relations with other religious traditions (notably Judaism). Among western Europe's many tribulations between 1300 and 1500, the Black Death and its emotional, psychological, and spiritual reverberations (with those of subsequent visitations) impacted significantly on religious and spiritual life.

These were also traumatic years in the western church's institutional history, especially for the papacy. Yet this remains a difficult period to encapsulate. The twelfth and thirteenth centuries had been years of foundation: the creation of the papal monarchy; the growth of new religious orders (including the friars), and awareness of the lay potential for Christian fulfilment in the so-called 'medieval' or 'twelfth-century' Reformation; the new intellectual currents and innovations of the twelfth-century Renaissance; and the consolidation of European Christianization in the thirteenth-century 'pastoral revolution'. In the sixteenth century came the Reformations. In between, from 1300 to 1500, occurs a crossing of paths. Preceding evolutions continued and were consolidated, but there was also reaction as obscured tensions and ambiguities became more apparent, revealing fissures and forces which threatened the church's status and its claims to catholicity within Europe. In 1500 the likely resolution of those tensions remained unpredictable; but the structures inherited from 1300 clearly no longer met the demands being placed upon them.

The Later Middle Ages. Isabella Lazzarini, Oxford University Press (2021). © Isabella Lazzarini.
DOI: 10.1093/oso/9780198731641.003.0004

Identifying 'the church'

Just how 'the church' should be defined was much debated. The term was ambiguous, with varying usages and meanings. Jean Gerson (1363–1429) summed up the key divergence: '"The church" chiefly indicates the universal congregation of the faithful, and hence is said to be catholic, that is, universal; yet that same noun is in common usage restricted to the clergy.'[1] That fundamental dichotomy was not the only ambiguity. 'The church' might refer solely to the institution, impersonally (although perhaps always presuming that it included the clergy, if not necessarily the laity). 'The church' also had more local significations, at national, diocesan, or parochial level. Yet as national churches grew and papal control weakened, very few actively sought to deny 'the church' its universalist aspect. During the Great Schism (1378–1418), debates about the definition became intense, lasting until around 1460.

Terminological debates were largely intellectual (despite massive practical repercussions), and actually affected few people. For most, the church's reality, as experienced, was of more immediate concern. In these centuries, the church was in constant flux. That was perhaps unremarkable. New dioceses were created as Latin Christianity's frontiers expanded—in Lithuania after 1386; in southern Spain after the conquest of Granada; eventually in the New World. Elsewhere, frontiers retreated, the Palestinian crusader states being eliminated in 1291 and Turkish advances in the Mediterranean forcing withdrawal. The church relinquished territory, but not claims: memories and aspirations were sustained by appointing nominal bishops to lost sees. Thus Simon de Cramaud became patriarch of Alexandria without leaving France, while bishops of Sebastopol and Beersheba acted as episcopal dogsbodies in Lichfield and Rodez respectively without ever seeing their titular dioceses.

Other changes occurred inside the frontiers. There were changes in rank and status, as when Prague and Florence became archbishoprics in 1344 and 1419. Diocesan boundaries might be redrawn (Pope John XXII divided certain southern French sees in the final onslaught against Catharism). Political concerns also impacted on ecclesiastical geography, with Calais being subjected to the archbishops of Canterbury after its capture by the English.

---

[1] P. Glorieux (ed.), *Jean Gerson: Oeuvres complètes*, 2 (Paris, 1960), p. 234.

Most alterations occurred at parish level, with a general trend for division as chapelries and small settlements sought full parochial status. Such developments—with their attendant tensions and conflicts—occurred across Europe. Perhaps their clearest manifestation is the fragmentation of the ancient Italian *pieve* into smaller, separate parishes. However, there were also amalgamations, notably in the wake of the Black Death. In England, local economic changes left many parishes unviable, leading to adjacent parishes being united to provide a decent income at least for one priest.

Regionalism was important in the late medieval church; it could not be a monolith. This is most evident in the liturgical variety. In England, despite the spread of the Use of Sarum (adopted by most of Canterbury province), variations survived. Hereford, as a diocese, and York, as a separate province, kept their liturgical identities. Elsewhere, for instance in southern France, individual dioceses retained their own practices, despite the growing influence of the Roman rite. There were also the differing rites of the religious orders, sometimes highly idiosyncratic. The Brigitines claimed that their liturgy resulted from direct revelation to their foundress, St Brigit of Sweden, and her confessor. Moreover, whatever the prescriptive wording of liturgical texts, in practice standardization was unattainable. Uneven resources meant parochial celebrations could not match those of cathedrals. Parishes had their own priorities, and their own devotions. In some sense, every parish had its own liturgical identity, but the differences are usually overlooked.

Many other aspects of late medieval religious life were similarly diverse, without provoking division. Saints' cults, and devotional foci, maintained their own catchment areas, ranging from devotion to a local holy figure to the international and universal saints. (Local cults also frequently revolved around unofficial devotions, notably in Italy to local *beati* who attracted devotion without being formally canonized.) Differing devotional and institutional contexts created local or regional practices. France, for instance, had its *prêtres-filleuls*, societies of priests who clustered in their birthplaces to celebrate masses for the souls of members of their natal community. Beguines appear primarily in the Rhineland and Netherlands, yet shared characteristics with other groups of holy women across Europe, especially in Italy and Catalonia. Devotional idiosyncrasies stimulated even greater regional diversity.

This church and religion were evolving and ever-changing, yet—perhaps paradoxically—they anticipated their own demise. Prophecy and millenarianism were important components of medieval Christianity, occasionally erupting in fervent preparations for Christ's Second Coming, or the appearance of the Antichrist. Successive late medieval crises, especially the Black Death and Great Schism, fed such expectations. The prophecies of Joachim of Fiore (d. 1203) remained potent, as did those of Hildegard of Bingen (d. 1179). John of Roquetaillade (d. 1362) and 'Telesphorus of Consenza' produced influential works in the fourteenth century, while millenarian expectation erupted among the Taborites in Hussite Bohemia. Expectations of the end of time appeared in the notion of the Last World Emperor, uniting crusade fervour, the pacification of the west, and hopes for the Second Coming in anticipation of a monarch who would rule all of Latin Christendom and reconquer Jerusalem, before Christ's return. Such expectations were intermittently attached to France's Valois kings (notably Charles VIII) or to Holy Roman Emperors (especially Sigismund).

The papacy

All catholics were members of the church as the universal congregation of the faithful, for which they regularly prayed in the Mass. As individuals, however, they unavoidably worried about their own souls: the church was universal, but salvation was personal. The church's history as a history of spirituality must be a history of individuals—even if collectively—searching for security in the afterlife. Its institutional history reflects different concerns: the practicalities of existence in a world of politics and economics, of threats and challenges. It directs attention towards administrative and practical issues.

The papacy was central in the church's institutional history between 1300 and 1500. Earlier centuries had created the 'papal monarchy'; developments in law, theology, and political thought had consolidated an ideology of papal supremacy over the world (not just catholics) which, if its basic premisses were accepted, was irrefutable. Alongside there occurred an expansion of papal administration; papal authority extended into the localities through control of religious orders, taxation, and intervention in clerical careers with papal provisions; and localities were anchored to the centre by allowing exploitation of the papal machine to secure spiritual benefits, practical privileges, and justice. The papal system thereby permeated the western church, even if sometimes resented.

Boniface VIII, the pope in 1300, might have been a great pontiff. Instead, despite the success of the first Jubilee (held precisely in 1300, and swamping Rome with pilgrims), he appears a failure. He struggled to control the papal states. He faced up to kings, repeatedly clashing with Philip IV of France. He defended church liberties, notably in his bull *Clericis laicos* (1296) seeking to prevent state-imposed taxes. His *Unam sanctam* (1302) was the pithiest summary of papal claims ever issued. But words were not mightier than the sword. On 7 September 1303, in the 'outrage of Anagni', French and Colonna troops invaded the papal palace and threatened Boniface's life, demanding his resignation. Although liberated, he died shortly after.

Initially, the aftermath of Anagni suggested that little would alter. Clement V's election in 1305 changed everything. Rather unwillingly, he summoned the Council of Vienne (1311–12). Its most memorable act was the suppression of the Order of Knights Templars, largely in response to French pressure. The council also condemned recent outbreaks of heresy, and decreed a network of language schools across Europe to teach Oriental languages to aid missionary work (nothing came of this). Clement V died in 1314, in southern France: he never reached Rome. In 1309 his court had stopped at Avignon. Then formally in the empire (but with France just across the Rhône), the city was almost surrounded by the Comtat Venaissin, papal spoil from the thirteenth-century Albigensian Crusade; but itself belonged to the king of Naples. Avignon provided a secure base for the papacy until 1376, and from 1380 the stronghold of one line of papal claimants in the Great Schism.

These decades of voluntary exile from Rome were the so-called 'Babylonian Captivity' of the papacy. For Petrarch, papal Avignon was a sink of iniquity; but he was not an impartial witness. There was intense faction and nepotism among the cardinals, and pro-French diplomatic bias, all unsurprisingly resented and bewailed by those excluded or adversely affected. The papal curia was increasingly gallicized, with the French almost monopolizing the cardinalate; but the cardinals had their own regional and familial rivalries.

Despite such failings, the Avignon papacy was not a failure. John XXII's administrative overhaul arguably made this period the apogee of the papal monarchy. Avignon had many advantages for a Europe-wide church: centrally located, with easy communications, few health risks, and relatively peaceful, it was potentially a much more effective ecclesiastical capital than Rome. Successive popes declared a wish to return to the Eternal City, but stability had attractions. Benedict XII began work on a massive papal palace; and in 1348 Clement VI bought Avignon outright from Joanna I of Naples. City and Comtat remained papal territory until the French Revolution.

Italy, however, could not be forgotten. John XXII poured a fortune into military actions meant to facilitate his return. Distant and ungovernable, the papal states had to be reconquered. That required mercenaries, who cost money. War was prohibitively expensive, its results negligible. Other issues caused distractions: conflict with Louis IV of Bavaria over the empire, the Franciscans' insistence on apostolic poverty, and the challenging political theories of Marsilius of Padua and William of Ockham.

Marsilius and Ockham provided ammunition for Louis IV, the imperial claimant whom John XXII desperately fought to exclude from Italy. Louis invaded in 1327, and captured Rome. He declared John deposed in 1328, appointing an obscure Franciscan as 'Nicholas V', the last imperially-appointed antipope. Having crowned Louis emperor, Nicholas decamped in the imperial baggage train; he was captured and imprisoned in 1330.

John XXII's successors continued his work. Benedict XII was something of a reformer, especially of religious orders. Even Clement VI had redeeming features. He sought to uphold the papacy's status, faced the Black Death with some dignity, and balanced French and English demands during the Hundred Years War. On his death the cardinals agreed an 'electoral capitulation', proposals to control whoever among them became pope. Once elected, Innocent VI annulled the pact, but this was not the last attempt to bind prospective popes.

Avignon's security and stability allowed consolidation and sophistication in papal administration; but Rome remained the pope's titular see, and ideal seat. Whatever its benefits, Avignon was not Rome; but return to Italy was inconceivable without assurances of papal security. In the 1350s and 1360s, Cardinal Albornoz reconquered the papal states and restored a semblance of control. In 1367 Urban V left Avignon, and entered Rome. In 1370 he died, back in Avignon. His successor, Gregory XI, likewise travelled to Rome, entering the city in January 1377. He died, still there, on 27 March 1378.

Gregory's death precipitated disaster. Several cardinals and much of the administration had stayed at Avignon. The cardinals in Rome were split by faction, yet had to choose Gregory's successor. The Roman people, having tasted the economic benefits of the returned papacy, were anxious not to lose them. The conclave, begun on 8 April, occurred in the midst of a riot.

Urban VI emerged as pope, but proved a poor choice. He rapidly alienated many cardinals, and clearly had no intention of returning to Avignon. The disorderly conclave gave his opponents their excuse: declaring his election coerced and invalid, most of the cardinals then in Italy renounced their obedience. On 20 September 1378 they elected a rival pope, Clement

VII. Thus initiated, the Great Schism would last until Martin V's election in November 1417. Even then division continued, until the resignation of Clement VIII in July 1429.

Following Clement VII's election, the church divided. He returned to Avignon, to oversee a governmental machine which had not been seriously disrupted. In Italy, Urban VI established his own administration. Across Europe, kingdoms and governments declared their loyalties, often affirming political rivalries. France defected to Clement VII; unsurprisingly, England stayed with Urban VI; equally unsurprisingly, Scotland chose Clement. Most of Italy and Germany supported Urban. The Iberian realms eventually chose Clement, but a revolution in 1385 carried Portugal into the Urbanist camp.

The split, and the loyalties, became more entrenched when Boniface IX succeeded Urban VI in 1389. With Benedict XIII replacing Clement VII in 1394, and Boniface IX being followed by Innocent VII in 1404 and Gregory XII in 1406, reunion became increasingly remote. Rival colleges of cardinals, separate (even duplicate) ecclesiastical hierarchies, generated irreconcilable interests. The division gave convenient cover to the complexities of inter-national politics. Urban VI encouraged Charles of Durazzo to invade Naples to overthrow Joanna I. John of Gaunt's attempts to become king of Castile masqueraded as an Urbanist crusade. Owain Glyndŵr's revolt sought to create an independent Wales with Benedict XIII as pope, severing ecclesi-astical ties with England. Yet while the schism caused difficulties, they were surmountable. In 1395 Boniface IX and Benedict XIII both supported the venture which became the crusade of Nicopolis; dispensations were granted for marriages across the divide, as when Richard II of England married Isabella of France in 1396.

Exasperation developed slowly. Before his election, Benedict XIII had supported negotiation, even papal abdication, to resolve the issue. His failure to act swiftly as pope spurred French attempts to force negotiation, and in 1398 a formal withdrawal of obedience. That lasted until 1403, when a coup in Paris restored recognition. Few Romanists supported the policy of with-drawal, despite French pressure: only Liège abandoned Boniface IX, in 1399, returning to his successor in 1405.

Innocent VII was the first Romanist pope to promise negotiation, but he did nothing. In 1406 Gregory XII swore to act, even to the point of resignation. Both rivals apparently recognized the need to prevent the division becoming per-manent, but neither would act decisively. Exasperated, Gregory XII's cardinals revolted: urging Benedict's cardinals to join them, they called a general council, to meet at Pisa in 1409.

That revolutionary act owed much to ideas about the church's structure which had developed during the Schism. The Council of Pisa acted with speed and determination; but without securing the desired outcome: its chief result was a third papacy, under Alexander V. Meanwhile, Gregory XII and Benedict XIII had called their own councils, which predictably reaffirmed their legitimacy as popes.

Most of Europe recognized Alexander V, but not all. In 1410 John XXIII succeeded Alexander, and the stalemate seemed set to endure. However, in 1414, under pressure from the emperor-elect, Sigismund of Hungary, John XXIII summoned another council, to Constance in Germany. He expected it to confirm his position; most of those present wanted reunion and major church reform. The council opened in November 1414; in March 1415 John XXIII fled, doubtless hoping that the council would descend into chaos, and possibly dissolve. Instead, it seized the initiative: the decree *Haec sancta* proclaimed that a council held authority immediately from Christ, not the pope, and that all (including popes) were under its authority in matters of faith. John XXIII was captured, imprisoned, and deposed. After negotiation, Gregory XII resigned. Benedict XIII was again declared deposed, but again held out. Slowly, however, his obedience melted away. Scotland finally abandoned him in 1418, but he retained adherents until his death in 1423.

At Constance, events became increasingly confused. Disputes about the agenda, national rivalries, and widespread distrust of the cardinals all impeded progress. In June 1417 the atmosphere changed: a new papal election became the priority, and on 11 November Odo Colonna became Pope Martin V. He presided over the council until it dispersed in April 1418, and then began the papacy's slow return to Rome.

Martin V's election is the customary terminal date for the Great Schism. However, only on the abdication of Clement VIII (Benedict XIII's successor) in 1429, and Martin V's election in his stead, was full unity restored. Martin thereby became the legitimate pope in the Roman, Avignonese, and Pisan lines, and through all three the rightful successor to Gregory XI.

Martin V returned to Rome in 1420, and began the process of papal restoration. Thereafter the papacy was emphatically Italian. Apart from two Catalans (Calixtus III and Alexander VI), all the popes were Italians. They all stayed in Italy, so that the century's biggest threat, posed by the con-ciliarists at Basle between 1431 and 1449, was tackled at a distance.

The return to Italy was a return to depleted resources. For much of the fifteenth century, despite wars and attempts at reconquest, the papal states eluded full control. In towns and cities dominated by despots the popes secured formal recognition of overlordship, and some financial return, but conceded actual authority to the local rulers as papal vicars. Only in the 1490s was recovery emphatically initiated, as Cesare Borgia began a reconquest.

The papacy's return to Rome brought many problems, not least that of relations with the civic authorities. Generally, however, Rome needed the popes more than they needed Rome. Yet there were tensions; from 1434 to 1443 Eugenius IV was exiled in Florence following a popular rising. That crisis aside, relations between popes and city were generally sound. Rome's fortunes revived, and extensive building programmes began to transform the city into a capital for Christendom. Nicholas V had grandiose plans, even intending to rebuild St Peter's basilica. A start was made, but real progress was delayed until the reign of Julius II (1503–13). By 1500 Rome, and particularly the Vatican, was definitively the chief papal residence, the city a fitting stage for a leading Renaissance prince. Here humanism could hold sway, the curia providing posts (or sinecures) for many. Pius II was one of the century's most notable humanists, at least before he became pope; while the building projects, and the official foundation of the Vatican Library by Sixtus IV in 1475, reflected the impact of the Renaissance.

The popes operated increasingly as princes, primarily within Italy's dynastic and political contexts. Straddling the peninsula, the papal states were always vulnerable, to attacks from north and south. Throughout the 1400s, relations with Naples were a chronic problem. The Neapolitan succession was a running sore, the popes favouring Angevin claimants against the Aragonese, and facing the latter's wrath when Alfonso V eventually won. To the north, fifteenth-century emperors were no threat, but the Medici of Florence sought influence, and the Venetians nibbled at the Adriatic coast. The centrality and vulnerability of their lands encouraged popes to intervene in Italian politics, yet militarily they could not be major international players. That was made brutally obvious when Charles VIII of France marched through the papal lands to invade Naples in 1494–5.

The restored papacy's Italian focus was matched by Italian dominance in the curia. The college of cardinals was increasingly under Italian control, partly because of a change during the Schism. Until then, cardinals were expected on appointment to abandon their previous careers and join the papal court, as Simon Langham did in 1368, quitting Canterbury for the curia. By 1417, that had changed; new cardinals no longer had to leave lucrative bishoprics for Rome, so few non-Italians did. In England, Henry Beaufort kept his see of Winchester (the country's wealthiest bishopric), and

John Kemp retained York: there were no fifteenth-century English curial cardinals. The increasingly Italian college at Rome also became more and more oligarchic, as the cardinals enhanced their status as princes of the church (only resident cardinals shared in the common fund). Dynasticism, fostered by papal nepotism, made pope and cardinals an increasingly homogeneous group, even if split by personal and factional rivalries.

The popes actively joined in the curia's factional intrigues, especially Sixtus IV and Alexander VI. The latter's reputation (owing more to his political enemies than to reality) offers the stereotype of a pre-Reformation pope, favouring his offspring and maintaining an allegedly dissolute lifestyle. Whether that reputation was much known outside Italy is doubtful: for most, the papacy was a remote institution, an administrative machine useful for providing spiritual and bureaucratic services (notably dispensations, indulgences, and judicial decisions), but with little direct spiritual impact.

This made the fifteenth-century papacy's situation somewhat paradoxical. While few formally rejected it, there are scant signs that it inspired great loyalty. Stability at Rome allowed the bureaucratic machinery to develop and expand. The 1400s saw greater refinement and expansion in record-keeping, clear testimony to the papacy's continuing international role. Yet rising national governments acted to curtail papal claims in key areas, notably finance, appointments to benefices, and jurisdiction. As finances became tighter, the popes exploited other sources of income. The pacification of central Italy could only aid this process. In 1462 the discovery of significant alum deposits (used in clothworking) at Tolfa proved a temporary but substantial windfall. Fees and other expedients served to bridge the gap, the sale of offices securing immediate cash in exchange for long-term salary payments.

Ecclesial ideas

The fifteenth-century papal court, like other Italian centres of power, attracted humanists. Part of their function was precisely to provide the intellectual decoration characteristic of a princely court. The broader humanist project, especially its philological element, opened the prospect of major changes in the church. Lorenzo Valla's linguistic analysis of the Donation of Constantine, a title deed of papal political power, exposed it as a forgery. That, however, did not fundamentally undermine the papacy's status, based ultimately on the Petrine commission in Matthew's gospel.

Potentially a more serious challenge was philological analysis of the biblical text itself. Again, Valla showed the way, his *Annotations on the New Testament* suggesting changes with significant theological and doctrinal implications. Unpublished in Valla's lifetime, they were used by Erasmus for his revised biblical text in the early sixteenth century. While Valla's methodology was only latently threatening, the potential for radical change had been shown in England around the same time. Reginald Pecock also analysed the Donation of Constantine, and likewise declared it a forgery. Applying the same methodology to the Apostles' Creed (the foundational statement of Christian belief), he demonstrated that part of it was a late interpolation. Like Valla's, these discoveries had limited impact, Pecock being silenced when found guilty of heresy.

While theological arguments sowed seeds for later debates, perhaps the most portentous intellectual threats confronting the papacy in this period, and indeed the whole church, derived from ecclesial thought. By 1300 the hierocratic notions which had underpinned European perceptions of papal authority from the time of Gregory VII (1073–85) were facing major challenges from the ideologies of secular monarchy. The Anagni incident clearly showed the papacy's practical weakness: popes might fulminate, but force would carry the day. After 1302, words and ideas were definitely not enough.

The papacy's status was challenged from many directions. Old ideas of imperial authority still circulated. Dante's *De monarchia* exemplified such arguments, urging the creation of a unitary universal ruling authority, but its practical significance was limited. Emperors—or aspirant emperors—did still invade Italy to secure coronation. Pope John XXII's struggle against Louis IV of Bavaria, which dominated the 1320s, has been called the last real battle between empire and papacy. Arguably, though, that final conflict occurred during the Great Schism, when traditional imperialist arguments were revived in the search to break the impasse caused by the events of 1378. Arguably, indeed, imperialism won that round, with Sigismund's success at the Council of Constance—but he was not actually emperor then.

Overall, traditional imperialism was a relatively weak factor in late-medieval anti-papalism. In the 1300s the ideas of Marsilius of Padua and William of Ockham (and their heirs, notably John Wyclif) offered the most serious challenge. Working from first principles, and questioning the whole ecclesiastical system rather than just papal powers, they undermined claims that the papal monarchy derived its authority directly from God and held universal powers above those of temporal rulers. Developing ideas of a strict separation of spheres of interest, these thinkers denied any temporal role to church hierarchs—especially the pope—and asserted the church's subjection to secular authority. Unsurprisingly, such ideas were speedily anathematized (in the cases of Marsilius and Ockham, partly because they also supported Louis IV). Condemned, the ideas went underground, surfacing sporadically (often without attribution) in later crises and debates, and still available to be invoked in the Reformation. Absorbed into the general intellectual tradition, they contributed to the later debates on ecclesiastical authority.

Conciliarism's rise as an alternative to papal monarchy is a key intellectual and practical evolution of this age. The years from 1400 to 1460 can be called 'the conciliar period', with assemblies at Pisa (1409), Constance (1414–18), Pavia–Siena (1422–4), and Basle (1431–49). (Eugenius IV's council at Ferrara in 1438, later moved to Florence, is not normally included.) Conciliarism dated from the late 1200s, its classic early exposition being the tract *On the method of holding a general council*, by William de Durandis, bishop of Mende. Despite its radical implications, this was no revolutionary statement: Durandis happily attended the papally-summoned Council of Vienne.

Conciliarism radically relocated the basic source of authority within the church. For extreme papalists, the 'Petrine commission' in Matthew 18:16–19, by which Christ granted Peter power to bind and loose in both heaven and hell, was a strictly personal commission, transmitted from Peter to his papal successors, and validating a monarchical—potentially autocratic—mode of ecclesiastical governance in which all power and authority emanated from the pope. For conciliarists (but not only for conciliarists), Christ's promise that the faith would never fail was one made to the church in general. For them, the complete church was the ultimate repository of authority; the pope was a minister, exercising powers conditionally delegated to him by the universal church, and necessarily answerable to it. Practically, the totality could not convene to exercise its powers, but it could assemble through representatives, in council. Such a general council then became the ultimate repository of authority, *vice* that universal church, with the pope accountable to it.

The ideas of accountability derived from early conciliarism became entangled in the fourteenth century with the new political thought of Marsilius and William of Ockham. In the Great Schism, conciliarism slowly emerged as the preferred route to restore church unity. Notions of papal accountability were voiced before the Pisan assembly of 1409; but Constance made conciliarism's revolutionary implications overt, in the decree *Haec sancta*. Actually a manifesto to validate a coup, the decree became the rallying point of politicized conciliarism, especially at the Council of Basle.

At Constance, conciliarism had solved an immediate crisis. The next council—at Pavia and Siena in 1422–3—met under papal auspices, and posed few threats. The ending of the schism had seemingly pulled conciliarism's teeth. Martin V doubtless assumed so when he called a further council at Basle in 1431. Eugenius IV, in whose reign that council met, thought likewise, but was soon disabused. A bitter dispute exposed the fundamental opposition of hierocracy and conciliarism. An increasingly radical council, basing its stand on *Haec sancta*, challenged Eugenius and his plan to move the assembly to Italy to facilitate discussions for union with the Greeks. In 1437, after acrimonious debate, Eugenius IV decreed the transfer: at Ferrara (and later Florence) his council achieved formal reunification with the Greeks (and other eastern churches) in 1439—short-lived, because Constantinople fell to the Turks in 1453. The staunch conciliarists had remained at Basle, consolidating their revolt, deposing Eugenius IV, and appointing an antipope, Felix V. Their conciliar revolution consumed itself in increasing radicalism. Largely isolated from the wider church (conciliarism never discovered how to ensure ties between the council and the church it supposedly represented), its projected reforms rarely adopted, riven with internecine bickering, and increasingly considered a threat to princely authority, the council harangued itself into oblivion. In 1449, after Felix V's abdication and a transfer to Lausanne, the rump elected Nicholas V (Eugenius IV's successor) as its new pope, and accepted voluntary liquidation. In 1460 Pope Pius II declared conciliarism anathema, marking its effective demise as a threat to the papacy. The ideas survived (they were used in 1511 to justify another Pisan assembly in revolt against Pope Julius II), but their impact on the church was strictly limited.

The 1511 Pisan gathering, like that of 1409, was summoned by rebellious cardinals. The cardinals' rising status presented a significant practical challenge to papal authority in the church at this time. It was a continuous process, dating back at least to the thirteenth century. The cardinals had long had a sense of corporate identity, especially as papal electors. They considered themselves the hinges (*cardines*) of the church's structure, linking the pope to the wider church. Their oligarchic tendencies developed greatly during the Avignon papacy, as their role in church government increased. Their developing claims and sense of identity congealed in the attempted 'electoral capitulation' of 1352. That pact aborted; equivalent fifteenth-century agreements also foundered on the basic clash between the aspirations of electing cardinals and the powers of a pope in office.

The Great Schism gave the cardinals a real opportunity to extend their influence. Yet they had to tread carefully, for they had caused the problem. From 1394 cardinals of both colleges were prominent in the search for union, initially trying to bind would-be popes by oaths promising resignation, and in 1408 rebelling and calling the council at Pisa. Yet the cardinalate after 1417 differed little from that of 1378. It had been chastened, the Council of Constance having vented considerable hostility on the College, questioning its relevance and role within the church, and urging major reforms. At the conclave of 1417 the cardinals lost their exclusive right of election, with others being brought into the process. That, however, proved to be a unique occurrence: under the increasingly princely restored papacy the cardinals became increasingly magnatial, entrenched as church leaders both nationally and internationally.

National and local churches

Contests over papal theory reverberated across Europe; the practicalities of church governance were mainly local concerns, reflections of local issues and local contexts. Localized sovereignties replaced the empire as the papacy's secular rival, whether national monarchies, lesser princedoms, or self-governing cities. As such governments defended and extended their claims over their subjects, including clerics, confrontation with universalist and separatist ideas of the church and clerical status proved unavoidable. The outcome was decentralization, and the emergence of national churches.

While the church's spiritual claims were never formally challenged (save by heretics), there was much debate about the extent of its immunity from secular obligations (especially taxes), privileged legal status, and freedom from the lay authorities in other areas. The hardest-fought battles, and the most public, occurred between lay rulers and local hierarchs, often backed by the pope. Three areas were especially contested: jurisdiction, finance, and clerical patronage.

Lay governors sought to extend their jurisdictional authority over the clergy as their subjects. They particularly tried to restrict, if not end, the abuse of 'benefit of clergy'—whereby clerics evaded punishment in secular courts just by being clerics. By definition this privilege was restricted to males; but it could cover all with clerical status, no matter how lowly. The practical details varied from place to place. In England, the right to benefit was effectively based on literacy, with a reading test administered by the royal judges replacing formal proof of ordination (although this changed slightly under Henry VII). Such lay administration created a paradox: England's church authorities had to accept as clerics those whom the royal courts so identified, on pain of fines.

Lay rulers also sought more say in other areas of the church's structure and organization, especially clerical appointments. The appointment of bishops was obviously a political issue; but the concern was more general. Attempts to limit papal influence were directed (at least in the 1300s) against perceptions that the popes were intruding foreigners into major posts and extracting revenues against local interests. Directed at papal provisions (the power to appoint regardless of local rules) and claims to annates (the first year's revenues from any benefice to which the papacy had appointed), this secular assault curtailed the powers without formally denying the rights. In England, patronage issues were judged in the royal courts; and papal provisions, which primarily affected benefices in the gift of religious institutions and individual prelates *ex officio*, were restricted by parliamentary legislation. Papal attempts to secure its repeal were ineffective. Similarly, in France, benefice matters were increasingly overseen by the Parlement of Paris, and papal rights of provision restricted. The chief French weapon was the Pragmatic Sanction of Bourges of 1438. Like the English statutes, it became the focus of contention between the French authorities and the papacy. Concordats, as in 1472, occasionally redefined the relationship, without completely overturning the limitations. Popes resisted such restrictions, yet recognized that bargaining worked. Temporary or partial surrender was a useful ploy, as with the Concordat of Redon (1441), which bought Breton support against the French, or the concessions which in 1443 secured German allegiance against the Basle conciliarists. Everywhere, regional issues affected developments, not always negatively. The Medici maintained close ties with the papacy to sustain their influence over Florentine ecclesiastical patronage: better to exploit papal authority to secure their aims, than undermine it and face their own subversion.

Finally, there was money. The papal curia was the hub of a complex financial operation. Lay rulers resented such transfers: the very fact of papal taxation, however identified, impugned their sovereignty; the transfer of bullion was disliked; even worse, popes might spend the money against national interests. Again, papal rights were effectively negated but not explicitly denied. England loyally paid Peter's Pence, but the amount was negligible. Real papal taxation, if formally levied nationally rather than disguised as curial fees, was another matter. After 1336 formal papal taxes were rarely levied in England, despite intermittent papal pleas, and only collected with royal approval. Promotion fees, especially annates, were frequently criticized, and produced bitter complaints in the conciliar period. Much resented, by 1400 they were a major source of income for the papacy (and for the cardinals). Schemes to abolish them generally foundered on unwillingness to provide adequate alternative funding for the church's central structures.

Nevertheless, a balance was maintained. English bishops, while effectively crown nominees (but always technically papal appointees), still paid the fees due on their promotion, in effect giving the pope financial compensation for abandoning his right to nominate to such posts.

The lower clergy

The papacy headed the ecclesiastical structure; its administrative and financial tentacles permeated the church. At its base, the parishes on which the whole structure rested and depended, were the ordinary clergy. For them, as for the popes, 1300–1500 was a time of turmoil.

One aspiration of the thirteenth-century pastoral revolution had been to revitalize the clergy as an effective Christianizing force in the catholic world. By 1300, diocesan synods were the basic means to that end, disseminating appropriate information via the clergy. At a higher intellectual level, the papal decree *Cum ex eo* of 1298 allowed clergy time away from their benefices to attend university. Clerical education and quality were matters of great concern: the fifteenth century saw particular emphasis on securing benefices for university graduates, following the Council of Constance, but little practical actually happened. Nevertheless, at the higher levels, clerical learning was improving: the percentage of graduates appointed to key posts, perhaps even ordinary parishes, did increase.

However, most clerics lacked university experience, and did not need it. University-level theology was generally too abstruse for pastoral care. Most clerics were probably trained by work experience alongside an established priest; most would not secure full benefices, but spend their careers as hired auxiliaries. Despite concerns about clerical quality, there were no seminaries as formal training colleges, although a few Italian experiments moved in that direction.

By 1300 the numbers of these lower clergy were high, with available evidence on ordinations indicating massive recruitment. Whether this reflects real commitment and vocations, or merely recognition that a clerical career might avoid the economic pressures caused by an increasing population approaching the limits of available resources, may be debated. The Black Death changed things dramatically. Initially there were enough ordained clerics to fill the benefices vacated by the plague, but the changed socioeconomic outlook reduced the pressures to take orders, and recruitment plummeted. In England the nadir occurred around 1440, but thereafter, as the population rose, so did ordination figures. In 1500 they were still lower than in the early 1300s, but were rapidly rising—much faster than the increase in the total population.

The Black Death also affected clerical incomes. It cut receipts from offerings made at purifications after childbirth, marriages solemnized in church, and funerals. It changed the pattern of tithes received from rural agricultural produce; population change also undermined the finances of many urban parishes. The changes varied, their detail reflecting regional economic regimes and general trends, but they were considerable. Other factors, notably the depredations of war (in France during the Hundred Years War, along the Anglo-Welsh border because of Owain Glyndŵr's revolt, or in Bohemia during the Hussite wars) also affected the value and viability of parochial livings. In extreme cases the decayed parish was united with a neighbour to secure continued spiritual provision for its remaining inhabitants. However, population growth and economic strength also encouraged local chapels to demand autonomy and higher status, the arrangements for provision (especially payment) of their clergy often provoking disputes.

The Black Death did not bring unremitting gloom for all the lower clergy. The greater preoccupation with death and with provision of *post mortem* commemorations to ease souls through Purgatory increased demand for priests for such tasks. The resulting high wages could make such short-term appointments more attractive than the responsibilities of a parish.

The religious orders

In contrast to previous centuries, the fourteenth and fifteenth were primarily the age of the secular clergy, those working in the world. The religious orders lost their earlier prominence, and move into the background. Monks, friars, and nuns were not unimportant or inactive, but the focus had shifted. Spiritual innovation was now reflected in lay and non-regular movements, whereas previously it was manifested in religious orders—although new orders were still established during the period.

The religious orders still attracted vocations (but fewer than before); still produced writings of intense spirituality (like the meditations of the Monk of Farne); still made important contributions to theological and intellectual life. However, the regular life had lost its earlier vitality and pioneering spirit, becoming regular in a mundane rather than technical sense. Monasteries (and nunneries) were economic machines and places of security, embroiled in the world rather than avoiding it. The friars had also lost their edge, and often now competed with the local clergy for lay loyalty. Their status, and their claims, provoked much debate, and frequent hostility as they were accused (not unjustly) of undermining the authority of the parochial clergy for their own financial benefit.

Against that negative tendency, these were still years of intellectual growth. Members of religious orders, especially friars, contributed greatly to the varied (and competing) theological strands of the pre-Reformation period, and to the intellectual milieu which produced Martin Luther. Other evolutions were also important. The Augustinian canons in the Netherlands and Germany were revitalized by the *devotio moderna*. Initially a clerical and lay movement, anxiety to ensure its supervision led to attempts to channel its energies into traditional structures. Many houses of the movement adopted Augustinian practices and joined the order, among them the leading German branch, the Windesheim congregation.

These Augustinian developments in part reflected a trend generally labelled 'observance', seeking a return to the original rules to rediscover the pristine motivations of the orders. 'Observance' especially affected the mendicant friars, who became influential after 1350, but was not limited to them. The observant movement created tensions: it was hard to reconcile the divergences between those wishing to restore lost ideals and those content with the status quo. Formal divisions were almost inevitable. Perhaps predictably, the Franciscans were most troubled. The Franciscan Observance seemed to revive the earlier split between Conventuals and Spirituals (as it did, to some extent). Centring on the assertion of absolute poverty as demanded by St Francis, and rejecting the accommodation with institutionalization resulting from becoming an order, that dispute had wracked the Franciscans between 1260 and 1330.

The Observants were always a minority; their appeal varied regionally, but adequate explanations for the variation are lacking. In England, only the Franciscan Observants established themselves, somewhat tenuously, in the late fifteenth century.

Perhaps more significant for the orders were the centrifugal tensions caused by states seeking more control over their local churches, including the international religious orders. In the Hundred Years War, the English dependencies of French houses, the 'alien priories', were effectively nationalized, their contacts with their continental mother houses varying with the state of Anglo-French relations. The Great Schism encouraged separation: when England and France obeyed different popes, ties between the English houses of orders like the Cluniacs and their French headquarters were unavoidably weakened. They were more definitively sundered in the fifteenth century, when smaller alien houses were dissolved and their possessions transferred to endow new English foundations (especially schools and university colleges), while larger ones saved themselves by seeking denizen status and reducing ties to the French centres. Only the Order of St John, the Hospitallers, avoided these developments, with its special role as bulwark against the Turks in the Mediterranean. In its case the tensions of the Schism were not allowed either to exacerbate divisions or to prevent transfers of funds.

Political forces elsewhere similarly affected the orders. In fifteenth-century Italy the development of formal ties of association and dependence between Benedictine houses, the congregations, was constrained by political considerations. The Medici rulers of Florence ensured that the houses on Florentine territory formed a single body, without external influences, to enhance their own control.

It is unclear that such evolutions were actually detrimental to the orders; international contacts were not totally ended. The English Premonstratensians remained formally subject to the French mother house into the sixteenth century, yet enjoyed de facto autonomy under a vicar general. England's Cistercians maintained regular contact with Cîteaux, and remained fiscally subject. The internationalism of the mendicants also continued, the powers of general chapters affecting houses across the continent.

The traditional view (now significantly modified) of the late Middle Ages as an era of stagnation or decline in the religious orders, especially among the monks, partly reflected their necessary accommodation to changing circumstances. After the Black Death, houses could not support as many members as before. Institutional evolutions, with less communal living, greater integration with the seigneurial and rentier economy, and more personal private property, also undermined their appeal. Monasticism was frequently criticized in reformist literature, with debates about its validity for the contemporary world. By 1500 such doubts were perhaps widespread even among the laity, as the monks' spiritual functions, notably their intercessory and commemorative roles, passed to secular chantry priests. Yet the monastic life remained attractive, particularly for those past the most energetic stages of their lives, or seeking particular types of spirituality. In England both these trends appear in the significant expansion of the Carthusian order, which stressed personal seclusion and meditation. In 1340 there were only two houses; by 1450 there were nine. Their later recruits were often clerics seeking a deeper spirituality, or laymen wanting to abandon a world of which they had already experienced more than enough. While always a small order, the Carthusians became a major force in late medieval spirituality.

The regular life retained an appeal. The observant movement attested continued spiritual vitality, as did the establishment of new orders. In the early 1300s the Celestines, founded by Pope Celestine V, offered one rigorous form of spirituality, which remained attractive on a small scale throughout the period. Pope Benedict XII in 1336 set the pattern for subsequent Benedictine development by imposing significant reforms (although their implementation and observance proved problematic). Later, the Benedictine congregational movement sought both spiritual and institutional renovation.

Alongside the male orders, the nunneries require comment, but the evidence for them is poorer, and the imperatives were rather different. Pope Boniface VIII's decree *Periculoso* (1298) addressed a major medieval concern about religious women, ordering their claustration and separation from the world. Women maintaining an independent and uncontrolled spiritual existence were considered a major problem; the standard response (not always successfully imposed) was to transform them into enclosed nuns. Late medieval nunneries seem to have maintained their numbers, and apparently remained popular; but that popularity was ambiguous. In Italy, nunneries solved the problem of surplus daughters; they restricted marital availability (and, for the nuns' families, the costs of dowries) without necessarily demanding a vocation. Some Italian houses were notoriously ill-disciplined, but as they served their social purpose, that was tolerated.

Vocations did still matter. Independent groups of women leading spiritual lives would attach themselves to an order and gradually coalesce into a formal nunnery. This happened often in Italy, where women retained considerable freedom in defining their regular life, and changes of affiliation were not unusual. Elsewhere, especially in the Netherlands and Germany, groups which earlier would have formed beguinages now became nunneries, often Augustinian canonesses. Women could still lead independent spiritual lives, as beguines or unmarried Franciscan or Dominican tertiaries (or as relatively uncommitted vowesses), but the drive for claustration was relatively relentless.

One significant development was the founding of a wholly new order, the Brigitines. Named for and founded by St Brigit of Sweden (1303–73), the order reflected the search for a profound spiritual life characteristic of fourteenth-century lay piety. It contained both men and women, but its abbesses were the rulers. The men provided spiritual counsel, as subordinates. The order was small, but influential: its sole English house, Syon Abbey, was among the country's leading spiritual centres.

Spirituality

Alongside the dogma and intellectual religion of the theologians there existed another Christianity, of practice and pragmaticism. Here, people used and manipulated religion to their own ends, through votive masses, benedictions, and the many sacramentals—holy water, blessed candles, and such like—which purified and protected. Fluid, vital, easily confused with (or dismissed as) superstition, able to absorb trends and evolve in response to newly perceived needs, such practices provided the bedrock for people's personal spirituality. It was highly lay-dictated, even if dependent on clerical sacramental power and status. Laicization, the extension of lay control, encouraged closer integration between the church and the lay world. Urban rulers, guilds, parish governors, and even individual, sought to direct and supervise local churches. Towns took control of hospitals and charitable bodies; guilds and fraternities hired priests and dictated liturgical performances. In parishes across Europe, communal representatives equivalent to English churchwardens assumed much of the financial responsibility, especially funding the church fabric and paying chantry priests. Even individuals became directors: by appointing priests to celebrate for souls (and so imposing their ideals of clerical behaviour); by funding posts and decreeing the liturgical demands; by undertaking charitable works and thereby defining spiritual priorities.

Intensely practical, as practised this was a religion of considerable but varying spiritual depth. Anchorites like Julian of Norwich, entombed in their cells, sought intense personal contact with the divine. In her case (but not in all), the search was successful. In the Netherlands and Rhineland, beguines maintained their own distinctive religious life, despite hostile church authorities fearing possible heretical deviation.

A notable feature of the period was the strand of mysticism. The early years were dominated by Meister Eckhart and his Dominican circle, with its intensely Christocentric piety. Later came the so-called English mystics, with Richard Rolle (d. 1349) as the leading figure, and Margery Kempe included somewhat uncertainly. Women are particularly notable in this period, individuals like Catherine of Siena and Brigit of Sweden, or groups like the nuns of Engelthal.

The emotionalism of aspects of this medieval spirituality can appear excessive, especially when emphasizing the immensity and horrors of Christ's redemptive Passion. The Passion, and the enormity of an incarnate God submitting to crucifixion to redeem humanity, was central to medieval catholicism. With the Passion at its heart, and the Mass as its focal point (commemorating and re-enacting the Passion, and through transubstantiation allowing God to be experienced on earth), late medieval catholicism became a religion of widespread devotional extravagance, superficially one of unrestrained emotion and gross display. It was against this appearance that the sixteenth-century reformers rebelled. From a distance it appears highly superstitious, but for its practitioners it was a rational, practical, and valid means of maintaining contact with divinity, and gaining results.

Accordingly, this was a religion of saints, shrines, and pilgrimage; where 'sacramentals' can seem more important than the actual sacraments; in which the afterlife pains of Purgatory could be reduced by acquiring indulgences. Shrines, especially Marian shrines, proliferated across Europe, attracting throngs of pilgrims. Cults rose and fell, rapidly. Margery Kempe, an inveterate pilgrim, is extraordinary for her extensive wanderings: to Rome, Compostela, and the Holy Land (the main foci—in Italy she also visited Venice and Assisi); Cologne (the shrine of the Three Kings), Aachen, and Wilsnack in Germany (the last famed for its Precious Blood, a controversial host relic); in England her tally included Hailes, Syon, York, and Norwich. The period's new saints include Catherine of Siena, Brigit of Sweden, Osmund of Salisbury (finally canonized some 350 years after his death in 1099), and Bernardino of Siena. Others did not make the grade, among them England's Richard Rolle and King Henry VI.

The religious responses to the period's continuous traumas often suggest that it was dominated by death. After 1350, awareness of death and implicit (often explicit) awareness of the afterlife shrieks from all forms of art. This is Johan Huizinga's 'autumn of the middle ages', an age of cadaver tombs depicting rotting corpses, of images like the Three Living and the Three Dead, of the Dance of Death, and of texts advising on the *ars moriendi*—the craft of dying. Much of this material is ambiguous, but the last is distinctive in stressing death not as an end, but a preparation for an afterlife which would continue until the Last Judgment.

That continuum was both communal and personal: if the Church Militant consisted of living Christians, the dead—those not consigned to Hell—were the Church Dormant, awaiting judgement and inclusion among the Church Triumphant in Heaven. The Church Dormant was not a Church Inactive: its members were in Purgatory, and had their own role in the scheme of salvation.

The development of the doctrine of Purgatory, and its identification as a specific location, was largely completed by 1300, although formal doctrinal definition was delayed until the Council of Florence in 1439. Its torments were almost as terrible as Hell's, but not quite: it would end, with guaranteed admission to Heaven. To speed the process, merit could be accumulated in advance through indulgences. Postmortem commemorations, through Masses said by chantry priests and the prayers of the living, offered other ways to reduce the suffering.

Crusades

Late medieval spirituality was marked by novelties, but there was also continuity. Crusading ideas remained influential, despite the westerners' expulsion from the Holy Land in 1291. Subsequent crusading hopes essentially had to restart from scratch: future crusades required reconquest, not reinforcement. Crusade planners now faced a more complex political context, especially the chronic Anglo-French hostilities and their ramifications in European politics. Plans existed aplenty, but little was actually achieved—although Alexandria was briefly taken by Peter I of Cyprus in 1365; Smyrna was captured and held from 1344 to 1402; and the Hospitallers controlled the castle of Bodrum on the southern Anatolian coast. Schemes foundered on politics, and on the recognition that a crusade with realistic prospects of regaining the Holy Land was no longer a practical proposition.

Scheming nevertheless continued, crusading aspirations being exploited for international propaganda purposes. Kings still paid lip-service to the idea; popes still exhorted them to act. The bathos of late medieval crusading is encapsulated in the death of Pius II. Having urged a major anti-Turkish crusade, he died at Ancona in August 1464, awaiting a crusading force which would never appear.

Yet crusade was still idealized. Philippe de Mézières (d. 1405) concocted grand plans for an international crusading coalition. Crusading's chivalric aspect was shown in 1395, when a cavalcade of knighthood took the land route to Constantinople and met disaster at Nicopolis. Other schemes were less altruistic. In the Great Schism, crusades defended partisan loyalties and claims, like the English expedition to support Urban VI in Flanders in 1383, or John of Gaunt's 'crusade' to gain the Castilian throne. Successive crusades were launched against the Hussites, and later against the Vaudois heretics of southern France. Crusading ideas supported Christian advances against Granada; the Teutonic Knights used them to maintain their hold on Prussia and justify wars against the Poles and Lithuanians. They were also used against papal enemies in Italy.

The numbers joining such ventures were always limited, and responses to the call usually highly regionalized. For most, participation was limited to a cash donation, in exchange for an indulgence. The low numbers do not mean that the crusading ideal, as a religious obligation and aspiration, was actually eroding. However, as the Turks increasingly menaced southern and central Europe—they briefly held Otranto in 1480—so crusade became defensive rather than offensive, despite the rhetoric.

Jews

The extinction of the crusader states in the Holy Land stimulated a hunt for scapegoats. The shock also focused attention on those perceived as the internal enemy, especially Jews.

Christian hostility to Jews had complex origins. Some of its motivations were economic and social, identifying Jews with exploitative moneylending and associating them with monarchical fiscal pressure. Much derived from religious stimuli, especially after 1095: popularly, in tales that Jews murdered Christian children for their own purposes; among the learned, in hostility to the continued vitality and evolution of a religion which Christianity considered obsolete. Charges of Jewish host desecration appeared across Europe after the first major case in Paris in 1290, partly exploiting anti-Jewish prejudices to reinforce the doctrine of transubstantiation.

All these factors persisted through to 1500, enhanced by specific contemporary conditions. Paranoia and scapegoating made the Jews easy victims: in 1349 they were even charged with spreading the Black Death. Accusations of host desecration and ritual murder regularly recurred. Indeed, they persisted even where there were no Jews. Edward I expelled England's Jews, yet Chaucer's Prioress's Tale centres on Jewish child-murder, and the Croxton *Play of the Sacrament* portrays Jewish host desecration. On the Continent, massacres and trials were frequent. The German Armleder movement of the 1330s, reacting to rumours of host desecration, took many lives. In 1475 Jews were blamed for the death of young Simon of Trent, with predictable results (including the child's veneration as a martyr).

While a latently hostile mentality towards Jews was seemingly endemic among Christians, actual violence was intermittent and episodic. The reality of relations depended on local circumstances and contexts. The evolutions in Spain provide a distinctive variant in the general theme. Fourteenth-century pogroms and zealous anti-Jewish preaching in the early fifteenth created a large group of converts, the 'conversos'. Usually poorly integrated into Christian society (although some became prominent churchmen), the conversos were viewed with suspicion by the Old Christians. From the 1450s, particularly in Castile, a 'converso problem' developed, mixing social and economic tensions with doubts about the conversos' faith and fears that they were undermining Christianity. The Spanish Inquisition was established in 1478 to tackle the issue; in 1492 came the final solution: Spain's remaining Jews had to convert or leave.

Witchcraft

If anti-Jewish hostility partly reflected Christian insecurity and attempts to bolster orthodoxy by creating an 'Other', so did the rising fear of witchcraft after 1400. The existence of powerful supernatural forces which could affect human beings for good or ill was widely accepted, most obviously in debates about astrology. Sorcery, and the supernatural powers of wise men and women who could cure illnesses, discern thieves, or locate lost property, were widely tolerated—or if not condoned, not repressed. However, attitudes changed significantly in the fifteenth century. A dualism which acknowledged the Devil's power as Christ's opponent in the battle for human souls coupled magic with diabolism in a potent and fearsome pairing. No longer seen as harmlessly harnessing natural gifts and powers for beneficent ends, witches became the Devil's agents, willing minions in the assault on Christendom. Witchcraft allegations appeared in prominent political trials, like those of Joan of Arc and Eleanor Cobham (wife of Humphrey, duke of Gloucester), but such cases were exceptional, probably more important for their overt political and propagandistic aspects than as witch trials. More sweeping purges, originating later in the century in southern France, laid the foundations for the witch craze of subsequent centuries. A landmark was the publication in 1486 of the *Malleus malificarum*, the classic handbook of witch-detection.

Heresy

By 1300, the church had long experience of dealing with heresy and heretics, even if recent scholarship has suggested that the heresy was largely imagined by its would-be repressors, and their victims essentially scapegoats or collateral damage. Whatever the truth, the church continued to hunt both heresy and heretics in the succeeding centuries—actions which provoke similar academic uncertainties. Old heresies lingered in Waldensianism and Catharism; by 1400 Lollardy was spreading in England; by 1420 Hussitism was rampant in Bohemia. Other manifestations were mainly academic, products of excessive speculation. Perhaps distinctive was the case of the Spiritual Franciscans, still a problem in the early 1300s.

Cathar dualism allegedly survived in southern France in 1300, despite repression. Although the Inquisition remained vigilant, the heresy was nearing extinction. The most explicit evidence on Catharism appears in the records of the processes at Montaillou in 1318–25. In contrast, Waldensianism was widespread, notably in Germany and Bohemia. Its overall coherence and unity are unclear: as an underground movement, whose members often attended catholic services without being overtly heretical, it remains obscure. Possibly there were regional variants, divergent despite attempts to maintain contact and some uniformity in belief and doctrine. Some of its ideas matched those of Wyclif and Hus— Waldensianism's integration into the Hussite revolution in Bohemia was important. It leaves few independent records, despite being the only sect in continuous existence throughout the period. Waldensianism surfaces most coherently in the alpine regions of southern France and northern Italy late in

the fifteenth century, among the Vaudois. Here, again, there was persecution, and inquisition; but this group has left texts which reveal its religious
mentality, suggesting continuing evolution and perhaps (simply by their
being written) a sense of security. Waldensianism in this form lasted until
the Reformation, finally dissolving in 1532.

Major developments occurred in England and Bohemia. In England the
ideas of John Wyclif (d. 1384) were seen as the springboard for Lollardy,
which lasted until the Reformation as an undercurrent intermittently persecuted by both church and state. In Bohemia, a local reform movement
similar to the *devotio moderna* was galvanized by Jan Hus (d. 1415)—
influenced by Wyclif, and a leader of Bohemian resistance to German
domination—as a movement for religious change which became a nationalist revolution. Military confrontation could not defeat the Hussites. In
1436, in a compromise solution, they re-entered the catholic fold as a
distinct, and tolerated, regional variant, which survived until the seventeenth
century.

Heresy was not always collective. Many individuals were charged for their
personal opinions: this was almost an occupational hazard of academic
theology. Those condemned included the great names of William of
Ockham, John Wyclif, and Jan Hus, and lesser stars like Uhtred of
Boldon, Jean Petit, Nicholas of Autrecourt, and Reginald Pecock. Even
popes were not immune. In 1332, as a private theologian rather than as
pontiff, John XXII preached on the Beatific Vision—on whether the justified
see God immediately after death, or not until the Final Judgment. Some
thought his views unorthodox, bringing attacks from extremist Franciscans
(who sought his deposition), from Parisian theologians, and from King
Robert of Naples. John partially retracted his views on his deathbed, leaving
his successor, Benedict XII, to issue a definitive ruling.

Anticlericalism

The intensity of late medieval spirituality, with its focus on the mass, on
penance, and thereby on priestly sacramental powers, stands in marked
contrast to a strand of apparently highly vocal opposition to clericalism.
'Anticlericalism' has been detected in many major writers of this
period, including Dante, Boccaccio, Langland, and Chaucer; it seems more
overt in political theorists like Marsilius of Padua and Wyclif.
'Anticlericalism' is also seen in bitterly-fought contests over jurisdiction in

Italian and German cities, and in legislation like the English *Statutes of Provisors* and *Praemunire*.

However, 'anticlericalism' is a seductive term, too easily misapplied. Criticism there certainly was, much from clerics themselves. Typical was Nicholas de Clemanges, whose *On the ruin and restoration of the church* (1400–01) lambasts contemporary abuses while urging reform in response to the Great Schism. Yet criticism with a positive intent (as most was) is not actually anticlerical. Few critics aimed to abolish church or clergy; most, whatever they said, wanted a better church, with good clergy, not bad. They sought reform, change for the better, without necessarily altering the basic structures.

Other attacks on the clergy require similar qualification. Many suggesting opposition—including tithe disputes, and complaints about pastoral care—were aimed at individuals, not all clergy. They reflect not rejection of priesthood, but a demand for good priests, and certainly do not indicate widespread rejection of the catholic priesthood and its ministrations as a prelude to Reformation.

The church in 1500

The late medieval church must be treated in its own terms, yet is over-shadowed by Reformation. Traditions of confessionalized historical scholarship have long affected assessments of pre-Reformation catholicism, tinged (or loaded) with notions of decadence and decline. The search for seeds of the Reformation, the desire to make Wyclif and Hus Protestants before Protestantism, has generated value judgements which are now increasingly untenable.

The church of 1500 was clearly no longer that of 1300. Its economic, social, spiritual, intellectual, and political contexts had changed, and forced adaptation. Yet, while it was a different church, it is impossible to say that it was actually stronger or weaker. It was spiritually vibrant, catering to contemporary aspirations, accommodating varied interpretations of and responses to the faith and its demands. Some were contradictory, but not sufficiently so to cause fissure—or were not recognized as being so. Even Hussitism had been accommodated, its challenge confined as reintegration threatened to stifle its independent vigour. Academics debated theological issues, but diversity had not yet produced adversity. The printing press, the novel agent of uniformity and stability, served the church well, pouring forth devotional tracts, liturgical texts, and mountains of theological and canon-istic writings to explain, affirm, and reinforce catholicism. From massive tomes by Augustine, Aquinas, and Gratian to single-sheet indulgences and cartoon-strip depictions of the Ten Commandments, the presses under-pinned international catholicism. Their threat was not yet evident.

The papacy's role had unavoidably evolved—without undermining its theoretical spiritual supremacy and character. After the traumas of the Great Schism and the conciliarist challenge, and the struggle to re-establish itself in Italy, the papacy was a very different institution. In bargaining for political support, it had surrendered prerogatives and practical authority for short-term benefits: outside Italy (indeed, often inside) it frequently exer-cised power on suffrance, subject to the whims of the local rulers. Yet the papacy could not be ignored. Despite criticism, and the seeming erosion of status, it was still respected, and had clout: in 1493 Alexander VI divided the world with a compass, delimiting the imperial ambitions of Spain and Portugal. Even if 'the papacy' was often treated as an administrative con-venience, its spiritual status remained high. As long as the appeal to the biblical Petrine commission retained its force, underpinning the Vicariate of Christ and all that it might mean, the papacy's spiritual primacy and supremacy was unassailable. Catholicism would lose half of Europe with the Reformation, yet in 1500 it seemed set for a period of dynamic expan-sion, in the Americas and Africa. Crystal-gazers then would surely have expected continued growth of this papal church, even if anticipating changes in its message, role, and relations with the faithful to meet the needs of this suddenly globalizing world.

Plate 5. Jan van Eyck, *The Arnolfini Portrait* (1434)

4

Culture and the arts

Alexander Lee

Jacob Burckhardt's *Die Kultur der Renaissance in Italien* (1860) marked a
watershed in historical perceptions of European culture in the fourteenth
and fifteenth centuries. In contrast to the French scholar Jules Michelet
(1798–1864), who had conceived of the period on a rather grand scale,
Burckhardt drew a sharp distinction between the 'medieval' outlook he
believed had prevailed north of the Alps and the 'rebirth' of classical
antiquity he saw taking place in the Italian peninsula. Though he recognized
that the Latin classics had continued to be studied in France and the Low
Countries, for example, it was, he believed, only in the self-governing
communes and despotisms of northern Italy, where men had cast off the
veil of 'faith, illusion, and childish presupposition' and fashioned a new
sense of man as a 'spiritual individual', that an attempt had been made to
revive the ancient past—not piecemeal, but *tout court*—as a model for the
present, and to apply classical ideals to every area of cultural activity, from
poetry and painting to architecture, sculpture, and even music.[1]

In the decades following its publication, Burckhardt's essay did not want
for critics. While some challenged his dismissive attitude towards the 'medieval' past, others took issue with his emphasis on classicism, and his quasi-
Hegelian conception of the 'spirit'. But his division of Europe into two
distinct cultural spheres was nevertheless greeted with wide approval.
Though often cast in rather different terms, it quickly became a commonplace of historical scholarship. In *Herfsttij der Middeleeuwen* (1919), for
example, the Dutch historian Johan Huizinga contended that, while the
cultural life of Italy was distinguished by a joyful sense of optimism and
rebirth, that of the French and Burgundian courts was marked by a weary
nostalgia for the chivalric past and a morbid preoccupation with death.
Similarly, in *Renaissance and Renascences* (1960), Erwin Panofsky pointed

---

[1] J. Burckhardt, *The Civilization of the Renaissance in Italy*, trans. S. G. C. Middlemore
(London, 1995), pp. 87, 111–15.

The Later Middle Ages. Isabella Lazzarini, Oxford University Press (2021). © Isabella Lazzarini.
DOI: 10.1093/oso/9780198731641.003.0005

out that one need only compare Leon Battista Alberti's design for the church of Sant'Andrea in Mantua with the choir of the Sebalduskirche in Nuremberg—both completed in 1472—to recognize that there was a fundamental difference between the art of Italy and that of the rest of Europe.

Over the past 60 years, however, the validity of such a contrast has been called into question. In distinguishing between a 'medieval' north and an Italian 'Renaissance', Burckhardt and his intellectual heirs assumed that cultures could be treated as discrete, monolithic units, and separated from one another with the same ease as lines could be drawn on a map. But scholars have increasingly come to realize that the reality was more complex. In the first place, cultural developments were anything but uniform. As Ernst Gombrich pointed out in a now-classic paper, artistic and literary innovations were accomplished not by 'a spirit or mentality shared by everyone in a society', but by small groups of individuals whose commitment to—and interpretation of—their professed ideals varied, often quite radically.[2] As a result, styles and techniques were diffused irregularly; towns and regions tended to follow their own lights; and every field was marked by a kaleidoscope of subtle differences. In the second place, cultural change showed little respect for borders. Although it is true that cartographers began incorporating frontiers into their designs from the late fifteenth century onwards, recent research has demonstrated that these neatly drawn boundaries neither contained discreet cultural domains nor precluded cultural exchange. Quite the reverse. Thanks to the growth of international trade, the proliferation of conflict, and the growing ease of communication, the diverse parts of Europe were brought into closer contact than ever before—thus dramatically increasing the opportunities for cultural commerce.

As a consequence, it is now generally accepted that the fourteenth and fifteenth centuries were characterized more by diversity than by division. Though some general trends can still be observed, it has become increasingly clear that, in every field of cultural endeavour, from painting and sculpture to poetry and music, there emerged a series of quite different, often heterogeneous trends. Originating in different parts of Europe, these were transmitted by various means across the continent, where they interacted with parallel developments elsewhere to assume ever more varied forms; and though some occasionally achieved a greater prominence than others, the

[2] E. Gombrich, 'Renaissance—Period or Movement?', in A. G. Dickens et al. (eds), *Background to the Italian Renaissance: Introductory Lectures* (London, 1974), pp. 9–30.

effect was less that of a concerto than of a rich and discordant symphony of competing voices.

Patronage and consumption

Underlying this diversity was a fundamental shift in the character of patronage. Though there was no sudden or dramatic break with the past, a combination of political, economic, and religious factors gradually transformed traditional patterns of consumption. The church, previously the principal agent of cultural production, saw its dominance falter. Despite laudable efforts to rebuild, first Avignon, then Rome, the papacy was too gravely weakened by schism, and too preoccupied with temporal concerns to play anything but a fleeting role in the cultural dramas of the day. Especially in Italy, dioceses became impoverished; the mendicant orders challenged the position of the monasteries; and across Europe, the growth of heterodoxy was accompanied by the emergence of more private and introspective forms of devotion. In much the same way, royal courts wavered. Though they continued to flourish as cultural centres, and even grew in importance as the business of government became more complex, the monarchs around whom they revolved found their patronage compromised. In England and France, the Hundred Years War emptied treasuries and sapped confidence. In Naples, an initial period of glorious stability under Robert of Anjou gave way to almost a century of civil strife. In the Holy Roman Empire, electors strove to minimize—or at least circumscribe—the authority of kings and emperors, thus preventing all but Charles IV of Luxembourg and the later Habsburgs from embarking on major cultural projects. And in Spain, the steady if uneven advance of the *Reconquista* imposed new burdens on divided and diverse kingdoms.

At the same time, new patrons emerged alongside the old, each with their own distinctive cultural needs, and their own desire for affirmation through consumption. Chief amongst these were the towns. Though theirs was already a long history, the growth of trade greatly increased both their economic importance and their political standing. In northern Italy, city-republics and *signori* consolidated the de facto autonomy to which they had become accustomed, and strengthened their organs of self-government. In the German lands, the free imperial cities (*Reichsstädte*) won progressively more rights and privileges from an enfeebled crown. And in England, kings granted a number of new charters. Between these, there was of course much variation, especially in the structure of public offices and the extent of urban liberties. But at the heart of every town lay a thriving bourgeoisie. Lower in standing than the old nobility (whom they often displaced), but more elevated than the disenfranchised masses, these 'burghers' were distinguished by their membership of guilds, their comparative wealth, and their dominance of civic government. By profession, they were merchants, lawyers, or speculators; by temperament, they were ambitious and ostentatious; but by inclination, they were often as deeply concerned with the personal as with the public.

Literacy and the vernacular

Of the many effects wrought by these changes, perhaps the most ubiquitous was the growing importance attached to the written word. As commerce expanded and secular government became more sophisticated, the need to keep accurate records became progressively more acute. Merchants relied on bills of sale and statements of account to transact business; public servants were required to minute council meetings and conduct correspondence; and even the most modest families found themselves obliged to resort to pen and ink to secure their property, or to impose order on their household affairs.

To meet these needs, there emerged a sophisticated system of elementary education, capable of instilling at least a basic level of literacy. Its structure and development varied considerably across Europe; but some general trends can nevertheless be discerned. Three main types of school existed: the 'communal' (paid for by urban governments, or, in some cases, by lay communities), the 'independent' (freelance teachers employed directly by parents), and the ecclesiastical (operated by monasteries or cathedral chapters). In the past, the last had tended to be in the majority. By the early fourteenth century, however, this began to change. Though in Germany, ecclesiastical schools still tended to prevail, they quickly proved unable to cope with growing demand. In the Low Countries, the crisis was severe. In Italy they collapsed entirely, due partly to monastic objections to child oblation, and partly to the gradual impoverishment of cathedral chapters. The gap this created was filled by communal schools and independent masters, each of which was increasingly staffed by specialized elementary teachers more attuned to the actual needs of their charges than to overarching religious concerns.

The accent was, above all, on practical literacy. Though Latin always played a prominent role in the curriculum, it did not always predominate. In Germany and the Low Countries, the vernacular was regarded as at least as important—if not more so. In Italy, the picture was admittedly more mixed. Whereas in Venice, primacy was accorded to the Latin grammar curriculum until well into the fifteenth century, a less conservative view held sway in Florence. There, the traditional Latin grammar curriculum increasingly coexisted with vernacular 'abacus' instruction—a new innovation, geared towards preparing students for business.

Despite some regional variation, literacy appears to have increased markedly over the course of the fourteenth and fifteenth centuries—no more so than in Italy. Writing in *c.*1338, the chronicler Giovanni Villani (*c.*1276–80 to 1348) claimed that in Florence '8000 to 10,000 boys and girls' were 'learning to read', '1,000 to 1,200 boys' were following the *abbaco*, and a further 550 to 600 were 'studying grammar and logic'—the equivalent of a male schooling rate of 67–83 per cent.[3] Incredible though this figure may seem, it is borne out by the Florentine *catasto* (tax records) of 1427. Given that the head of each household was supposed to make out a tax declaration in his own hand, or, if he could not, have someone else do it for him, it has been possible to calculate that at least 69.3 per cent of the adult male population could read and write.[4]

Partly as a result of this 'revolution' in literacy, the fourteenth and fifteenth centuries also witnessed the growth of vernacular writing. Whereas the common tongue had been used only infrequently in the past, it now became an indispensable part of written communication. Though there was, of course, some variation, its spread seems in retrospect to have been inexorable. Across Europe its status and authority grew; its applications, once few in number and limited in scope, multiplied; and its flexibility—not to mention its familiarity—made it possible for texts to address a much wider range of purposes than previously thought possible.

Naturally enough, everyday life provided the arena for most vernacular production. In some parts of Europe—particularly where Romance languages were spoken—vernaculars were brought to bear on almost every facet of ordinary experience. In Italy, for example, we find an extraordinary

---

[3] P. F. Grendler, *Schooling in Renaissance Italy: Literacy and Learning, 1300–1600* (Baltimore and London, 1989), pp. 71–2.

[4] R. Black, *Education and Society in Florentine Tuscany: Teachers, Pupils and Schools, c.1250–1300* (Leiden, 2007), pp. 1–42.

number of urban chronicles, private letters, account books, and *libri di ricordi* (a kind of diary), all written in local dialects. Elsewhere, the picture was somewhat patchier. In England, for example, business Latin was 'far too supple an instrument', too replete with French and English loanwords, 'to be easily replaced', and remained the lingua franca of commerce until well into the fifteenth century.[5] Even here, however, some notable vernacular letter collections (e.g. the Paston letters) and private devotional works survive.

Translations from Latin into the vernacular also became common. Books of the Bible and saints' lives were particularly popular, although in England there was some debate about whether rendering Scripture into the common tongue would debase God's word. There were also a number of important translations of classical texts. Towards the end of the thirteenth century, for example, Brunetto Latini (*c.*1220–94) prepared Tuscan versions of three of Cicero's orations, and began a similar translation of Cicero's *De inventione*.

Arguably the most important development, however, was the emergence of the vernacular as a literary language. This was, admittedly, not an entirely new trend. Strong vernacular traditions already existed in France, Germany, and Spain; and though Italy had lagged behind for a time, the poetic possibilities of everyday speech had been recognised by the Sicilian School in the mid-thirteenth century. After *c.*1300, however, the use of the vernacular began to assume a new vigour, reinforced in some cases by the hardening of patriotic sentiments amidst the vicissitudes of war, and in others by the proliferation of religious heterodoxy.

For the first time, the vernacular came to be regarded as a mode of expression equal in dignity to Latin—and strident efforts were made to defend its merits. Perhaps inevitably, it was in Italy, where scepticism was most pronounced, that the earliest and most striking justifications were produced. Dante Alighieri's *De vulgari eloquentia* is perhaps the best known; but the works of Leonardo Bruni (1370–1444) and Cristoforo Landino (1424–98) are no less worthy of remark. Other parts of Europe were not far behind, however. In 1549, for example, Joachim du Bellay proudly declared his belief in the superiority of French in *La Défense et illustration de la langue française*. With or without a theoretical underpinning, however, vernacular writings abounded. In Italy, the three 'crowns' each brought Tuscan to bear on a different genre: Dante to epic, Francesco Petrarca (1304–74)—known in English as Petrarch—to love poetry, and

[5] J. Catto, 'Written English: The Making of the Language, 1370–1420', *Past & Present* (2003), pp. 24–59, at p. 37.

Giovanni Boccaccio (1313–75) to *novelle*. In England, from the 1370s onwards, Geoffrey Chaucer pioneered a range of metrical innovations in works such as *The House of Fame*, while William Langland combined social commentary with mystical allegory in *Piers Plowman*. And in Germany, Johannes von Tepl (*c*.1350–*c*.1415) and Sebastian Brandt (1458–1521) each experimented with moralistic and satirical verse.

One of the principal effects of this was the solidification of 'national' languages. Just as Chaucer is sometimes said to have helped establish the variety of Middle English spoken in and around London as a 'standard' English, so debates about Italian's merits as a literary language ultimately served to consolidate the Tuscan dialect as the Italian vernacular. Similarly, Charles IV of Luxembourg consciously cultivated Czech literature as a means of strengthening 'Bohemian' identity. Yet at the same time, the emergence of vernacular literature also drew strength from cultural exchange between parts of Europe. At the same time as Latin works were being rendered into the common tongue, a growing effort was made to translate works from one vernacular into another—and thereby to accelerate the exchange of literary innovations. A good example is provided by Boccaccio's story of Griselda. Originally written in Tuscan, it was translated into Latin by Petrarch, into Middle English by Chaucer, and later into German by Heinrich Steinhöwel.

Humanism

Alongside vernacular literature, there emerged a new interest in the study and emulation of the ancient classics, known as humanism. Though its roots have been hotly debated, two principal points of origin can be discerned. Its first manifestation appeared in Padua, in the final decades of the thirteenth century. As Ronald Witt has shown, it developed out of the study of grammar, and was distinguished, above all, by a new approach to the learning of Latin. Whereas, in the past, so-called *dictatores* had placed greater stress on the inculcation of rules than on the reading of classical texts, the humanists believed that the study and imitation of Latin *auctores* was the best way of learning how to write Latin correctly. From this essentially pedagogical insight, there arose not only a scholarly appetite for the accuracy of Latin texts but also a new-found enthusiasm for composing works in an authentically 'classical' style, and an inkling that, in the culture of the ancient past, there might lurk a model for the present. An early pioneer was Lovato de' Lovati (c.1240–1309). Boldly announcing his desire to 'follow in the footsteps of the ancients', he composed a number of Latin poems, often dealing with political questions, in the style of Ovid, Propertius, and Statius (amongst others), and wrote an essay on Seneca's tragedies which marked a watershed in the study of ancient prosody. But it was only in the generation which followed that the potential of this new approach was fully realized. As the practice of *imitatio* was extended to new genres, it was quickly realized that the works of Latin moralists and historians could be viewed not simply as stylistic models, but also as repositories of precepts which could be applied meaningfully to the challenges of the present day. In this a leading role was placed by Albertino Mussato (1261–1329). Though he penned a number of occasional verses and even some priapic poetry, it was in defence of Padua's liberty that he wrote his most important works. His best known is the *Ecerinis*. Modelled on Seneca's tragedies, this was a dramatic (if rather fanciful) dramatization of the commune's struggle against Ezzelino da Romano a few decades earlier. Mussato also wrote a number of histories in both poetry and prose, each replete with classicizing devices, such as set-piece speeches and topographical digressions.

A short time later, however, a second, subtly different, strain of humanism appeared in nearby Verona. Centred on the cathedral library, this was more antiquarian and philological in focus. It was concerned almost exclusively with the recovery of 'lost' texts, the preparation of accurate redactions, and the pursuit of ancient history. Perhaps because of the relative disinterest in the emulation of a classical style, the church fathers continued to be revered, and a marked continuity between the luminaries of ancient Rome and patristic literature was perceived. Among its leading lights was Giovanni de' Matociis (d. 1339). A notary and sacristan by calling, he is particularly noteworthy for having been the first to distinguish between the two Plinies.

Though early attempts at synthesis were made by Giovanni da Cermenate (c.1280-post 1344) and Convenevole da Prato (c.1270/5–c.1338), it fell to Petrarch (1304–74) to bring these two strains together with the completeness they deserved. Born into a Florentine family, Petrarch was, by his own confession, something of a wanderer. Though much of his life was spent in Provence, near the papal court in Avignon, he passed many years flitting between the cities of northern Italy, often as the guest of local *signori*. This rootlessness gave him a rather different perspective to his predecessors. Whereas, in decades gone by, the humanists' literary activities had been tied to the interests of their native cities, or pursued with scholarly abstraction, Petrarch made Rome the focus of his endeavours. Driven by a lifelong fascination with the city's ancient glory, he believed that it was his task to help restore the classical past to 'light' after a long period of darkness. The first person to be crowned poet laureate on the Capitol in over 1,000 years, he strove to imitate classical Latinity more closely than ever before, and extended the classicizing impulse to a wide range of other literary forms. As well as epistles in both poetry and prose, he wrote epic verse, moral treatises, penitential psalms, public orations, invectives, and dialogue— many of which would go on to be recognized as models of their kind. In the avidity with which he sought out 'lost' works, and in the sophistication of his textual methods, he far excelled his predecessors. He reconstructed the surviving decades of Livy's *Ab urbe condita* from fragments in different manuscripts, rediscovered Cicero's letters to Atticus in Verona cathedral library, and exposed the so-called *Privilegium maius* as a crude forgery. Perhaps most importantly, he also strove to make Rome once again the true *caput mundi*. After briefly supporting the ill-fated Roman 'revolution' of Cola di Rienzo (1313–54), he repeatedly urged Charles IV of Luxembourg to make Rome the capital of a renewed empire, and exhorted successive popes to return the papacy to its proper home.

After Petrarch's death, this form of humanism continued to flourish in Milan, Padua, and Bologna. But it was in Florence that the fires of the new learning burned most brightly. Of those who fed its flames, the most significant was Coluccio Salutati (1331–1406). A long-time admirer (and sometime correspondent) of Petrarch, Salutati was in some respects a faithful continuator of his work. Though they differed on a number of points (e.g. allegory, predestination, free will), Salutati's private cultural interests were cut from a similar cloth. He wrote extended treatises on fate and fortune, on the merits of the secular and religious life, on the rivalry of law and medicine, and on the labours of Hercules. But in other respects, Salutati propelled humanism along a quite different path. In his hands, humanism once again acquired a profoundly 'civic' character. As chancellor of Florence, he turned his back on Petrarch's dream of Roman renewal, and instead used his learning to defend republican liberty, first against the papacy, and then against Gian Galeazzo Visconti of Milan. At the same time, he also opened humanism up to the study of Greek. Though he, like Petrarch, had only the most rudimentary grasp of the language, he recognized that it was impossible to understand Latin literature without an appreciation of Greek culture, and to this end persuaded the Byzantine scholar Manuel Chrysoloras (*c*.1355–1415) to take up a position as a professor of Greek at the Florentine *Studio*.

These developments were to have a decisive impact in the decades that followed. Two individuals were to pursue their implications with particular vigour: Leonardo Bruni (1370–1444) and Poggio Bracciolini (1380–1459). Though they too had been nourished on Petrarch's legacy, they followed Salutati in adopting a far more critical approach to earlier generations of humanists—and to the classical figures whom they had held up as models for emulation. In Bruni's *Dialogues*, a fictionalized version of the bibliophile Niccolò Niccoli (1364–1437) attacks Petrarch for his impenetrable style, Dante for condemning Caesar's assassins, and Boccaccio for his flippancy—only to defend them all a little later in the same text. They were also more overtly 'republican'. Though the term 'civic humanism' should be used with caution, there emerged from their writings a sense not only of the superiority of republicanism to all other forms of government, but also of the virtues which citizens needed to cultivate in order to defend their liberty. What was more, they threw themselves into the study of Greek culture. Bruni translated Aristotle's *Nicomachean Ethics* and *Politics*, as well as the pseudo-Aristotelian *Economics*, while Bracciolini prepared Latin versions Xenophon's *Cyropedia* and the first five books of Diodorus Siculus' history, amongst others.

Humanism was, however, neither purely Florentine nor in any way homogeneous. By this point, it had already begun to put down roots elsewhere—and to assume a variety of different forms. In Milan, Antonio Loschi (1368–1441) and Pier Candido Decembrio (1399–1477) emerged as vigorous (if occasionally inconstant) defenders of signorial government. In Venice, patricians like Francesco Barbaro (1390–1454) and Bernardo Giustiniani (1408–89) strove to glorify the Republic, while also writing treatises on moral and social problems. And in Naples, the royal court was home to a remarkable group of poets, scholars, and historians. Of these none was of greater consequence than Lorenzo Valla (1407–57). Truculent, irascible, and almost compulsively argumentative, Valla pursued the textual practices of humanist scholarship further than any other. To his mind, the correct use of language was not merely a desirable end in itself, but the foundation of all intellectual enquiry. Its value to the study of history was obvious. In his most famous work, Valla used philological techniques to demonstrate that the so-called Donation of Constantine—which had long been used to support the papacy's claims to temporal as well as spiritual supremacy—was a forgery. So too was its relevance to biblical exegesis, a field previously neglected by humanist scholarship. By comparing the Vulgate to the Greek text of the New Testament, Valla was able to identify a number of previously unnoticed flaws in the translation, and to suggest appropriate emendations. But it was of greatest value to philosophy. In the *Elegentiae linguae latinae*, Valla explained that the reason why so many previous philosophers had erred was that they had lacked a *facultas loquendi*. Seduced by over-complicated, technical language and fruitless dialectic, he argued, they had been led far from truth—and had even come to contradict the precepts of the Christian faith. To Valla, 'ordinary' language, tempered by a thorough grounding in Latin and Greek grammar, was sufficient to comprehend everything—and on that basis he sought to make it the core of a new, humanistic vision of the world.

Yet it was in Florence that humanism still had its spiritual home. Under the patronage of the Medici, there emerged a marked predilection for Platonism. This was, to be sure, not entirely new. At Salutati's suggestion, Bruni had translated Plato's *Phaedo*, and had found in it a 'confirmation of the true faith'. But from the middle decades of the fifteenth century, Platonism's prominence increased exponentially—due partly to encounters with Greek culture at the Council of Florence (1439), and partly to the influx of Byzantine scholars after the fall of Constantinople (1453). It was, admittedly, not without opponents. Particularly during the middle years of the fifteenth century, George of Trebizond (1395–1486) saw Plato's revival as a harbinger of the Antichrist, and engaged in a lengthy dispute with Cardinal Bessarion (1403–72) about the 'errors' of his philosophy. By the 1470s, however, Platonism had found in Marsilio Ficino (1433–99) its most able exponent. Ficino not only provided authoritative translations and commentaries on Plato's dialogues, but also wrote a lengthy treatise (the *Platonic Theology*) in which he attempted to demonstrate the harmony of Plato's conception of the soul with the tenets of Christianity.

As this engagement with Plato suggests, humanism was never an introspective endeavour. At no point did it seek to isolate itself from other disciplines, or other intellectual concerns. Though Petrarch often decried the 'sophistry' of some schoolmen, for example, the humanists were never hostile towards either Aristotle or scholastic philosophy. Quite the reverse. Especially insofar as political theory was concerned, the humanists' debt both to Aristotle and to contemporary Aristotelians was often profound. Until Louis IV's ill-fated Roman expedition, Mussato maintained a close friendship with Marsilius of Padua and drew on Aristotelian terminology in outlining his understanding of the political community in his *De lite inter naturam et fortunam.* Similarly, Bruni's claim—in the *Isagogicon moralis disciplinae*—that human happiness required not just spiritual but also material goods was taken directly from the *Nicomachean Ethics.* Nor was humanism inimical to law—especially Roman law. Many humanists had some legal background, as either notaries or judges; and an appreciable number engaged in a lively, if not always explicit, dialogue with contemporary juristic thought. Cola di Rienzo, for example, delivered a famous oration on the *lex de imperio Vespasiani* in the basilica of St John Lateran in 1347; and Salutati's *De tyranno* is at least partly framed around arguments borrowed from Bartolus of Sassoferrato.

Nor, indeed, was humanism exclusively 'Italian'. Though it traced its origins to self-governing cities in Tuscany and the March of Treviso, it was from the first a cultural endeavour which reached far beyond the peninsula. Not only did Petrarch spend much of his life in Provence, but he also undertook diplomatic missions to Paris and Prague, where he found a number of ready admirers. Bartolomeo della Fonte (1446–1513) spent many years at the court of King Matthias Corvinus in Hungary; and thanks to the enduring intellectual strength of Italian universities, the fruits of humanism were carried back across the Alps by the students who enrolled. Already well-established in Bohemia and certain parts of Germany by the mid-fourteenth century, humanism had become a truly European phenomenon by the end of the fifteenth.

Architecture

The transformation of the built environment followed a less clear-cut path. For much of the twelfth and thirteenth centuries, architecture had been confined within narrow bounds. Its principal subject had been the church; and its style the stiff, unyielding French Gothic, known as the *rayonnant*. From *c.*1300, however, this pattern was broken. As patronage shifted from the ecclesiastical to the secular, and as political authority began to fracture, architecture was harnessed to a far wider range of purposes. Though churches continued to be a focus for innovation—especially in electoral bishoprics or self-governing cities—their dominance was contested by the proliferation of palaces (in preference to defensive castles), royal and private chapels, town halls, guild halls, and even lesser urban residences. This occasioned a dramatic transformation of style and manner. New settings required a new approach to structural design, while competition between patrons, each anxious to outdo the others, fuelled an almost pathological inventiveness. The staid formality of the *rayonnant* was gradually abandoned, and in its place there appeared a succession of more fluid alternatives, capable of accommodating regional idiosyncrasies, and sustaining an insatiable appetite for improvisation. The result was a proliferation of new architectural styles, so dizzying in their variety that few, if any, general trends can be observed, and so rich in novelty that only by breaking them down into their different forms can their characteristics clearly be seen.

Perhaps unsurprisingly, it was in France that the *rayonnant* survived the longest. Due partly to the demise of the Capetians, and partly to the destitution of the Valois kings, royal patronage was unable to furnish the impetus towards innovation that it might otherwise have supplied. Not until the stabilization of the new dynasty in the mid-fourteenth century did signs of a new style begin to appear. Known as the *flamboyant*, this was first seen in the fortified palaces increasingly favoured by the upper echelons of the French nobility. Partly because of the peculiarly hybrid nature of these structures, the *flamboyant* was characterized by its looseness and mobility. Florid tracery—set off by large blank spaces—was combined with undulating lines and double arches. Capitals disappeared; canopied niches abounded; and elaborately decorated portals came to the fore. By the beginning of the fifteenth century, however, its influence had begun to extend to other genres of building. Particularly noticeable examples include the west façade of Sainte-Chapelle de Vincennes (1379–1480) and the Hôtel de Cluny in Paris (1485–98).

In England, the *rayonnant* was initially supplanted by the so-called 'Decorated Style' (*c.*1290–1350). Often said to have been pioneered by Michael of Canterbury (*fl.* 1275–1321), this was a lively, even exuberant, rebellion against French norms which found its earliest expression in St Stephen's Chapel in the Palace of Westminster. Though it was, from the beginning, a loose collection of different elements, it was characterized by a greater intricacy of design. Continuities were interrupted, and tracery abounded. The bay—one of the most distinctive features of the Gothic cathedral—was broken up by lierne vaults, in which ribs were joined by intermediate bonds to give a star- or net-like appearance; ogee arches, consisting of two 's-shaped' curves meeting at the apex, were introduced into windows and niches; and canopies were used with joyful abandon.

Yet even as the Decorated Style was brought to its fullest potentiality, its limitations were already becoming apparent. For while its flamboyant disjunctures and filigree whimsy may have been a refreshing tonic after the austerity of the *rayonnant*, its richness tended towards spatial confusion. By the outbreak of the Hundred Years War, it had begun to be supplanted by the 'Perpendicular Style' (*c*.1330–*c*.1520). Claimed by some to have originated with William Ramsey's design for the chapter house of Old St Paul's cathedral (begun *c*.1332), this is perhaps best exemplified by the chapel of King's College, Cambridge (begun 1446). At its heart was an abiding concern for the coherence of design. Tracery was no longer allowed the free rein it had enjoyed in the past. Instead, it was reduced to a series of simpler, repeating patterns which could be stretched over the building like a web. Clear, sharp lines were given priority over florid complexity, and vertical harmonies were emphasized by slender columns and increasingly fine mullions. The triforium largely vanished, its place being taken by taller nave arches and an enlarged clerestory. And the lierne evolved into the fan vault—unquestionably England's most distinctive contribution to the architecture of the age.

In the German lands and the Low Countries, the *rayonnant* was subjected to more radical—and chaotic—reimagination. Though the influence of English trends can sometimes be strongly felt, political fragmentation and growing urban self-confidence fostered an abundance of styles, techniques, and even materials. Indeed, so varied were the innovations and so rich the inventiveness that scholars have rarely even tried 'to impose conceptual cohesion upon this tangle of forms'.[6]

As in England, some of the earliest efforts to break away from French influence were characterized by the profusion of tracery and ornamentation; but its application was almost relentless, culminating in enormous spires and surfaces crammed with jarring decorative elements. A good example is provided by the façade of Strasbourg Cathedral. Begun in *c*.1332, it a work of breath-taking complexity, an intricate mass of varied patterns, delicate statuary, and filigree canopies.

In the second half of the century, some measure of discipline began to be imposed by Peter Parler (1333–99). The son of an equally distinguished architect from Schwäbisch Gmünd, Parler had likely worked on the façade of Cologne Cathedral before accepting a commission from Charles IV of Luxembourg to oversee the reconstruction of Prague in 1356. His inclination was, naturally, towards the intricate; but his instinct was nevertheless orderly, and his designs governed by a subtle but unshakeable sensitivity

---

[6] N. Nussbaum, *German Gothic Church Architecture*, trans. S. Kleager (New Haven, CT: Yale University Press, 2000), p. 87.

for geometrical wholeness. Much later German architecture was undertaken in Parler's shadow, especially in the old heartlands of the Empire.

Elsewhere, however, a richer variation took hold. In Brabant, for example, churches—often built from a light and malleable sandstone—retained some elements of *rayonnant* design (e.g. bundled pillars), but were distinguished by elegant tracery friezes, strong vertical lines, and lierne vaults, while town halls—such as Leuven (1448–69) and Brussels (1402–54)—were covered in a superabundance of tracery and statues, and often topped with highly elaborate turrets.

In the Iberian kingdoms, the *rayonnant* style was generally repudiated. There, capaciousness—rather than ornamentation—was paramount. Partly due to the pervasive influence of the mendicant orders, cathedrals and churches tended to be wide and tremendously tall. Transepts disappeared, and naves were often encased by side-chapels. Though frequently topped with spires (e.g. Burgos Cathedral), and incorporating decorative elements borrowed from Islamic architecture, façades tended to be comparatively uncluttered, with elements of tracery being balanced by broad, flat surfaces (e.g. León Cathedral).

In Italy, the picture was rather more confused. Though elements of the *rayonnant* did survive into the fourteenth century, it was refracted through a kaleidoscope of local tastes, prejudices, and pretentions. In Milan, for example, Gian Galeazzo Visconti's new cathedral—built partly to strengthen his claims to a ducal title—combined a typically Lombard plan with ostentatiously French features. The façade of Orvieto Cathedral, meanwhile, combined a rather restrained French design with glittering polychromatic mosaics. And in Pisa, the little church of Santa Maria della Spina was laid out on an unassuming rectangular plan, but faced with banded marble and adorned with a complex network of tympana, cusps, rose windows, and statues. From the beginning of the fifteenth century onwards, however, architects endeavoured to include more 'classical' elements in their design. This tendency was especially pronounced in Florence. Though his style was perhaps more 'Tuscan' than 'Roman' in many respects, Filippo Brunelleschi (1377–1446) has long been credited with pioneering a new architecture *all'antica*. His major works—such as the Ospedale degli Innocenti (1419) and the Pazzi chapel (*c.*1440)—incorporate elements such as round arches, slender columns, pilasters, Corinthian capitals, and hemispherical domes. A little later, Leon Battista Alberti (1404–72) took this still further. A diligent student of Vitruvius' recently rediscovered *De architectura*, Alberti not only grasped the essentials of classical orders but also wrote an influential

treatise—the *De re aedificatoria*—laying down rules for the design of buildings which were to have a lasting effect on the development of architecture
in later centuries—and which were eventually to enjoy a European
readership.

The visual arts

The development of the visual arts mirrors that of architecture. Although it
used to be thought that the fourteenth and fifteenth centuries witnessed a
transition from French Gothic to Italian classicism, recent research has
shown that the period was characterized more by diversity than by displace-
ment. Out of the maelstrom of social, economic, and religious change
sweeping Europe, there emerged not only a demand for new art forms but
also new expectations of the function(s) art should perform. This, in turn,
provided the impetus for technical and stylistic innovation. As in so many
other fields, there was, admittedly, no sudden break with the past. For the
most part, change was gradual; and in each halting step, continuity was at
least as evident as rupture. Nor indeed was there much common purpose.
Though it is difficult to avoid using rather broad terms to describe aspects of
style, each city or region tended to follow its own light. Each favoured its
own forms and styles, and when it adopted another's insights, adapted them
to its own needs. And as the exchange of artworks and ideas gathered pace,
so the admixture of different styles gave rise to an infinitude of subtle
variations.

In previous centuries, the dominance of court and church had tended to
limit the visual arts to a relatively narrow range of forms, such as altarpieces,
manuscript illuminations, stained glass, tombs, portal statuary, and portable
devotional pieces. Though chivalric romances and courtly themes were, of
course, occasionally tackled in secular pieces, most works tended to address
religious themes. In these, a certain strain of naturalism was already beginning to make itself felt. In depictions of the Virgin Mary and the Passion of
Christ, for example, the humanity and intimacy of the scene was made
vividly apparent; rich fabrics fell in folds; and even in the romances which
dominated the secular imagination, there were hints of genuine emotion.
But this was nevertheless restrained by an overarching emphasis on simplicity. Due partly to the persistence of earlier religious practices, compositions
tended to rely on the reduction of the represented world to its most basic
elements, and on the arrangement of elements in a narrative form.

Beginning in *c.*1300, a gradual process of evolution was set in motion. The transformation of old patterns of consumption and the emergence of new classes of patron created new contexts for production; and this in turn gave rise to a corresponding demand for new art forms and subjects. One such shift occurred in towns. Having now consolidated their de facto independence, self-governing cities began adorning municipal buildings and public spaces with works celebrating their liberty, extolling their strength, or fostering their civic virtues. Yet arguably the most important change in the secular sphere was the 'domestication' of the visual arts. As aristocratic patrons grew in confidence and members of the urban bourgeoisie rose in status, defensive castles and urban *case* gave way to luxurious palaces. This led to the development not only of highly decorated rooms defined by function, such as the *studiolo* (study) and the *camera* (bedroom), but also of new art forms tailored to those settings, like the *cassone* (a wedding chest, one or more panels of which constituted a painted scene) and the *lettuccio* (a high-backed bench). Though frescoed walls remained popular, tapestries became more elaborate and ambitious; and freestanding paintings and sculptures also came to be viewed as suitable, even normal decorations for the home. This, of course, had a knock-on effect on subject matter. Though the religious was a constant presence, secular themes—courtly romances, ancient myths, tales from vernacular literature, interior scenes, even landscapes—gradually assumed a greater prominence; and portraiture also became common.

At the same time, shifts in devotional practices led to the 'privatization' of religious works. Following the promulgation of the doctrine of Purgatory (1274), a more introspective form of worship had emerged. The individual was now encouraged to reflect more seriously on his own sinfulness, and to take whatever spiritual measures were necessary to alleviate the punishments he was liable to suffer in the next life. Particular emphasis was laid on the *meditatio mortis* and the intercession of saints. One effect of this was the proliferation of private commissions for churches and the foundation of a growing number of private chapels, a trend which was facilitated by the growth of the mendicant orders. But a far more important consequence was the emergence of a range of new art forms and subjects designed to focus contemplation, encourage immersion, or even solicit prayers after death. Though there is considerable variation between regions, these included *Andachtsbilder* (devotional images), often small enough to be used in private meditation and prayer, chantry tombs, and non-narrative iconic representations, especially of the Passion of Christ, the Veronica, the Man of

Sorrows, and the Pietà—many of which commonly featured portraits of, or at least allusions to, the patrons who had commissioned them.

These developments helped stimulate the development of new methods of artistic representation during the fourteenth century. Across Europe, the growing preoccupation with the personal and the emotive gave rise to a greater lyricism, a fineness of line, and a delicacy of shape. But in certain parts of Italy and southern France, the impulse towards naturalism first glimpsed in the Gothic of the previous century also began to be developed in a more radical—and far-reaching—direction. In this process, two figures were of particular importance. One was Giotto di Bondone (c.1267–1337). Building on the work of Cimabue (c.1240–1302) and Pietro Cavallini (1259–c.1330), Giotto succeeded in endowing his scenes with a sense of depth and space, and his figures with a truly three-dimensional quality. This allowed him to employ entirely novel compositional techniques. Whereas before there had been a tendency to fill the painted area with figures, carefully arranged to relate a narrative sequence, Giotto was now able to establish a more dynamic relationship between personalities, and to capture the intensity of a single moment. But his was not the only solution to the challenges of the day. Of equal notes is the Sienese artist Duccio di Buoninsegna (c.1255/60–c.1318–19). Working predominantly with panels, Duccio used the interplay of lines, colours, and planes—rather than a sense of volume—to convey the impression of spatial depth. His style was more delicate; and the relationship between his figures more intricate. Such is apparent in the Rucellai Madonna; but the effect is even more clearly evident in the work of his continuators. Simone Martini's *Annunciation* (1333) is a particularly good example. Though the figures are still, to some extent, artificial in appearance, and their emotions rather strained, the flowing nature of lines gives them a sense of depth, and a remarkable immediacy.

Though Giotto and Duccio are most closely associated with Florence and Siena, their contribution to the development of artistic style was anything but parochial. At various points in his career, Giotto worked in Padua, Assisi, Rome, and Bologna—as well as in Provence and the Regno. Simone Martini was similarly peripatetic, spending significant periods of time in both Naples and Avignon. This ensured that their innovations spread rapidly throughout Europe, combining with local traditions to produce distinctive and idiosyncratic variants of the new realism.

It was, however, only in the early fifteenth century that the potential of these new methods were fully realized. Despite their differences, Giotto and Duccio had each demonstrated that the 'problem of space'—essential to all forms of naturalism—was essentially a matter of mathematics, or rather of geometry. Though they had approached this intuitively, rather than analytically, Filippo Brunelleschi succeeded in developing their insight into a fully developed system of linear perspective. This made it possible to imitate reality more closely than ever before, and transformed pictorial representation into a truly mimetic endeavour. The effect is vividly apparent in Masaccio's *Trinity* (1425–7). Painted for the church of Santa Maria Novella in Florence, this is thought to be the earliest surviving application of Brunelleschi's principles.

The effect on style was dramatic. Though the earlier emphasis on slender, delicate lines did not disappear altogether—especially in northern Europe— linear perspective had robbed it of its utility. In its place, a greater monumentality began to take hold in both painting and sculpture. This did not, to be sure, entail a loss of grace. Far from it. One need only look at Mantegna's *Entombment* (*c.*1465–75) or Filippino Lippi's *Allegory of Music* (*c.*1500) to see an unmistakable elegance of movement. But figures were nevertheless invested with a weightiness, a solidity which they had not previously possessed.

These compositional and stylistic innovations were to interact powerfully with two further developments. The first was technological. Whereas, in the past, egg-based tempera had been the principle medium for painting, oils now became available for the first time. Often attributed, albeit rather dubiously, to Jan van Eyck (*ante* 1390–1441), oils allowed for far greater depth of colour and subtlety of expression. As a consequence, the possibilities of naturalism were immeasurably enhanced. In the Low Countries, where painting *al olio* first emerged, van Eyck and his circle seized on oil's potential to produce a series of exceptionally vivid landscapes and domestic scenes. But yoked to the growing spirit of religious simplicity, it led to devotional works which combine a haunting, almost unsettling calm, with an arresting emotional intensity. Transplanted to Naples by the Spanish, it was adopted to remarkable effect by Antonello da Messina (*c.*1430–79); from there, it was later to endow Venetian painting with the rich colouration for which it is best known. But the compositional qualities it permitted were admired almost as much as the technique itself, and fuelled the growing appetite for Netherlandish art south of the Alps. In 1460, Bianca Maria Sforza sent Zanetto Bugatto to the Low Countries to be trained by Rogier van der Weyden; and in the 1470s, Federico da Montefeltro summoned Justus of Ghent to work in Urbino.

The second was a 'classicizing' impulse. Though Nicola Pisano (*c.*1220/ 4–84) had already begun to integrate features borrowed from Roman sarcophagi into his works at the end of the thirteenth century, it was during the Quattrocento that antiquity was brought to bear on the visual arts most fully. This was, in origin, closely related to the growth of humanism. Since Petrarch's friendship with Simone Martini in the early Trecento, humanists had enjoyed a close friendship with painters and artists. As a guest of the Medici, the young Michelangelo, for example, had rubbed shoulders with Marsilio Ficino and Pico della Mirandola, and later confided to his biographer, Antonio Condivi, that, in carving his relief of the *Battle of the Centaurs and Lapiths*, he had been encouraged by Poliziano. As this suggests, the classicizing effect was naturally felt in the growing prominence accorded to subject matter. But it was to have a much wider impact. Inspired by the recovery of Vitruvius' *De architectura*, architectonic elements—columns, capitals, arches, plinths, etc.—began to be introduced into scenes, often in a ruined state. Symbolism and allegory began to assume a fresh importance, particularly under the influence of Florentine Neoplatonism; and works of extraordinary iconological sophistication—such as Botticelli's *Mystical Nativity* (*c*.1500–01) started to appear. Perhaps most importantly, a concerted effort was made to imitate the remains of classical art, alongside—or sometimes even in preference to—the natural world. Ancient statues were avidly sought, carefully studied, and assiduously emulated, often to great effect. According to Condivi, Michelangelo's *Sleeping Cupid* (1496) was so classical in appearance that, at the suggestion of his patron, Lorenzo di Pierfrancesco de' Medici, it was sold as a genuine antique.

Music

The development of music in this period parallels that of architecture—and, to a lesser extent, the visual arts. Although a great many pieces which were performed, sung, or played were too incidental—or too reliant on interpretation—to be written down, it is evident from those which have survived that the demand for music expanded greatly as a result of the refinement of courtly culture and the emergence of an urban bourgeoisie. New contexts for composition and performance were introduced; new, more secular forms emerged; and, as technical innovations proceeded apace, a proliferation of new styles were developed, tending first to the vibrant, then to the ornate, and finally to the measured. Innovation was centred predominantly on France and the Burgundian Low Countries, with lesser outposts in northern Italy and Spain; but the increasingly peripatetic lifestyles of composers and musicians ensured that technical and stylistic developments were rapidly diffused, reaching from England to Cyprus, and from Sweden to Sicily.

Three main phases can be identified. The first is known as the *ars nova* (the 'New Art'). This had its origins in northern France and Burgundy, but was from the outset a 'European' phenomenon. It began in *c*.1315 with the appearance of the *Roman de Fauvel*—an allegorical verse romance, inter-spersed with 169 short pieces of music—and is usually said to have ended in around 1375. Its name most likely originated with Philippe de Vitry's treatise *Ars nova musicae* ('The New Art of Music', *c*.1322), the title of which was deliberately chosen to set the innovations of the day apart from the earlier school of polyphony, known as the *ars antiqua* (the 'Old Art'). Found particularly in a courtly context, it was a far more vibrant style, which contrasted with the restrained, even staid, forms which had gone before. At its heart were a series of notational innovations, which allowed for richer harmonies and more elaborate modes of composition. Thirds and sixths were preferred over octaves, parallel fifths, and unisons; isorhythms—a technique involving a repeating melodic and/or rhythmical pattern—became common; and secular subjects were accorded a dignity they had not previously enjoyed. Its greatest exponent was Guillaume de Machaut (*c*.1304–77). An ordained priest, he spent much of his life in the service of John I of Bohemia, Jean de Berry, and Charles II of Navarre, amongst others. He is perhaps best known for his sacred works, the most notable of which is the *Messe de Notre Dame*, the first setting of the entire Mass to polyphonic music by a single, identifiable composer. But he also left behind a significant number of secular pieces, the best known (and most representative) of which is perhaps his courtly *virelai*, *Douce dame jolie*.

After Machaut's death, the *ars nova* gradually gave way to the *ars subtilior* (the 'More Subtle Art'; *c*.1377–*c*.1420). In contrast to its predecessor, it was predominantly a southern European phenomenon, focussed on Aragon, Provence, and the states of northern Italy. Though many of its most prominent practitioners—such as Jacob de Senleches (*fl.* 1382–95) and Philippus de Caserta (*fl.* late fourteenth century)—found employment at the papal court in Avignon during the Schism, it was likely a response to the demands of a secular, or at least secularized, social elite, which held the new humanistic learning in high esteem and cherished the ideals of chivalric culture. Much as the English Decorated style was to the *rayonnant*, the *ars subtilior* was a far more complex variation on the themes of the past. Its quick, intricate rhythms pushed the notational innovations of Machaut and

Vitry to their limits, and imposed unfamiliar burdens on performers. Though sacred settings are not unknown, it found expression predominantly in secular songs (*ballades, virelais*), often in French, which took for their subject classical myths or chivalric romance, and was probably intended for recitation in intimate settings, rather than before larger audiences.

The limitations of the *ars subtilior* were, however, all too apparent. Just as the English Decorated style had ultimately proved too florid and ornate for most tastes, so the over-rich complexity of Jean de Senleches and Philippus de Caserta were abandoned in favour of a more measured and refined style. The differences were, in some ways, subtle. Supported by the further refinement of notation and a slowing of tempos, a higher premium came to be placed on harmony. The effect was, however, dramatic. Writing in 1477, Johannes Tinctoris (1435–1511) even went so far as to claim that, so completely had music been transformed that anything written before *c*.1430 was scarcely worth listening to. For the first time, settings of the Ordinary of the Mass were arranged around a common theme (known as 'cyclical Masses'); madrigals were transposed to the sacred sphere; and a host of new secular forms (e.g. the *frottola* and the *villancico*) came to the fore. Once again, the impetus for this new style came from northern France and the Burgundian Low Countries; but so varied was the employment of its practitioners, and so widely circulated were their works, that it is difficult to speak of either centres or peripheries.

According to Tinctoris, the origins of the new style could be traced to John Dunstaple (*c*.1390–1453). A pioneer of the so-called *contenance angloise* ('English countenance), Dunstaple's works were distinguished by their lightness and melodic elegance. The majority of his surviving works are Mass sections, isorhythmic motets, and Marian antiphons; but he is perhaps most remarkable for producing the first known cyclical Mass. Among the others singled out by Tinctoris was Guillaume Dufay (*c*.1397–1474). Born in all likelihood in Beersel, Dufay was among the most itinerant of all composers in this period. Though his heart was always in Cambrai, he spent time in Rimini, Pesaro, Bologna, Florence, Ferrara, Rome, and Savoy. Endowed with unusual virtuosity, he experimented with most of the musical forms then in use. Many of his works were written for specific occasions or to commemorate particular events (e.g. his *Lamentatio* on the fall of Constantinople). He was particularly notable for his use of fauxbourdon, a novel technique of harmonization. Of no less importance was Gilles Binchois (*c*.1400–60). Based at the Burgundian court, he was an accomplished, if restrained, composer whose pieces bordered on the austere. While he wrote some sacred music, most of his surviving works are secular songs—such as the haunting *ballade, Ma dame que j'ayme et croy.*

By the end of the fifteenth century, however, greater complexity was again beginning to creep in, especially in the works of Johannes Ockeghem (1410/25–97) and, later, Josquin des Prez (*c.*1450/5–1521). Though harmony was still preferred above all else, there was a move towards contrapuntal sophistication and virtuosity; while efforts were being made by those such as Tinctoris to distil these innovations into precise 'rules' for composition. Taken together, these were to have a determining influence over the direction of music throughout the sixteenth century.

Printing

Arguably the most important cultural development of the fourteenth and fifteenth centuries was the invention of printing by Johannes Gutenberg (*c.*1400–68). As Francis Bacon later noted in his *Novum Organum* (1620), printing was one of the three innovations 'unknown to the ancients' which could truly be said to have 'changed the appearance of the whole world'.

It was, to be sure, not a bolt from the blue. As literacy had expanded and the demand for books had grown, people had begun looking for ways of speeding up the copying process. During the early thirteenth century, universities had introduced the *pecia* system, whereby books necessary to the curriculum were divided up into short pieces (*peciae*) by licensed stationers and hired out for copying to students or scribes. In the late fourteenth century, there may also have been some attempts at printing short texts using hand-carved wooden blocks. Such techniques were, however, painfully slow and punishingly expensive. They were also woefully inflexible (in the case of 'block books') and prone to error (where copying was done by hand).

Gutenberg's process represented a gigantic leap forward. Its key characteristic was the use of movable metal type. This allowed any text to be set with ease—and any number of copies to be printed. Coupled with the use of paper in preference to vellum and a new, more adhesive ink, movable type made it possible to produce books more quickly, at lower cost, and with greater consistency. Though Gutenberg's 42-line Bible still cost around three times the annual wage of an average worker, it was still far more affordable than a comparable manuscript; and, crucially, the text of each copy was identical to that of all the others.

Having begun in Mainz in c.1450, printing quickly spread throughout Europe. Over the next 20 years, presses were established in Bamberg (c.1457), Strasbourg (1460), Cologne (1464), Subiaco (1465), Basle (c.1467), Rome (1467), Augsburg (1468), Nuremberg (c.1469), Venice (1469), Milan (1470), Paris (1470), and Naples (1470). And by 1500, over 100 more had been founded across the continent. The towns in which presses were established followed no obvious pattern; but in this diffusion, a central role was played by German printers, who were either moved to set up presses on their own or invited to do so by wealthy patrons. The Subiaco press, for example, was established by Conrad Sweynheim and Arnold Pannartz, both from the Rhineland; while Venice's was founded by two brothers from Speyer, Johannes and Vindelinus de Spira. Needless to say, some presses fared better than others. While many lasted only for a few years at a time, some—such as those founded by Anton Koberger (c.1440/5–1513) in Nuremberg and Nicolas Jenson (c.1420–80) in Troyes—achieved a position of European dominance, helping to fuel the growth of a truly international trade in printed books.

Printing was at first directed towards religious—rather than secular—texts. Latin and humanistic works were, on the whole, slow to appear, and did not at first find a ready market. Though the first two books printed by Sweynheim and Pannartz were a *Donatus* (a Latin grammar) and Cicero's *De oratore*, for example, they failed to generate enough interest to prevent the Subiaco press from closing a few years after it was set up. This was not untypical. In Strasbourg, no more than 9 per cent of all the books published in the last two decades of the fifteenth century were 'classics'.[7] It was much the same story with vernacular literature. Though the English printer William Caxton (c.1422–91) published editions of Chaucer's *Canterbury Tales* (1476) and Sir Thomas Malory's *Le Morte d'Arthur* (1485), such texts generally did not appear with any regularity until the later sixteenth century.

Within this general scheme, there was considerable geographical variation—particularly insofar as the types of secular books were concerned. This tended to reflect the interests of different cities, rulers, and elites, but there were nevertheless some peculiarities. In the period 1450–1500, Florentine printers, for example, showed far less interest in 'scientific' subjects (such as medicine and botany) than their counterparts in Ferrara or Venice. Somewhat surprisingly, they also neglected Latin literature; but—

[7] M. U. Chrisman, *Lay Culture, Learned Culture: Books and Social Change in Strasbourg, 1480–1599* (New Haven, CT, 1982), p. 298.

as a result of the growing popularity of Greek amongst the city's humanists, and the presence of a number of leading scholars at the *studio*—they did produce pioneering editions of Homer, Plato (in Ficino's Latin translation), Euripides, and Callimachus.

As the rather uneven progress of 'secular' works suggests, printing was not always greeted with the enthusiasm we might expect. Although Aeneas Sylvius Piccolomini (1405–64)—later Pope Pius II—had admired the clarity of Gutenberg's 42-line Bible in 1455, early readers did not necessarily share his excitement. Manuscripts remained popular, especially among the well-to-do. Incunabula, meanwhile, were viewed with scepticism, even outright hostility. In 1473–4, for example, the Venetian monk Filippo de Strata wrote a violent polemic against printing, in which he complained that the 'plague' of books was 'sweeping away the laws of decency'.

Nor, at first, did printing bring with it any improvement in textual accuracy. Quite the opposite. Precisely because texts were prepared in haste by printers, rather than scholars, defective readings were often preserved, and new errors were introduced—much to the chagrin of readers. In 1470, the Florentine humanist Niccolò Perotti observed that the books then coming off the presses contained so many mistakes that the world would have been better off without them. Hitherto unknown market forces only compounded the problem. Such was the excitement generated by the *editio princeps* of a classical text that the early appearance of a bad edition could consign a superior—but later—version to obscurity. In the case of new works, this could assume a more insidious character. Driven by intense competition, dishonest printers are even known to have stolen page proofs from their competitors and rushed out inferior 'bootleg' editions, festooned with misspellings and omissions.

Such flaws were, however, to prove the making of printing. Partly because inaccurate editions were prone to appear, printers quickly realized that one way of winning over sceptical readers was to produce more accurate versions. With growing frequency, they employed distinguished scholars and humanists to act as proofreaders. Perhaps the best example of this is the Venetian printer Aldus Manutius (1449/52–1515), who employed Desiderius Erasmus (1466–1536) to check his books at the beginning of the sixteenth century. Other innovations were quick to follow. Since many early incunabula could often be confusing—especially for new groups of readers—printers started introducing new features to aid understanding, such as indices, lists of contents, and marginal summaries. Most importantly, the growing competition between presses—and the superabundance of inferior houses—endowed printers with a hunger for the new. With growing fervour, they strove to disseminate new ideas as widely and as quickly as they could. This was never more evident than in the case of Christopher Columbus's letter announcing the discovery of the New World. Within a year, versions of this had been printed (in various languages) in Barcelona, Rome, Florence, Paris, Antwerp, Basle, and a host of other cities around Europe. But much the same process occurred in almost every field of cultural endeavour—from music (the first sheets of which were printed by Ottaviano Petrucci in 1501) to architecture and the visual arts.

Printing was arguably the fuel which fed the fires of cultural creativity in the latter part of the fifteenth century—and long into the future. It nurtured the diversification of styles and techniques, exposed local varieties to new influences, and shared the fruits of innovation with far-flung regions. And in doing so, it pointed the way to the emergence of a shared, but infinitely varied, 'European' culture in the centuries which followed.

Plate 6. Nicholas Oresme, *De Coelo et Mundo* (fourteenth century)

5

Space, time, and the world

Matthew Kempshall

Conceptions of space and time have conventionally lent themselves to characterizations of late medieval Europe as an 'Age of Discovery'. Mongol expansion prompted Dominican and Franciscan missions in the 1240s and 1250s (John of Plano Carpini, William of Rubruck) and then the journeys of Niccolò, Maffeo, and Marco Polo in the 1260s and 1271–95. It was two-way traffic thereafter, from John of Monte Corvino, Odoric of Pordenone, and Jordan Cathala of Séverac in the 1310s and 1320s, to Niccolò de' Conti in the 1420s and 1430s, and from Portuguese exploration of the Canaries in 1336, and Madeira and the Azores in the 1340s, to Cape Verde in 1444 and the Gulf of Guinea in 1470–75. This dynamic, initially ecclesiastical but increasingly mercantile and political, culminated in the rounding of the Cape of Good Hope by Bartolomeo Dias in 1488 and the landing of Christopher Columbus on Hispaniola in 1492. The fourteenth and fifteenth centuries thereby discovered a world well beyond the frontiers of Christendom and, it is argued, a new understanding of geographical space. This transformation is charted, literally, through maps, from the Ebstorf and Hereford *mappae mundi* of *c.*1220 and *c.*1285 to the terrestrial globe of Martin Behaim in Nuremberg in 1492. A 'medieval' geography centred on Jerusalem, with physical locations for Eden, Gog and Magog, and 'monstrous races' of monopods, cyclops, and mouthless creatures who lived off the smell of apples, is replaced by increasingly accurate depictions of the Mediterranean, north Atlantic and African coastlines all the way to the Arabian Gulf, Indian Ocean, and Caspian Sea. As a mode of representation, this production of images with a better 'fit' to the physical world was paralleled by a discovery of pictorial space. From the volumes of Giotto's frescoes at Padua in the early 1300s, through the architecture and landscapes of Ambrogio Lorenzetti at Siena in the 1340s, to the invention of perspective by Alberti in the 1430s and its mathematical deployment by Piero della Francesca in the 1450s and 1460s, the mimetic naturalism of 'humanist' art

The Later Middle Ages. Isabella Lazzarini, Oxford University Press (2021). © Isabella Lazzarini.
DOI: 10.1093/oso/9780198731641.003.0006

is provided with an analogous narrative of the development of 'modern' spatial realism.

This discovery and representation of 'real' space is often correlated with the development of an absolute scale with which to measure time. Between 1250 and 1500 the 'natural' day was rationalized and standardized into units of 24 equal ('equinoctial') hours and subjected to increasingly accurate measurement by mechanical clocks. This process, too, can be charted: from the weight-driven escapement mechanism of the late thirteenth century, through the installation of striking clocks and regulation of hours by political authorities in the fourteenth century, to the invention of the spring-driven mechanism, dials with pointers, and the dissemination of a new, 'public' time via ever smaller and more portable clocks in the fifteenth century. Again, an ecclesiastical construction of the physical world is usually identified as the chief casualty of this new ordering, as the canonical hours of the liturgy were transformed and then supplanted by hours whose measurement and promulgation lay beyond the control of the church. The result was, not just a desacralization, even secularization, of time, but its appropriation as something to be bought, sold, used, saved, and wasted—a commodity, in other words, and, as such, an instrument of power for new political and mercantile elites. Viewed in these terms, a 'crisis of time' in the fourteenth and fifteenth centuries is seen to adumbrate modern capitalism and industrialization by anticipating both Weberian rationalization and Marxist alienation.

These characterizations of space and time underpin an account of historical 'progress' which is as much technological as intellectual and social, where the catalysts were provided by the 'mechanical' arts of metal-working and navigation—the magnetic compass, the verge and foliot escapement mechanism, the caravel, and the lateen sail. These were the technical instruments (and not just the astrolabe, the quadrant, and the arabic numeral produced from the more 'scientific' disciplines of astronomy, geometry, and arithmetic) which challenged exclusively clerical conceptions of space and time. Coupled with other retrospective and capitalized 'modern' projections—Renaissance Humanism and The Rise of the State—they are proffered as some consolation for an otherwise uniform picture of demographic stagnation and economic downturn, from dissent and schism within a fissiparous church, from endemic violence within and between kingdoms and city-states, from the Black Death, the Hundred Years War, and the fall of Constantinople. Space and time, in short, yield at least one reassuring narrative of empirical, rational, and scientific discovery in the autumn, even the end, of 'the Middle Ages'.

Assumptions and approach

A mechanistic interpretation of the understanding of space and time has clear attractions. It is not unreasonable to draw some connection, for example, between spatial realism and the study of optics or the invention of reading glasses (1266). The 'new' quadrant, meanwhile, invented at Montpellier by Jacob ben Machir ibn Tibbon (Profatius Judaeus, c.1236–1305), was used to determine the hours from precise observation of the sun. The torquetum provided the time of an astronomical calculation and the exact coordinates of a star in space. The cross-staff ('Jacob's staff'), invented by Levi ben Gerson (Gersonides, 1288–1344), measured angles and altitudes and (in conjunction with solar tables) the means of establishing degrees of latitude at sea. On the other hand, as studies in the diffusion of technology have challenged assumptions of epistemological determinism, attention has shifted to why such instruments were developed at certain times and places. Contacts with China are certainly suggestive of the potential influence of people who had already constructed, in the twelfth century, elaborately geared, water-driven astronomical clocks, and scaled grid-maps of large geographical areas. The same is true of the expertise of Muslim Cordoba and Alexandria, exemplified by the twelfth-century geographer Al-Idrisi, where it remains a striking conjunction that the most technically advanced cartography in Europe was produced on the Mediterranean littoral, by Genoese and Catalan workshops (the Balearic Isles were conquered by Aragon in 1248). Hard evidence for *direct* influence from exogenous sources is, however, notoriously difficult to pin down. The diffusion of Chinese and Arabic know-how, continuity with classical Roman technology, and autochthonous developments in weight-drives and in the gear-trains of medieval water mills, are *all* possible causes for the appearance of the mechanical clock and the portolan chart. The availability of technical instruments also forms only part of the picture. A theory of planispheric projection, for example, existed at Constantinople from the twelfth century and there are three surviving Greek manuscripts of Ptolemy's *Geography* from the thirteenth century which contain maps. Jordanus de Nemore wrote *De Plana Sphera* in the 1220s and Roger Bacon discussed the need for a system of coordinates and planispheric projection in his *Opus Maius* of

1268. However, the Byzantine maps of Maximus Planudes and Nicephorus Gregoras did not have any wider impact on cartography until Ptolemy's text was translated into Latin between 1406 and 1410. Classical manuals for field and estate surveyors (*agrimensores*) had likewise been copied well into the twelfth century. However, their description of how to use solid geometry to measure irregular land boundaries and inaccessible objects (typically towers) did not result in the production of scaled-down representations of physical space, even though treatises on such practical geometry were composed in the twelfth century by Hugh of St Victor, in the thirteenth by Leonardo Fibonacci, and in the fourteenth by Dominicus de Clavasio. The uses to which technology was put—in other words, the needs which it met— are just as important to identify as its existence.

Progressively more accurate conceptions of 'real' space and time are also now subject to heavier qualifications on the immediacy of the relationship between the world 'out there' and the world as subjectively experienced. This is particularly significant for the forms which representations of reality may have taken in the past, be they linguistic (when language is regarded as instrumental and strategic, rather than a transparent medium of description) or iconographic (when images are not regarded as direct transcriptions of what they 're-present'). The conception, depiction, and experience of space and time are no exception. Familiar terms can, in this respect, prove misleading. Representations of the physical world could bear several labels— diagram (*figura*), image (*imago*), picture (*pictura*), description (*descriptio*)— whereas the word 'map' simply meant 'cloth' (*mappa*). These alternative terms denoted schematic, verbal, and visual depictions of what exists, often as mnemotechnical devices, but very few reflected a deliberate attempt to represent reality with the spatial verisimilitude and scale that the modern term 'map' implies. A medieval understanding of space, meanwhile, is more accurately conveyed by the notion of place (*locus*) and the relation *between* places. This is clear from the ten Aristotelian categories which were fundamental to how anyone thought and wrote in the Middle Ages. The fifth category is 'where' (*ubi*, *locus*), the seventh is 'position' (*positio*, *situs*), and, whereas position can move, 'place' is fixed. The term 'space' (*spatium*) was therefore, strictly speaking, confined to the notion of 'area' and thus to the discipline of geometry. In the fourteenth century, this extended to a distinction between *plenum* (an area filled with some permutation of the four elements) and *vacuum* (an area without matter, a void). Time, meanwhile, was classified by Aristotle as a measure of motion and under the second category of quantity (*quantum*). It was therefore distinct from the sixth category of 'when' (*quando*). The semantic field for 'time' (*tempus*) or 'times' (*tempora*) accordingly included the extensive range of referents listed by Isidore of Seville, developed by Bede, and then disseminated by writers such as Bartolomeus Anglicus. These encompassed atom (the 'indivisible' unit), moment (one 40th of an hour), part (one 15th of an hour), minute (one tenth), point (one quarter), hour, quadrant (one quarter of a 12-hour day), day (24 hours), week, month, season, lunar year, solar year, cycle (*not* century), era (*saeculum*), and world age (*aetas*). It was axiomatic that these divisions of time represented measurements that were either natural (the 365-day year) or customary and conventional (the 30-day month) or of divine and human institution (the 7-day week, the 15-year indiction, the 4-year Olympiad).

Reconsidering the presuppositions behind technological and scientific progress and linguistic and iconographic representation has important methodological repercussions for space and time. In particular, it invites a closer reading of anthropological and sociological studies for how such seemingly transhistorical notions could be conceived, described, and experienced in different ways and by different groups. The result has been pluralism and fragmentation, as monolithic generalizations about a 'medieval' understanding of space and time are replaced by an appreciation of the plethora of forms which it could take. The measurement of time, for example, varied according to the particular activity being performed by particular agents in a particular context. Ecclesiastical time was thus, at its most comprehensive, an overarching scheme of six ages of the world— infancy (Adam to the Flood), childhood (the Flood to Abraham), adolescence (Abraham to David), young adulthood (David to the Babylonian Captivity), mature adulthood (the Babylonian Captivity to Jesus Christ), old age (the Crucifixion to the Second Coming). This linear scheme was dovetailed, however, with a liturgical cycle of fixed and movable feasts within each calendar year, a system which was arranged around Easter and Christmas in order to provide Christian communities with a repeating commemoration of the life and ministry of Christ, as well as an education in Christian doctrine (Trinity Sunday, for example, was instituted in 1334). This liturgical year, moreover, was arranged according to two concurrent cycles: the fixed *sanctorale* began on the Feast of St Andrew (30 November) and was based on the Roman reckoning of solar months and days (kalends, ides, and nones); the *temporale* began on the first Sunday of Advent and was based on Advent, Christmas, Epiphany (all fixed), Easter, Ascension, and Pentecost (all movable). Days of the week could be denoted with reference to these major feasts or to the particular liturgical season in which they fell, or simply with reference to the preceding Sunday, to the scriptural text assigned to that day, or to its particular saint. The liturgical year was further harmonized with the temporal seasons—the Feast of the Annunciation, for example, needed to fall *after* the vernal equinox (the beginning of the astronomical year) because, just as Light came into the world to overcome Darkness, so Christ was made flesh only *after* daylight hours started to become longer than the night. The liturgical day was similarly accommodated to the unequal variation of the 'artificial' day throughout the solar year. Of the eight canonical hours (Psalm 119: 'at midnight I rise to give you thanks'; 'seven times a day will I praise you'), the night offices of matins and lauds could be moved to allow sufficient time for sleep. The daily offices of prime, terce, sext, none, vespers, and compline, meanwhile, divided a nominal 12 'hours' of daylight between them, such that the actual length of these 'hours' would vary constantly, from the shortest day (the winter solstice) to the longest (the summer solstice), depending on geographical latitude. These hours also changed relative to one another, most clearly in the case of 'none', which migrated over the course of the thirteenth and fourteenth centuries from the 'ninth' hour (three-quarters of the way through the day) to midday ('noon'), thereby displacing the 'sixth' hour or sext.

Agriculture was the most straightforwardly seasonal and cyclical temporal order of time, dividing the year according to its own particular rhythms of birth, growth, and decay. However, the labours deemed appropriate to each month (chopping wood, breaking ground, pruning, hunting, mowing, shearing, reaping, threshing, winnowing, harvesting, sowing, ploughing, and slaughtering) varied according to the climate of a region and therefore to geographical latitude. Such labour could be coordinated with markers drawn from the liturgical calendar ('on St Urban's day, harvest your walnuts'), but duration was measured according to the activity being performed (sowing, winnowing, and reaping lasted as long as it took to complete the task). Legal time, academic time, mercantile time, and musical time were different again. Lawyers had their own units of reckoning—terms, 'return days', regnal years, 'times of war and peace', and 'time immemorial'. Legal process required the precise calculation of the particular saint's day on which an act had been committed, what time within that day, and when that day began (the civil day commenced at midnight, but other methods started from dawn, midday, or the sunset of the day before). Lawyers needed to establish an individual's age (for the purposes of office-holding), to measure when and whether 'a year and a day' (or indeed the duration of any calibrated tariff for penance and punishment) had elapsed, and to record an equitable allocation of irrigated water to farmers, millers, and fullers. In schools and universities, the length of lectures depended on their subject matter, but also on whether they were in the morning or in the afternoon. University statutes may have gradually adopted regular hours (Merton College, Oxford, installed its own clock in 1387), but clock-time did not sweep everything before it. In part for reasons of reliability (the most accurate mechanical clock lost at least 15 minutes each day), in part because some activities remained conventional, the sandglass remained just as important a means of measurement. If a generalization is to be made, therefore, then it lies in the illustrations to Henricus de Susa's *Horologium Sapientiae* (*c.*1334), which reveal just how many different means of calculating time were available depending on the particular activity being measured.

Conceptions of space were likewise conditioned, first and foremost, by function. The topography of rural and urban landscapes was as much social and mental as it was physical. Most obviously, space was relative to the time taken to traverse it—in societies for which water was the primary means of transportation, this gave places linked by rivers, coasts, and open seas much greater proximity than their 'actual' physical distribution might suggest. The islands of Britain and Hibernia, for example, were described facing the coasts of Germany and France, but also of Spain. Similar effects were produced by communication overland, where mountains, forests, marshes, roads, and bridges put a different spatial configuration on the landscape when the function was travel. Political space, sacral space, gendered space, and networked space were different again. Public buildings and piazzas in urban communities; sanctuaries, choirs and shrines in churches; female quarters in castles: these were all spaces defined by access, by the identity of the people who could use them, rather than simply by physical form. The list can be multiplied. Space and time were relative to use and, as such, both their comprehension and representation varied according to the purposes they served. A 'real' physical dimension amounted only to one of several meanings with which they could be invested. Indeed, it might be, in some respects, the *least* important feature of an individual place or event when the physical universe—Creation—could be read figuratively as well as literally, when historical existence in space and time was overlaid with tropological, anagogical, or allegorical senses. Whilst the precise signification might not be immediately apparent, there remained more than one way of identifying, interpreting, and representing the literal and physical reality of the world.

Faced with such a fragmented picture—conceptions of space and time not only varying between individuals and groups but also overlapping (such that the same people could deploy different categorisations in different circumstances)—it may seem moot whether it is possible to do more than simply replicate this variety with a series of micro-historical studies of particular categories in particular contexts. As Bartolomeus Anglicus acknowledged, 'nothing is more uncertain than time because, as Isidore states, time is not known in itself but through human activities' (*De Proprietatibus Rerum* IX.2; *Etymologies* V.31.9–10). Judicial records, in this regard, furnish an index of just how wide the range could be for how individuals, in practice, measured space (the length of a bow-shot), time (with reference to a significant event, to the person by whom they were employed, to a particular feast day, to the birth of a child), and duration (the length of a Mass, the time it took to walk a mile or to recite a prayer such as the Paternoster). If conceptions of space and time *did* change between 1250 and 1500, therefore, either responding to or themselves stimulating processes of empirical discovery and technological change, then the possibility of finding a grand narrative for this process depends on explaining, not just how and why these changes might have taken place, but also what *form* these changes were given. In other words, it requires an examination of the relationship between the conception and experience of space and time and the means by which they were represented.

Evidence and extent

The first challenge is the typicality of the evidence which has survived. Much has been made of a conflict between 'church' time and 'merchant' time, largely on the basis of a small number of well-documented cases (notably Aire-sur-la-Lys, in 1355) where ecclesiastical authorities disputed control of the measurement of hours and therefore the time for which labourers worked. Other evidence suggests that churches not only actively supported the introduction of public clocks striking regular hours (by housing them in church towers) but actually took the initiative (at Reims, for example, Chartres, or Tours), integrating these hours with the temporal hours of their liturgy (St Mary's, York) or supplying the clock hours by which work and market activities were regulated. It is accordingly a striking feature of fourteenth-century almanacs that they provided tables by means of which one type of time could be converted into another so that the different systems could be used side by side. Nor was the diffusion of new technology simply, or even primarily, at the initiative of mercantile elites and commercial networks. In 1370, Charles V of France installed the *horloge du palais* at the Louvre explicitly to regulate the business of the *parlement* and of the citizens of Paris in a more orderly manner. In 1392, the king of Aragon sanctioned a striking clock at Barcelona on the grounds that it would counter sloth and promote an orderly life. Jean, duc de Berry (1340–1416), installed clocks in several of his residences, paid for the cathedral clock at Bourges in 1372, and subsidized the building of a clock tower at Poitiers. Thus, whilst the earliest and best-attested evidence for the installation of public striking clocks may occur in cities in northern Italy (Visconti Milan 1336, Carrara Padua 1344, Monza 1347, Genoa 1353–4, Florence 1353, Siena 1360), the fact that they appeared simultaneously in churches, monasteries, and royal palaces (Canterbury 1292, Norwich 1323–5, Windsor 1351–2), and the rapidity with which they spread (Prague 1354, Avignon 1374–5, Santiago de Compostela 1395, Moscow 1404), suggest that regular hours represented a practical solution to a social problem of urban order, not an ideological battleground between ecclesiastical and mercantile power. Clocks did become an important symbol of communal authority and, as such, could be removed as punishment for disobedience. However, statutes governing the multifarious trades and activities within urban communities reveal just how complex such regulation had been before such a uniform method of measuring time was introduced. The 'working day', for example, could begin and end, not at sunrise and sunset, but when there was sufficient light to distinguish between two coins or recognize someone in the street. The standardization of aural time-signals throughout a city was also far from straightforward. In the first instance, public clocks merely added to the variety (in number, duration, and tone) of bells that were striking throughout the day, each of them for different groups and activities (Milan in 1288, for example, had over 200 bells ringing from 120 towers). At the end of the fourteenth century, by contrast, the municipal statutes of Cologne were using clock hours to regulate the beginning and ending of selling-times and work-times for a number of different markets and trades, as well as access to those markets for different groups. Regulation of time was, in this regard, no different from the standardization of weights and measures—an aspiration and a practice to which, from Bede onwards, it had been explicitly connected, both because of Scripture (Wisdom 11:20: 'God created everything in measure, number, and weight') and through its similar numerical proportions of 12 (12 can be divided by 2, 3, 4, and 6; 60 can be divided by 2,

3, 4, 5, 6, 10, 12, 15, 20, and 30). The implementation and regulation of each of these duodecimal or 'uncial' systems certainly had consequences for public power, but enforcement did not divide neatly along temporal and ecclesiastical lines.

Similar issues of typicality are raised by medieval 'maps' and, in particular, the number of *mappae mundi* relative to navigational charts, city plans, regional maps, or local cadastral (estate or field) surveys. By their very nature, the former stood a better chance of preservation. In 1423, for example, a guide, notary, and painter journeyed through the counties of Diois and Valentinois for Charles VII and spent four days producing a *figura ad modum mappae mundi*. The map itself is now lost. Thus, whilst the employment of urban surveyors is attested from the early thirteenth century, scale maps and street plans drawn up for official purposes survive only from the fifteenth century (at Verone in the 1450s, for example, or the bird's-eye view of Venice by Jacopo de' Barbari in 1500). This leaves regional maps such as the Gough Map (*c.*1360) something of an anomaly when so much of the context surrounding its depiction of principal roads and towns (and the distances between them) is unknown. Even then, with certain notable exceptions (Ebstorf, Hereford), it is those *mappae mundi* composed in (or edited down and copied into) manuscripts which have been preserved. We know of many more *mappae mundi* on walls, tapestries, and tables which have *not* survived. Matthew Paris records wall paintings at Westminster and Waltham Abbey in the 1240s; Ambrogio Lorenzetti accompanied his depiction of the seasons and the labours of the months at Siena with a 'map of the world' in the 1340s; Jan van Eyck (d. 1441) painted a *mappa mundi* for Philip the Good, duke of Burgundy, which was described as so consummate that it could be used to measure the distances between places; Mantegna painted one for the Gonzaga villa of Marmirolo in 1494.

Mappae mundi raise a further question of category or type. World maps derived their appearance from the round diagrams or wheels (*rotae*) which accompanied manuscripts of Isidore's *De Natura Rerum*. As such, they were one of several schematic methods—all of them circular—which were used to convey information about the physical world. These representations include division into seven climates, three continents (the so-called T-O maps of Europe, Asia and Africa which were typified by the orb held by Christ Pantocrator), five zones, four elements, four cardinal directions, 12 months, and 12 winds. Some round maps have the island of Delos in the centre (on the basis that it was first to emerge after the Flood), others the city or mountain of Arim (the meridian on which al-Kwarizmi's astronomical tables were based). Maps which chose to place Jerusalem in the centre were therefore making, not a geographical, but a theological point (Ezekiel 5:5; Psalm 73:12), in the same way that the Ebstorf map surrounded the inhabited world with the head, hands, and feet of Christ, or the Hereford map with the Last Judgment at the top and the word 'DEATH' (M–O–R–S) on the circumference. Climatic diagrams, zonal maps, city plans, and itineraries likewise had their own conventions and approaches for the physical reality they conveyed. So too the moralized maps of Opicino de Canistris in the 1330s, which combined 'accurate' coastlines with personifications of southern Europe and northern Africa as a man and a woman in a Mediterranean sea of sin. *Mappae mundi* were no exception. This differentiation was acknowledged by contemporaries. Hugh of St Victor produced, not one, but two images or descriptions of the world—an all-encompassing moral and allegorical theology of the ark of Noah, integrating human existence in the physical world with the salvific dynamic of Creation and Redemption, but also a strictly 'historical' depiction, complete with provinces, rivers, mountains, and names.

When *mappae mundi* presented monstrous races in the remoter parts of Africa and Asia, this was therefore as much a matter of genre as it was of understanding. The information was taken, directly or indirectly, from Pliny's *Natural History*. Having opened book II with a digest of astronomical knowledge on the planets and a discussion of the shape and nature of the earth (including inequalities in the duration of daylight), Pliny laboriously listed the place names, sizes, and distances of provinces and peoples ('the Chinese [Seres]', he writes, 'although mild in character [. . .] shun the company of the rest of humankind and wait for trade to come to them'). Towns, mountains, seas and rivers (books III–VI) were followed (book VII) by some of the more remarkable variants on human nature which had been reported on the margins of the habitable world. Coupled with the popularity of twelfth-century vernacular romances on Alexander the Great, Pliny's compendium (and its epitome by Solinus) provided the model for combining literal chorography with marvels (*mirabilia*) and fables (*fabulae*). Its influence continued well into the thirteenth century and, above all with the *Travels* of Sir John Mandeville, the fourteenth. Rather than use this classical material to construct a peculiarly 'medieval' view of the world, it is more apposite to pair such science fiction with the functions served by marginal grotesques in ecclesiastical sculpture and illuminated manuscripts. Or simply repeat the reservations of Augustine. 'It is not, of course, necessary to believe in all the kinds of humans that are said to exist,' he writes, either because the evidence is unreliable or because they are monkeys and apes. Even if they are human, they are still descended from Adam, however unusual they may seem in shape, colour, motion, sound, capability, composition, or nature. For Augustine, the variety of 'monstrous races', like Siamese twins, was primarily a theological question. 'Perhaps,' he suggests, 'they were created by God so that our own monstrous births should not be thought of as the work of an imperfect craftsman, so that we should not think He has erred' (*City of God* XVI.8).

Questions of typicality and typology also inflect one of the more difficult aspects of 'medieval' space and time—its end. Dating historical events depended on the purpose of the text. Writers could choose accordingly from the year of the world (*annus mundi*), the year of the incarnation (*annus domini*), the foundation of the city of Rome (*ab urbe condita*), a particular indiction, or the reigns of individual consuls, kings, bishops, and dukes. Even when a single system of dating events to before, as well as after, Christ's incarnation was developed (as a means of synchronizing different chronologies of events in the ancient world), the pluralism of chronological systems remained driven by function. Amidst this diversity, there was a long-standing ecclesiastical prohibition on using this chronography to calculate the end of time (Mark 13:32; 1 Thessalonians 5:2). Yet the Bible had also listed the signs which would herald Antichrist and the Second Coming. If Augustine's Six Ages left the world in its dotage (*mundus senescens*), with all the travails that old age brings (material decay and death), a reading of Eusebius' chronography (dating the age of the world at Christ's birth to 5,198 years) prompted some writers to calculate exactly when the end would come. There were six days in Creation and, since 'one day is like a thousand years' (Psalm 90:4; 2 Peter 3:8), the world should end in 6000 AM/802 AD. Mindful of the dangers of such presumption, Bede followed his computation of a coordinated lunar/solar calendar with a chronicle of the world which radically revised Eusebius' figure downwards to 3,952 years. Not only did this mean that the world would not end around 800 AD (nor, necessarily, 2048 AD), but, to reinforce the point, Bede provided Easter tables as far as the year 1064.

Tension between chronography and eschatology resurfaced throughout the Middle Ages, not least after Joachim of Fiore's apocalyptic exegesis was posthumously furnished with a precise date (1260) by Franciscans such as Gerard of Borgo San Donnino. Such speculation continued into the 1290s with Ubertino da Casale and Arnau of Villanova, the latter fusing Joachimism with Jewish apocalyptic exegesis of Daniel 12:8–12. It was no less intense 200 years later for Girolamo Savonarola or Giles of Viterbo.

Identifying signs of the last times, however, was not the same as predicting how soon the end of the world would actually follow. As Gregory the Great demonstrated, use of apocalyptic language is not, in itself, proof of anything other than an urgent argument against a false sense of security or in favour of regeneration and reform. It is in this context that the apocalypticism accompanying the Black Death should be set. Following the famine of 1315–22, the devastating plague outbreaks of 1347–53, 1362, and the 1370s could not help but be interpreted in eschatological terms. Earthquakes, famines, troubles, sorrows, nation rising against nation— 'when you see these things come to pass, you will know that the kingdom of God is at hand' (Luke 21:31). By the same token, famine, war, and plague also represented the retributive justice which would always be visited by God on a disobedient and sinful people (Psalm 50). Penitential preaching and intercessory processions were thus the required response. This was also not the only language with which such chastisement (*plaga*) could be met. Alongside calls to reform came political, medical, meteorological, and astronomical explanations for its outbreak—the murder of Andrew of Naples, the distribution of air-borne pollution, and the conjunction of Mars, Jupiter, and Saturn. For a world that was old and infirm, the effects of sin, physical corruption, and the cycle of nature were not mutually exclusive explanations. Numerical calculations of the age of the world and numerological speculation inspired by Joachite prophecies or cabbalistic mysticism could certainly encourage a belief that the end of the Sixth Age was imminent. Such responses, however, should not be given undue weight. Like the location of Jerusalem and of monstrous races, apocalypticism made a theological point for a specific moral purpose.

Evidence for conceptions of space and time requires assessment of typicality and genre but also an appreciation of the integration of Latin and vernacular learning and the reciprocal influence of 'high' and 'low' culture. The classical cosmography and chorography made available through Martianus Capella or Macrobius was not obscure or recondite knowledge, still less when it was itself epitomized by encyclopedic manuals such as Bartolomeus Anglicus' *De Proprietatibus Rerum* (*c.*1245) or Vincent of Beauvais' *Speculum Naturale* (*c.*1250), least of all when these manuals were actually composed in the vernacular, such as Brunetto Latini's *Livre dou Tresor* (*c.*1260). Bartolomeus became the most widely circulated scientific compendium in the Middle Ages—translated into French in 1372, English in 1398, and most other western European vernaculars by the fifteenth century. His text (including its summary of cosmography and astronomy in book VIII, its account of time and computus in book IX, and its alphabetical list of places on the earth in books XIV and XV) was so popular that 11 Latin and 6 French editions were printed between 1472 and 1500. The circulation of such works of synthesis means that certain ideas about space and time can be presumed for individuals beyond an intellectual and Latinate elite. These include: the spherical nature of the earth ('like a ball', *comme une pelote*, according to Nicole Oresme); its division into climatic zones; its location as the fixed centre of a hierarchy of rotating planetary spheres under the heaven of the fixed stars; the difference between the solar and the lunar year; the variation in length of days and nights on either side of the two solstices; the inequality of these daylight hours according to geographical latitude; and the diversity in customary practice over exactly when days and years are reckoned to begin. These ideas extend to the relation between the physical and temporal properties of the spherical earth—almanacs included the longitude of places so that allowance could be made for the same hour occurring at different times in two different places; in the fourteenth century, Nicole Oresme even suggested establishing one place on the earth when a particular day would officially begin. If an idea of flatness was mentioned at all, it was merely one of several refutable misconceptions listed by Aristotle and Pliny. This is how Martianus Capella treated it. It was also the approach of the thirteenth century. As Bonaventure observed, when Psalm 104:2 speaks of heaven as a 'skin' (*pellis*), i.e. a 'roof' (*camera*) or 'tent' (*tentorium*), this is language chosen to communicate with simple people, describing the heavens as they appear to the senses.

Teaching within the university likewise permeated much further than the confines of the schools themselves. Alongside the armillary sphere (introduced in the fourteenth century as a teaching aid), the core text was John of Sacrobosco's *Treatise on the Sphere* of *c*.1220 (a distillation of Ptolemy's *Almagest* which became the most widespread textbook on the nature of the heavenly and earthly spheres), supplemented by the *Theorica Planetarum* of *c*.1290 (possibly by Campanus of Novara) and the Latin translation of Aristotle's *De Caelo et Mundo*. Within the universities, these texts were given extensive commentaries and provided the basis for teaching alongside more specialized treatises translated from the Arabic. They were also progressively refined. At Vienna, for example, Henry of Langenstein (*c*.1325–97) began a pedagogic tradition culminating in Georg Peurbach (1423–61) and Regiomontanus (1436–76), the latter compiling a *New Theory of the Planets* whose observations were to underpin the work of Copernicus and Tycho Brahe. These texts also reached a still wider audience by being translated into the vernacular. Sacrobosco was rendered in both French and German in the early fourteenth century, whilst in 1377 Charles V commissioned Nicole Oresme to write a translation of, and detailed commentary on, *De Caelo et Mundo*. Set alongside the Ptolemaic and Aristotelian ideas already propagated by Bartolomeus Anglicus, this dissemination indicates a wide currency indeed for the concepts such teaching contained.

This process was not simply a matter of intellectual communication outwards and downwards. In the case of the uniform measurement of a day as 24 equal hours, it is certainly tempting to attribute its introduction exclusively to the intellectual influence of astronomy, a discipline for which such units (and, indeed, sub-units such as the 60 'minutes' into which Ptolemy had divided the equal, equinoctial hour) were an intrinsic part of its science. The extraordinary astronomical clocks developed by Richard of Wallingford at St Albans in the 1330s, and Giovanni de' Dondi at Padua in *c.*1365, suggest such a stimulus. So too does Oresme's comparison of God to a 'clockmaker', and the universe, not to a *machina mundi* (the phrase from Lucretius cited by Sacrobosco), but to 'clockwork'. And yet evidence is lacking for a direct causal correlation between these complex inventions (they showed solar time, sidereal time, planetary motions, the date of Easter, sunrise, sunset, the phases of the moon, and the motions of the tides) and the development of much simpler, striking tower-clocks. The relationship is, if anything, the reverse. In his 1271 commentary on Sacrobosco, Robertus Anglicus lamented the fact that astronomers had been trying—and failing—to have clockmakers construct a sufficiently constant and reliable motor wheel for the accurate mechanical simulation of the movement of sun, moon, and stars. When Richard of Wallingford and Giovanni de' Dondi succeeded in building their *astraria* some 60 years later, it appears that they used a mechanism which had been developed by manufacturers of clockwork automata and striking bells. The degree of precision and sophistication to which these two astronomers then took this technology was certainly exceptional (even in the fifteenth century, the duke of Milan could find no one to repair Dondi's *astrarium*), but the responsibility for its invention lay with blacksmiths, organ-makers, locksmiths, and armourers—in other words, makers of mechanical and musical instruments. The iron clock which Philip IV commissioned in 1301 for the abbey at Poissy was built by a crossbow-maker, Gilbert de Lupara. It is no accident that Richard of Wallingford was himself the son of a blacksmith.

The fact that so significant a development as the verge and foliot escapement has undocumented origins, moreover, has striking parallels with the contemporaneous appearance of the portolan chart. According to William of Nangis, Louis IX was shown his distance from the Sardinian coast after his fleet had been scattered by a storm; later in the 1270s, Giles of Rome mentions a 'map of the sea' (*maris mappa*) produced by sailors to provide a 'proportional' depiction of ports, seas, and other details to enable them to locate their position and identify the route they should take. The first surviving portolan actually to support these literary references—the Carte Pisane—dates from *c.*1300. And yet how, and why, these navigational charts should have been developed, together with the connection of their rhumb lines and scale-bars to use of the magnetic compass and sandglass (*horloge de mer*), remain unclear. Whether portolan charts mark a direct link with classical *periploi* or with expertise learned from Arab merchants, the accuracy with which they represented the Mediterranean, Black Sea and Atlantic coastlines remains remarkable. As early as *c.*1320 this knowledge was used by Pietro Vesconte, a Genoese working in Venice, to produce portolan charts and a *mappa mundi*, as well as a grid-map of Palestine, in order to illustrate Marino Sanudo's appeal for a new crusade. By 1375, with the production of the Catalan Atlas by Abraham Cresques, portolan coastal outlines of place names (inscribed almost exclusively in the vernacular) started to cover the Baltic and include features such as rivers and mountains. By the fifteenth century, this combination of coastline with inland information produced a sub-genre of island maps (*isolarii*), of which the earliest and most influential was by Cristoforo Buondelmonti in *c.*1420. If the influence of portolan charts on *mappae mundi* became progressively more marked, culminating in the Genoese world map of 1457 (perhaps by Toscanelli) and in the world map of Fra Mauro (drawn in 1459 for the king of Portugal but extant only in a copy made for the government of Venice), this did not mean that existing conventions were abandoned. Traditional forms of representation still underpinned the work of Giovanni Leardo or the 'Borgia' world map from the mid-fifteenth century. Nonetheless, when it came to how the physical world was represented, it remains the case that, as with the regular measurement of time and its relation to astronomy, physics, and music, the techniques behind the portolan mapping of place originated in the practical demands of navigation—in a mechanical art, not a scientific discipline.

The patronage of intellectual culture by the laity may have reached an exceptional level with Charles V, but his interests were shared by other rulers in their courts. The king's concern with *De Caelo et Mundo*, moreover, with spheres and other astronomical instruments, with the division of his own day into three parts by means of a 24-hour candle, with a portable clock (*horloge portative*), and with the public and private installation of mechanical clocks in Paris and in his palaces, did not reflect a deliberate 'desacralization' of time. On the contrary. The popularity of Books of Hours in the fifteenth century gives sufficient indication that 'ecclesiastical' time continued, in certain contexts and for certain purposes, to exercise a powerful influence on the laity, even if these canonical hours were observed in practice only at the beginning and the end of the day or during Mass. Indeed, works of this genre demonstrate how widespread a basic knowledge of calendrical computation could be. As devotional texts, Books of Hours provided pared-down, paraliturgical offices of prayer for the laity (Hours of the Virgin, Penitential Psalms, Hours of the Cross, Hours of the Holy Spirit, the Office of the Dead), but they were prefaced (like many missals, breviaries, and psalters) by a calendar which indicated feast days throughout the church year, 'red-letter days' marking the most important, the letter D marking two *dies mali* ('dismal') each month. The provision of lunar phases, dominical letters, and nineteen golden numbers, moreover, enabled both the identification of Sundays in any given year and the calculation of the date of Easter (and, by extension, of the movable feasts dependent upon it). Although this information was sometimes also presented in tabular form for an entire sequence of years in the future, or made accessible in a separate almanac, in theory it was possible for lay patrons to perform these calculations for themselves. Some Books of Hours contained other material too, most famously in the case of the *Très Riches Heures* commissioned by Jean, duc de Berry, who also owned a copy of Oresme's *Livre du ciel et du monde*. The *Très Riches Heures* illustrated the (rural) labours of the months, adapted from earlier iconographic traditions, but they also identified the signs of the zodiac through which the sun would pass along its ecliptic in the course of the year. It is this all-inclusive aspect of the calendar which explains why knowledge of the Ptolemaic and Aristotelian universe should have been so extensive—the movements of the heavenly bodies were integrated with actions and events on the earth, and to an extent which went well beyond the creation of the four seasons by the passage of the sun and the motion of the tides by the phases of the moon.

Cosmography

Strictly speaking, the term 'world' (*mundus*) meant the combination of the heavens (*caelum*) with the earth (*terra*) and, as such, medieval conceptions of space and time are better understood in terms of cosmography than geography. As the liturgical calendar demonstrated, there was nothing intrinsically antithetical between 'linear' Christian time and cyclical astronomical time. Yet, from patristic denunciations of astral determinism onwards, the content of that astronomy proved highly problematic territory. This was particularly the case from the twelfth century, when Latin translations of Ptolemy's *Tetrabiblos* (*Quadripartitum*) and of Arabic treatises (notably by Alfraganus and Abu Ma'shar, as well as the compendium known as the *Liber Novum Iudicum* which was subsequently translated into French for Charles V in *c.*1360) began to spread throughout western Europe. Even though an ecclesiastical commission was appointed to differentiate works which were acceptable from those which were dangerous, the resulting report—the *Speculum Astronomiae*—was simply the first of many attempts to police the boundary between legitimate astronomy and geomancy. Even legitimate astronomy identified three ways in which the planets and the stars (either singly or in conjunction) could affect the sublunary sphere: cause, action and influence. The degree to which generation and corruption was affected in sublunary bodies depended, in turn, upon their natures—animate or inanimate, rational or irrational. Even though it was argued that celestial bodies could only incline, not force, the will of human beings, the consequences for blurring the boundary between astronomy and astrology were profound.

In the first instance, a theory of astral and planetary conjunction meant that there was a *right* time, an *opportune* moment, to commence or perform certain actions so that they would be successful. This branch of astrology, 'elections', included wars and battles, but it extended to travel, writing, and medicine (hence the importance of identifying the precise moment of a child's conception and birth, or of timing surgery and blood-letting to coincide with the sign of the zodiac which was associated with that particular part of the human body). This is why John Lydgate records the exact time at which he began writing his *Troy Book*—4.00 p.m. on Monday 31 October 1412. It was the predictable conjunctions of planets and eclipses of sun and moon, not just irregular comets and shooting stars, which served as portents of important events. They could also be used to foretell the weather. The casting of a horoscope (literally a 'vision of the hour') or birth chart ('nativity') was the most practical manifestation. This is why, for example, we know the exact time of Charles V's birth (5.36 a.m. on Wednesday 21 January 1338) and why Alberti's *Libri della Famiglia* (1434) recommended noting the hour, day, month, year, and place of the birth of one's children.

Having the technical means of telling the time, therefore—a moment specific to a certain configuration of the sun, moon, planets and stars—was a subject whose practical impact was too important to be left to astronomers alone. If planets and stars offered the means of forecasting the weather and securing good health, then it is hardly surprising that knowledge of their movements, of the connection *between* space and time, was regarded as useful at every level of society, not just schools and universities.

If the motion of the planetary spheres relative to the sphere of the fixed stars had repercussions on the earth, both the nature and degree of this influence were subjects of controversy. Nicole Oresme wrote a treatise against astrological prediction, reinforcing the attack on astrology by John of Salisbury which had been translated along with the rest of *Policraticus* in *c.*1372. So too did Pico della Mirandola. Pierre d'Ailly, Oresme's successor at Navarre, tried to harmonize astrological conjunctions with God's providential governance of the universe, defending true astrology against its superstitious practitioners. This was one aspect of a whole series of disagreements. There was no scholarly consensus on the physical consequences of a geocentric conception of the universe. Ptolemy's *Almagest* and Aristotle's *De Caelo et Mundo* (by themselves, in the form of Arabic commentaries, or as digests in Sacrobosco and the *Theorica Planetarum*) may have constructed the universe as a series of rotating spheres, but this model left numerous points open to debate. Most obviously, some sort of reconciliation needed to be found between the theoretical physics of Aristotle's perfect concentric spheres and Ptolemy's practical observation of eccentric and epicyclic planetary motions. There was also the question of how many spheres existed in addition to those of the earth and the seven planets—was it 10, 11, or 12, if the total included the outermost, immobile empyrean (itself contained by nothing), the *primum mobile*, the crystalline heaven, and the firmament of the fixed stars? The most important stimulus to such debate was provided, perhaps paradoxically, by the condemnation of 219 propositions at the university in Paris in 1277. This list covered a vast range of subjects; and whilst the practical effectiveness of their proscription remains questionable, the theological motivation behind their cosmological content was clear— establishing the Aristotelian physics of the universe should not serve as a constraint on God's absolute power to act as He wills or do anything short of a logical contradiction.

In 1277, the most pressing of these issues was Aristotle's insistence that the world was eternal (propositions 4, 87–9, 98, 99), a principle which, according to Aquinas, could not be proved or disproved by exclusively rational considerations. Eternity, sempiternity (i.e. creation in time but aeviternity or perpetuity thereafter), and creation *ex nihilo* followed by the end of the world, were all logically tenable solutions. After 1277, philosophers and theologians used the reservation of God's absolute power to speculate on other conceptual possibilities that were, according to Aristotelian physics, natural *im*possibilities. Most famously, Jean Buridan and Nicole Oresme discussed the question, raised by *De Caelo et Mundo*, of parallel universes and whether God could create more than one world (cf. proposition 34: 'the first cause cannot make other worlds'). As a result, they investigated the nature of the 'space' or void (*vacuum*) that would therefore have to exist between these worlds (cf. proposition 49) and the possibility of an infinite void which existed before Creation, which now surrounds the universe and in which God is nonetheless omnipresent (cf. proposition 201). Likewise, questions of time raised the issue, not only of how God could foreknow future events that were contingent and therefore indeterminate, but also whether God could change what had already happened in the past. Speculation was not limited to God's absolute power. Both Buridan and Oresme extended what was at least thinkable and possible to the question of the axial rotation of the earth, Oresme concluding that a rotating earth and a fixed heaven were at least as plausible as a fixed earth and a rotating heaven—it just could not be proved conclusively by reason or experience.

Geography

Geographical speculation took place within a similarly dynamic intellectual context. Starting,again, from widely shared parameters (five climatic zones encompassing an orb differentiated by specific circles and tropics; seven habitable zones in the upper hemisphere differentiated according to specific latitudes and lengths of daylight hours), both the size and nature of the inhabited part of the earth and the size and nature of the remainder were debated. If the whole earth was divided into five zones (a torrid zone of extreme heat straddling the equator, two frozen poles at either end described by the arctic and antarctic circles, and two temperate zones on either side of the equator), the identity of the temperate zone between torrid equator and antarctic pole was open to discussion. Was it the expanse of a southern ocean or was there a habitable land mass and, if the latter, was it uninhabited or inhabited by *antipodes*, people with 'feet opposed' to our own? The existence of *antipodes* or *antigeni* ('born opposite') was part and parcel of the classical geography transmitted through Pliny, Macrobius, Martianus Capella, and Isidore. Although the possibility had been treated with ridicule by Lactantius and circumspection by Augustine, it continued to be aired. It was also not the only unknown but inhabited mass of land which was posited. Macrobius and Martianus Capella divided the sphere of the world into four populated quarters, each separated from the others by the torrid zone and by the ocean—the known inhabited zone and its opposed land mass inhabited by *antipodes* formed two of the four, but there was a similar pairing on the underside of the upper and lower hemispheres—the *anticthones* and the *antecians* respectively. What prevented such speculation from being tested was the impassability of the torrid zone (either it was simply too hot to be traversed or the extremes of heat caused its ocean to become solid salt—*mare concretum*). This did not mean, however, that circumnavigation of Africa was out of the question. Both Pliny and Martianus Capella insisted that it was possible to sail around the coast to Arabia and that the Carthaginian general Hanno had done so and left a written account. In the 1290s, the brothers Ugolino and Vadino Vivaldi set out from Genoa to do the same.

The spatial relationship of the known inhabited part to the remainder of the globe naturally depended upon an assessment of the circumference of the earth. A straightforward method was inherited from classical antiquity and at least two estimates recorded by Martianus Capella: according to Eratosthenes, the figure should be 252,000 stades (31,500 Roman miles); according to Ptolemy, it was 180,000 stades (22,500 Roman miles, a figure subsequently rounded down to 20,400 by Alfraganus). Given that Pliny provided the overall dimensions of Europe, Africa, and Asia, as well as the distance from Cadiz to India (figures repeated, again, by Martianus Capella), it was possible to calculate the distance from the west coast of Europe and Africa to the east coast of India, not just overland (i.e. eastwards), but also overseas (i.e. westwards). *De Caelo et Mundo* had cautioned against disbelieving those who argued that the pillars of Hercules (Cadiz) and India were relatively close, not least because of such shared characteristics as the presence of elephants. Pliny had described the vast wealth of India and 'Taprobane' (Sri Lanka) and the 'Gold' and 'Silver' islands (Chryses, Argyra), but also how the east coast of India faced the west coast of Gaul. Albertus Magnus wrote a commentary on *De Caelo et Mundo* (1241) in which he echoed the endorsement by Arabic commentators of Ptolemy's estimate of the circumference of the earth. In *De Natura Locorum* (*c*.1251-4), Albertus further suggested that, whilst the size of the ocean precluded effective communication, the fierce deserts separating the known world from the habitable southern hemisphere were difficult but not impossible to cross. These ideas were picked up in the 1260s by Roger Bacon and in the 1340s by Nicole Oresme. Their remarks were then incorporated by Pierre d'Ailly in his *Imago Mundi* (12 August 1410). The relative narrowness of the western ocean and the habitability and accessibility of the southern temperate zone were clearly open questions and d'Ailly returns to them on at least three occasions, appealing both to authority and to *experientia*, 'the sight of modern witnesses'. Whilst a circumference of 20,400 Roman miles would make the earth circumnavigable in just over four years (1,570 days), d'Ailly repeats Bacon's citation of Aristotle and Pliny to argue that the ocean between Africa and India is small (*mare parvum*) and, given a favourable wind, navigable in a few days (*paucissimis diebus*). D'Ailly had already composed a series of 14 questions on the *Sphere* of Sacrobosco and, as a cosmographical and geographical compilation, the *Imago Mundi* was not an original work. Nevertheless, it was very influential. Following its printed edition of 1480–83, one of its readers was Christopher Columbus, whose annotated copy survives.

Time and place

Late medieval cosmographic and geographical inquiry was driven by classical authority, logical extrapolation, and intellectual speculation. Disagreement over concentric, eccentric, and epicyclic circles of planetary motion or over the heliocentricity of Venus and Mercury demonstrates that such inquiry was also founded on discrepancies between Aristotelian theory and Ptolemaic observation. This involved measuring the movements of the sun, moon, and planets relative to the sphere of the fixed stars and, since the measure of this motion was time, observation of these cycles naturally drew attention to the accuracy of the existing lunisolar calendar. Because this calendar was constructed on the mathematical principles of computus rather than astronomical observation, it became readily apparent that, despite the intercalation of extra 'embolismic' lunar months and an extra day in a leap or 'bissextile' year, it needed to be adjusted. Most glaringly, the true vernal equinox was falling earlier and earlier than the date which was predicted and identified in the calendar (21 March). Bede's distinction between natural, customary, and humanly instituted time, together with Macrobius' account of the reforms which had produced the Julian calendar under Julius Caesar and then Augustus ('corrected to the fineness of a close-cut fingernail'), provided additional historical sanction for such changes. Sacrobosco and Grosseteste accordingly advocated reform of the calendar in the 1220s, Roger Bacon in the 1260s. Pope Clement IV died before reading Bacon's submission, but by 1344–5 the issue was again before the curia, and Clement VI got as far as summoning Firmin de Beauval and John of Murs before his priorities were changed by the Black Death. Pierre d'Ailly wrote a treatise calling for correction of the calendar in 1411 after the issue had failed to be resolved at the Council of Pisa in 1409—this time it was Schism which prevented the requisite changes being made. Likewise at the Council of Basle in 1437 and the Fifth Lateran Council of 1512. The fact that it took until 1582 for Pope Gregory XIII finally to add 11 days to realign the mathematical calendar with solar and lunar observation was the result of the vagaries of ecclesiastical politics, not of astronomical ignorance.

If measurement of planets and stars gave greater precision to astronomical time, it also precipitated more accurate calculation of place. The seven zones into which the habitable world was divided were distinguished according to the disparity between their longest and shortest periods of daylight over the course of the solar year. The particular configuration of planets and stars that was visible at any one time, meanwhile, most obviously during eclipses of the sun and the moon, was known to vary according to both the latitude and longitude of the observer. The altitude and azimuth of any star (i.e. its longitude and latitude on a celestial sphere) was known to depend on the place and time of the observation. Construction of astrolabes was based accordingly on the stereographic projection of points and lines from this celestial sphere onto a flat disc, but also required adjustments to be made according to the latitude of the place from which the sighting occurred, and included hour lines to calculate the time at which the observation was made. As a result, sundials and astrolabes were calibrated according to the geographical location of where they were used, whilst portable 'ring' sundials and astrolabes were adapted to the latitude of the observer. Ever more accurate tables of astral and planetary phenomena (above all, the tables commissioned by Alfonso X of Leon-Castile in 1272) were adjustable to particular locations, be this Oxford (as in the Merton almanac of 1341) or Genoa. These calendars and tables made it possible to calculate the positions of celestial bodies and to predict the occurrence of conjunctions and eclipses.

Despite their inaccuracies, the effects of such measurement on 'geography' were profound. Pliny went to great lengths to record the names of places, listing them, not alphabetically, but as they would be encountered on an actual circuit (*periplus*) of a coastline or a journey through a province, giving measured distances wherever they were available. Martianus Capella produced a summary of the art of geometry which took its etymology seriously as 'measurement of the earth', and his description of peoples, provinces, towns, mountains, and rivers was nearly four times as long as the account of strictly Euclidian figures which followed it. When Albertus Magnus wrote *De Natura Locorum*, the impact of astronomic sensitivity to locality is marked. Moving from a theoretical definition of place to consider the diversity of individual locations, Albertus produced a long list of the effects of place on plants, animals, and human beings. Appealing to both authority (*auctoritas*) and empirical investigation (*experimentum*), Albertus notes how different crops and animals flourish in different physical contexts, and how hard they are to transplant from their 'proper' location, their natural place of generation. On this basis, he discusses the influence of geographical positioning on the racial characteristics which are found in human beings and on the factors which influence human health. The attention Albertus pays to the different ways in which global positioning (latitude and longitude), climatic zone, and locality (weather, air, mountains, forests, and water) can affect human nature reveals just how much he depended on astronomy (cf. propositions 142 and 143: 'that the necessity of events comes from the diversity of places; that the differences of condition among men [...] are traced back to the diverse signs of the heavens'). Location in space and time was more than just a matter of contingent circumstance; it directly affected the nature of what lived in a particular place on earth.

Representation of place and time

Judged by modern criteria, Albertus Magnus' integration of geography and astronomy presents something of a conundrum when it comes to how this cosmography was subsequently represented. Given that knowing exactly where a place was located on the earth was so important in *c*.1250, to both astronomy and medicine, why did it take so long to translate this knowledge into a visual 'map' of the earth, as Bacon suggested in the 1260s and when the art of navigation was already producing such accurate depictions of coastlines? Part of the answer may lie in technology, given that Ptolemy's demonstration of how to plot a sphere onto a plane surface only became available to western Europe in Latin after 1406–10. The impact of his

Geography was certainly marked, in the map drawn by Pirrus de Noha in *c.*1414 to accompany Pomponius Mela's *Chorographia*, for example, in the Walsperger Map of 1448, or in the world maps of Henricus Martellus from the 1480s and 1490s. In 1427 Guillaume Fillastre, a fellow cardinal and close colleague of d'Ailly (who himself produced a tabulated summary of Ptolemy in 1414, giving coordinates of individual places arranged by climatic zone), had a manuscript illustrated with 26 regional maps and a *mappa mundi*. As the *Geography* was copied, new regional maps were drawn to accompany the text, as well as a composite of the whole. Such Ptolemaic world maps, however, do not in themselves constitute a *deus ex machina* for the transformation of cartography. They had their own peculiarities (a 'winged' Scotland, a landlocked Indian Ocean), their coastlines were not as accurate as portolan charts, and they needed to be supplemented with additional maps for those areas (notably the west coast of Africa and Scandinavia) of which Ptolemy himself had been ignorant.

As a theory of planispheric projection, a technique for transferring lists of places with coordinates, Ptolemy's *Geography* still raises a question of need. The measurement and representation of both space and time remained intrinsically connected to function, and the accurate plotting of these dimensions was therefore primarily determined by the purposes which it served. Portolan charts and Alfonsine tables may seem, from a modern perspective, perfectly natural companions, but even without the technical advance of planispheric projection enabling latitude and longitude to be spatially represented, navigation continued to be the purpose of the former, astronomy or medicine the latter. There was no reason for them to be put together. A list of coordinates which positioned places relative to the planets and the stars was sufficient for the requirements of an astrologer or physician. Likewise, with exclusively verbal lists of towns and distances for a traveller: a schematic itinerary with a sequence of towns with distances marked between them was enough—in the Peutinger Map, for example, a Roman road map copied in the thirteenth century, or in Matthew Paris's map for a pilgrimage from London to Palestine via Apulia or Sicily. Given the spatial possibilities for journeys across a sea such as the Mediterranean, compared to the more restricted routes of road and river, there are pragmatic reasons for a chronological disjunction in the accuracy with which nautical and terrestrial space were plotted. A schematic itinerary was simply a more practical guide to travel overland than an accurate topographical map. The reverse was true at sea. Different types of cartographic representation served different purposes and there was no necessary relation, or communication, between them.

Locating a particular place on the earth did not require the mode of scaled, pictorial representation which might seem 'natural' from a modern map. To ask why it took 'so long' to extend the accuracy of portolan charts and astronomical coordinates to terrestrial maps is therefore to ask the wrong question. It is instead a question of transformation, not in the conception of space, but in the way this space was represented. Astrology and medicine required a close connection to be made between celestial and terrestrial space, and thus required detailed knowledge of the connection between place and astronomical time. Medieval 'maps' served different intellectual functions, and when they did seek to represent the connection between space and time, it was with another type of time that they were concerned.

Realization that subjective human perception of time can be altogether different from the mathematical measurement of the motion of the universe is not a modern phenomenological discovery. 'What is time?' asked Augustine. 'I confess I am still ignorant,' was his answer. 'Who can easily and briefly explain it? Who can even comprehend it in thought or put the answer into words? Yet we refer to nothing more familiarly or more knowingly' (*Confessions* XI). Time, he observed, could not itself be the motion of the heavenly bodies by which it is measured, since not only was it created on the first day (i.e. before the sun and the moon on the fifth), but there was at least one occasion on which the sun stood still (Joshua 10:12). What particularly intrigued Augustine was the elusive nature of present time as distinct from time past and time to come. Past time exists in the present as memory (*memoria*), future time exists in the present as expectation (*expectatio*), and, as a result, except for one brief, instantaneous moment of immediate awareness (*contuitus*), present time 'exists' only as remembrance of what has just been or anticipation of what is just about to be. Since past and future do not exist except in the present, and since what does not exist cannot be measured, time itself is effectively an aspect of the soul. As such, human experience of time is permeated by the consequences of sin as a distension or 'stretching' of the soul. Only God experiences eternity, not as the divided, multiple, and successive duration of time, but as a single, instantaneous, all-encompassing moment, as a unified, indivisible present point, an instant now (*nunc instans*).

Augustine's analysis of past, present, and future time in terms of memory, experience, and expectation was as influential on a 'medieval' understanding of time as his classification of the Six Ages. Its significance was reinforced by Macrobius (whose syncretic solar theism comprised a three-headed Serapis symbolizing time present, past, and future) and Martin of Braga (for whom prudence had three faces—past, present, and future—corresponding to memory, intelligence, and foresight). This sequential conception forms one further explanation of why *mappae mundi* continued as a mode of representation 'so long' into the fifteenth century. The time in which their geographical space is located comprises the present but also the past and the future. The existence of all three temporal aspects is conveyed by the depiction of Adam and Eve in the terrestrial paradise, by the location of the tower of Babel, the city of Jerusalem, and the land of Gog and Magog, by the inclusion of Alexander the Great and Augustus, and by the figure of Christ around the circumference at the Day of Judgment. The Hereford *mappa mundi* describes itself accordingly as 'history' (*estoire*); it represents the concurrence of past, present, and future in a single image, a reflection of the *nunc instans* seen by God. Hugh of St Victor had already demonstrated how the literal existence of events in the physical universe, the historical sense of *imago mundi*, could be overlaid with moral, anagogical, and allegorical meanings, each of which might convey a theological point as a didactic and mnemotechnical device. For the Hereford and Ebstorf *mappae mundi*, a physical representation of the earth was the foundation for a narrative of Creation, Redemption, and Judgment expressed in God's eternal vision. The instrumental purpose of portolan charts and schematic itineraries was altogether different; so too was the particular sense of time—as distance travelled, as motion measured—which they needed, and sought, to convey.

Juxtaposing an Augustinian analysis of time relative to human perception and experience with a definition of time as an objective measurement of motion was a standard starting-point for discussion once Aristotle's *Physics* became available in Latin from the late twelfth century. A distinction between the various ways in which time could exist in human consciousness and the absolute nature of time as the measure of physical motion (particularly of the sun relative to the earth) accordingly provides a critical perspective from which to assess medieval representations of time. This applies to the conflation of past, present, and future in *mappae mundi*, but also to the recording of past time in written histories. It is sometimes argued that it took 'the Renaissance' to discover a sense of the past as something separate and different from the present. In 'the Middle Ages', by contrast, use of the historic present as a tense in which to narrate deeds of the past, together with the visual depiction of ancient people and scenes in contemporary dress and architecture, are cited as proof of the absence of a 'real' understanding of the past. Closer scrutiny of the distinction between conception of the past and the nature and purpose of its representation reveals this contrast to be over-drawn.

An acute awareness of the passage of time, of the transitory and fleeting nature of the things of this earth, was a familiar theme even before the Black Death gave it renewed, as it were, vitality, whether in *transi* tombs or the Legend of the Three Living and Three Dead. Comparing the sufferings of the present to the glories of the past was a commonplace rhetorical strategy for inducing pity and indignation in one's audience. *Ubi sunt* ('Where are they now?') accordingly became an established literary register, if not genre, from Ovid's *Metamorphoses* through to Petrarch's *Triumph of Time* (*c.*1370). If Saturn embodied the course and revolution of times and seasons, Chronos and his sickle formed an iconographic shorthand. This sense of the passage of time could also be given spatial and physical dimensions. The *translatio imperii* of four world monarchies (Daniel 2:37–40), for example, was given an east-to-west political trajectory by Pompeius Trogus and Orosius, as power moved from Assyria to Greece to Rome and then, according to Otto of Freising, from Romans to the Franks. Geographical lists, meanwhile, could include a record of the disappearance of towns, their changes in name and importance, the movements of peoples (according to Albertus Magnus, conquering Saxons called Britain 'Anglia' because of the Roman villas which were still called 'engelae' in the Saxony of his own day), and alterations in the landscape wrought by earthquakes and floods.

A sense of the past also underpinned interpretation of the written word. From *Accessus ad Auctores* in the eleventh century, asking who, what, where, when, why, how, and for whom a text was written became a standard approach, whether the text was biblical, classical, or late antique. Lorenzo Valla's forensic demonstration in 1446 that the Donation of Constantine was an early medieval forgery continued this tradition. It was not just a case of proving that the language was inappropriate for the time in which it purported to be written (as an issue of philological veracity); it was also a case of the impossibility of Constantine ever making such a grant in the first place (as an issue of plausibility or verisimilitude). The representation of what happened in the past, however, was always conditioned by the use to which it was being put, the function which it served. The writing of history accordingly followed classical antecedents in adhering to the demands of its moral-didactic genre—the purpose was to teach (*docere*), move (*movere*), and entertain (*delectare*), and therefore medieval historiography deployed the full panoply of linguistic techniques available from classical rhetoric. In order to be convincing, a narrative of past actions needed plausibility (*verisimilitudo*) and, in order to possess this 'likeness to the truth', such description needed to be invested with a number of qualities—it had to correspond with what normally happens and be adapted to the expectations or beliefs of the audience. Verisimilitude extended to making the narrative as vivid as if it were happening before the audience's eyes, a quality of 'being seen' which was termed *enargeia* or 'evidence' (*evidentia*). It also had to be described in language which was appropriate both to its subject matter and its audience, which avoided redundant or anachronistic terminology and too slavish an imitation of style from the past. As Macrobius recommended, 'let us show in our lives the *mores* of the past, but speak the language of our own day' (*Saturnalia* I.5).

Once the representation of past time is viewed as part of a narrative whose effective communication depended on using language that was plausible, 'evident', and suitable for its intended audience, the conventions governing the commemoration of history become much more readily apparent. A sense of past time as something separable and different is not mutually exclusive from a means of representation which makes that past both comprehensible and moving for a particular audience, where it needs to be translated into terms which make sense in the present. This is why Alexander the Great was portrayed in the form of a medieval knight. The principles governing narrative verisimilitude were intertwined with pictorial realism by the same manuals of classical rhetoric. This connection forms at least part of the reason why perspective was developed in painting—as a technique it may have owed its origins to the study of optics, but as a method of representation it owed its appreciation to the rhetorical effectiveness of 're-presenting' events as if they were happening before the audience's eyes. Spatial realism was not the only means of achieving this end—like portolan accuracy on medieval maps, perspectival naturalism remained one of several methods of representation and depended on the didactic purpose of the object being produced. This is not the same as seeking a more 'scientific' reproduction of the physical universe. Indeed, one of its aims was often to solve the narrative clutter which might otherwise result from depicting a continuous sequence of events within the same image. Perspectival depth enabled narrative to be introduced by having past and future described simultaneously, not by proleptic iconographic symbols, but with events taking place in the background of the present.

Discovery and rediscovery

The period 1250–1500 presents a necessarily plural and fragmented picture of socially and culturally conditioned ways of seeing space and measuring time. No one approach is absolute or all-embracing, many of them overlap, and all of them are distinguished by the use to which they were put, the needs which they served, and the function for which they were developed. In this respect, there is no reason to assume that the later Middle Ages were any less complex and variegated, or any less sophisticated, than the early modern or modern periods, either in their conception and experience of space and time or in the ways in which they chose to represent them, in word and in image. Indeed, the fourteenth and fifteenth centuries might reveal a greater degree of complexity and sophistication—in the absence of a single, uniform, all-inclusive scale by which every activity is measured irrespective of the particular rhythm of its nature; in the extent of mental numeracy produced by training in computus and the use of finger-reckoning; in the exercise of memory as a function of oral culture and a trained skill; and in the integration of a practical knowledge and observation of the celestial spheres with more mundane patterns of weather and human health. Above all, the period 1250–1500 reveals an understanding of place which did not stop at the literal, physical level, but accepted meanings invested with moral and allegorical significance, as *lieux de mémoire*. It indicates an understanding of time which *started* by distinguishing between the experiential relativism of past, present, and future and the scientific measurement of motion in the physical universe.

If changes did occur in the conception of space and time over the period 1250–1500, these do not represent the process of scientific empiricism and discovery which post–Enlightenment humanists might prefer. It was not simply a case of Aristotle's physical conception of time replacing Augustine's periodization of Creation, Redemption, and Judgment, nor of regular, equal, rationalized public hours replacing the irregular, unequal, sacral, ecclesiastical hours of the liturgy. Stripped of the teleological presuppositions of progress, freed from the assumption that a scientific conception of absolute time and physical space is the only true measure of reality, the relationship between *experimentum* and *auctoritas* reveals a more complex interaction than the master narratives of 'naturalism' and 'realism' would suggest. In the first instance, this process turned on the respective influences—sometimes separate, sometimes reciprocal—of 'high' and 'low' culture, academic and mercantile, Latin and vernacular, the 'scientific' disciplines of astronomy, geometry, arithmetic, and music, and the 'mechanical' arts of navigation and metalwork. In the second instance, it turned, not just on intellectual comprehension, but on the conventions which governed how different conceptions of space and time could be represented, both pictorially and verbally, to serve different purposes in different contexts. Using maps and clocks to assess how place and time were conceived depends fundamentally on the purposes for which such analogical representations were made and the use(s) to which they were put. There was more than one way, in other words, of seeing and understanding the same space or time—portolan charts or *mappae mundi*, Books of Hours or striking clocks. The physical or literal reality of an event or place was, in many ways, less significant than the meaning with which it was invested by different people at different times for different purposes. This applied to chronology too—an absolute, linear, numerical calculation of the *annus mundi* was one of several possible dating systems, but this quantitative measure was not the only, or most important, available. In the third instance, as repeated calls for reform of the calendar show, any process of transformation was as much about politics as knowledge. For Alexander the Great and Augustus, 'measuring the earth' was a practical as well as a symbolic function of power and, as representations of that measurement, 'maps' were created to serve military and economic needs. This was why Martianus Capella's personification of Geometry—holding a rod in her right hand and a solid globe in her left—underpinned the iconography of royal rulers throughout the Middle Ages.

The discoveries of the fifteenth century, in sum, were not the result of a brave new vision of the world, a shift from 'religion' to 'science', 'medieval' to 'modern'. The ecclesiastical and mercantile contacts with India and China which had been initiated by the Mongols became difficult to maintain after 1368 with the overthrow of Mongol China, even more so with the conquests of the Ottoman Turks before and after the fall of Constantinople in 1453 and the expulsion of the Genoese from the Black Sea in 1475. This precariousness provided a powerful political incentive for Genoese and Portuguese to find other routes to the East, but this was in order to *re*connect with what had *already* been known and traded in the period 1250–1350. The mindset of Christopher Columbus was firmly rooted in two centuries of geographical knowledge and debate. His reading of Pierre d'Ailly's *Imago Mundi* took him straight to the cosmographical and geographical learning of John of Sacrobosco, Albertus Magnus, Roger Bacon, and Nicole Oresme. His own *Book of Prophecies*, meanwhile, demonstrated that, like Franciscan and

Dominican missionaries in the thirteenth and fourteenth centuries, preaching the Gospel to all peoples of the world would serve both as preparation for a new crusade and a sign of the last times. Columbus was not to know that his journey to the east coast of India would mean that the *translatio imperii* would, in fact, continue ever westwards, even full-circle, on its trajectory. What led him to make that journey, however, was a combination of *experimentum*, mercantilism, mission, apocalypticism, and geographical understanding that would have been completely familiar 200 years earlier.

Plate 7. Bernardino Licinio, *Portrait of Arrigo Licinio and his Family*, (*c*.1530)

6

Society, family, and gender

Catherine Kovesi

In early September 1382, King Louis I of Hungary and Poland died without male issue. In east-central Europe women had no right to inherit land, let alone a kingdom, and so a curious solution was found to the succession of Louis's dual crowns. A week after Louis's death, on 17 September 1382, his daughter Mary was crowned as king with the Holy Crown of Hungary by the archbishop of Esztergom in the country's then capital of Székesfehérvár. Two years later, on 16 October 1384, Louis's youngest daughter, Jadwiga (Hedwig), was also crowned, in Kraków, as king of Poland (*rex Poloniae*). At first glance this dual monarchy of female 'kings' might suggest a radical revisioning of the power of women in late medieval Europe. But legally Mary and Jadwiga could not be queens. Their access to power could only be achieved through a transformation of their gender via a legal fiction—a fiction which only served to underpin the existing legal status quo. Moreover, in contemporary assessments of these women's respective reigns, their success or otherwise was premised on their perceived qualities as women rather than men. Mary was reviled as a bad ruler, and therefore became an exemplar of the fact that women, by their nature, are unfit to rule; whilst Jadwiga became the paradigmatic saintly female ruler, the beneficent mother figure, who converted her pagan husband to Christianity, died in childbirth, and was eventually canonized. Transformations of gender in these two cases had no real underlying value, but only reinforced their countries' entrenched social systems.

The two curious coronations of King Mary and King Jadwiga highlight some of the core issues involved in the social expression and understanding of gender in the later Middle Ages. They also underscore the difficulties involved in attempting to write synthetically about society, family, and gender more broadly. Indeed, one of the defining qualities of all three aspects of life in this period was their variability across the geopolitical, legal, and social divide, and their surprising fluidity. How might one

The Later Middle Ages. Isabella Lazzarini, Oxford University Press (2021). © Isabella Lazzarini.
DOI: 10.1093/oso/9780198731641.003.0007

meaningfully compare, for instance, the lives of Mary and Jadwiga with those of numerate and literate merchants' wives in republican Florence? or the experiences of a knight in the court of Philip III le Bon of Burgundy with those of an artisan in the imperial city of Nuremberg? or the experiences of a prostitute in Castile with those of an anchorite in Norwich? And how might one even compare the experiences of those within the one geographically defined community whose backgrounds were divergent? A courtesan, a noble girl married at 13, a nun, a mendicant friar, an oarsman, an unmarried young noble, and an elderly statesman, all in the same city of Venice, might have very different understandings and experiences of family and of gender and of sexual relations. And even taken individually, over a lifetime, understandings, experiences, and practices of these same concepts would change as men and women moved from one life stage to another. Such varieties of experience of men and women in the later Middle Ages were also occurring against a backdrop of extraordinary upheaval from prolonged war, catastrophic and then endemic plague, burgeoning economic expansion, and spectacular financial collapses, all of which placed great demographic and economic pressures on society, whilst allowing for new sociopolitical opportunities to emerge. These variables all need to be taken into account when approaching an understanding of men and women's lived experiences in this period, but they are also what make this period so intrinsically fascinating.

Despite these complexities, certain paradigms remained as touchstones throughout late medieval Europe against which normative values were constructed: a shared understanding of Christianity as the foundation of society in this life and in the next; a predominant acceptance of classical Greek texts for understandings of the human body and of sexual differences between men and women; an overwhelming dependence on patriarchal structures with implications for constructions and experiences of masculinity and femininity; and an ideal of family and of community relationships (whether secular or religious) from which no individual could readily claim isolation. Marginalized and often persecuted groups, such as Jews, sodomites, or heretics, were understood and defined against this normative backdrop. By the end of the period, increasing political and legal consolidation of societal structures led to their interrogation by those whom these same structures excluded or constrained. In particular the later Middle Ages saw an increasing audibility if not yet visibility of the voices of women, and the beginnings of the so-called *querelle des femmes*.

Gender

The case of Mary and Jadwiga is also useful for demonstrating the importance of gender as a category of analysis with which to approach relations between the sexes and the self, identity, and the nature of power. Gender is not, however, without contestation as an analytic paradigm. Its usefulness as a category is that it moves us away from seeing 'men' and 'women' as essentialist, timeless, classless categories, locked into to their sexual bodies. It assists us in looking at the differing ways men and women understood what it was to be male and female, masculine and feminine, across time and space, circumstance and lifecycle. It is a category which regards male and female identities as socially constructed rather than biologically given, and enables a richer disentanglement of men's and women's experiences rather than looking at them as simple binary opposites. However, some have argued that using the term 'gender' has led to too dramatic a softening of the differences in the situations between men and women, that it underplays the predominance of patriarchal structures constraining women, and that there is still too great a gap in research and knowledge about the lives of women in the Middle Ages in relation to that concerning men. Thomas Kuehn takes a more anthropological approach and argues instead for the category 'social personhood'. For Kuehn, social personhood emphasizes 'relations between individuals, or even between parts of an individual',[1] and recasts gender 'as a matter of contingent differences, not as a matter of absolute opposition'.[2] He warns against imposing our western notions of the individual back onto the past, when both men and women instead operated within kinship groups, households, neighbourhoods, and a range of social identities, which could also include race, nationality, and religion, or what Kimberlé Crenshaw usefully described as intersectionality. Gender in all its complexities is always present, in other words, but is rarely the sole determining factor in an individual's life experiences. Whether you look at this period in terms of men and women, gender, or social personhood, it is perhaps useful to remember Judith Brown's central question: 'what cultural

---

[1] T. Kuehn, 'Person and Gender in the Laws', in Judith C. Brown and Robert C. Davis eds., *Gender and Society in Renaissance Italy*, London and New York: Routledge, first edn 1998, second edn. 2014, pp. 87–106, and, Judith C. Brown, 'Introduction' in the same, pp. 1–16, p. 5

[2] T. Kuehn, 'Understanding Gender Inequality in Renaissance Florence: Personhood and Gifts of Maternal Inheritance by Women', *Journal of Women's History* 8.2 (1996), pp. 58–80, at p. 59.

constructs allowed women and men in the past to attach different meaning to similar circumstances?'[3]

Patriarchy

It might seem uncontroversial to describe late medieval European society, from the household through to legal, political, and religious systems, as patriarchal, and to assert that such a structure was seen as God-given. As the Sicilian writer Paolo Caggio expressed it in his dialogue on the governance of the family: 'all over the world, women follow the customs of their husbands as the law of their life; this rule is established by the Rector of Heaven, nature, and the holy institution of marriage.'[4] The male head of a household (pater familias) was deemed to have authority over his wife, his children, his household staff, and all dependents, including animals. Women were the legal property of their male relatives, with a monetary value attached. Men, with rare exceptions, held the principal positions of religious, political, and legal authority. Even men's bodies were usually seen as the primary God-given ideal and women's bodies as either a malformation of that ideal or, in Aristotelian terms, as an imperfect inverted version. But many historians have become increasingly uncomfortable with the unreflective use of patriarchy to describe societies in the past. Since the late 1980s in particular, it has been argued that the term 'patriarchy' is too static and ahistorical and does not adequately allow for the agency of women and alternative power structures. It is a term, moreover, that is too deterministic and simplistic in explaining women's subordination as caused by sexual difference, whilst ignoring differences in class, race, or even power relations between women. By emphasizing the repressive aspects of male power, it is argued, patriarchy underplays the often mutually beneficial relations between men and women,

---

[3] Brown, 'Introduction', p. 4.
[4] Paolo Caggio, *Iconomica del Signor Paolo Caggio gentil'huomo di Palermo nella quale s'insegna brevemente per modo di dialogo il governo Famigliare, etc* (Venice: Al Segno del Pozzo, 1552), Prima Parte, 19r: 'Et tutto questo facilmente sarà à tutte le donne del Mondo, s'elleno si porran dinanzi i costumi de' lor mariti come legge della lor vita, impostale, e dal Rettor del Cielo, e dalla mestra Natura, per la congiuntion sacra del Matrimonio santo.' Translation as given in A. Dialeti, 'From Women's Oppression to Male Anxiety: The Concept of "Patriarchy" in the Historiography of Early Modern Europe', in M. G. Muravyeva and R. M. Toivo (eds), *Gender in Late Medieval and Early Modern Europe* (New York, 2013), pp. 19–36, at p. 28 (Dialeti mistakenly identifies Caggio as Venetian).

and the influence of other societal bonds such as kinship networks between women as well as between men and women.

More recently, however, with historians' increasing focus on gender formation and masculinity studies, patriarchy has reappeared as a useful term in historical discourse concerning late medieval Europe. Men too, of course, are gendered beings with no single universal experience of manhood. Masculine identity in this period was constructed not just in opposition to feminine identity, but against a range of other men, other classes, age groups, and so on. Patriarchy needs to be approached from a male as well as a female point of view. Patriarchy might subordinate women to the benefit of men, but it also challenged men and provided a yardstick against which their effectiveness as men could be measured. If a patriarch was unable to be an adequate husband or father, or if he fell into financial ruin, or if he simply was not terribly successful, his very manhood and capacity for governance of self and others could easily be challenged. Whilst men were the prime beneficiaries of such a paradigmatic worldview, not all men were equally privileged by it, just as not all women were unilaterally subordinated by it. Like gender, therefore, patriarchy still has value as a category if we use it not as an absolute but as one with which other multiple categories of power, relationships, and identity intersect.

Roles of men and women

Sensitivity to the subtleties of gender and of patriarchy is crucial in appraising the respective roles of men and of women in late medieval Europe. When the radical English Lollard priest John Ball preached for social equality in his famous sermon on Blackheath in 1381, his argument contained an unquestioned assumption about the respective God-given relationships between men and women's work. 'When Adam delved and Eve span,' he famously asked, 'who was then the gentleman?' His argument was one for an end to bondage, but it made an unquestioning assumption about the respective relationships between men and women's work: men should labour outdoors (delve) and women should work in the confines of the home (spin). This was a view reinforced by many of the prescriptive advice manuals of the fourteenth and fifteenth centuries, which articulated an ideal of the marital home as one rigidly divided along patriarchal lines, with women and men assuming clearly defined roles. There is also plenty of evidence that men did indeed predominate in labouring tasks, and women in the sedentary crafts, including textile crafts and trades such as spinning of thread and finishing of cloth (if not necessarily its weaving). But if this might be the assumed norm, in reality male members of households were often absent for extended periods—fighting to fulfil obligations of vassalage in battles far from home (as during the extended war between the English and French crowns), or trading as merchants and bankers in companies set up in Europe and the wider Mediterranean world, or fighting as mercenaries in bands around Europe. During these absences, women of the household often assumed roles of responsibility that required detailed knowledge of the family's economic status and a relatively advanced ability at business, estate, and household management. Christine de Pizan's detailed advice regarding the duties and expectations of 'ladies and demoiselles living in fortified places or on their lands outside of towns' assumed that 'these women spend much of their lives in households without husbands. The men usually are at court or in distant countries. So the ladies will have responsibilities for managing their property, their revenues, their lands.'[5] The 252 extant letters of Margherita Datini to her husband, the wealthy merchant Francesco Datini, exist because he was absent for extended periods from the family home in Prato, and they detail a capacity and a knowledge of business management and household oversight in his absence that cannot have been unique. Indeed, Margaret Paston's letters from the family estate in Norfolk to her husband, John, in London recount a similar level of knowledge of household management and family business. More prominently, Isabella d'Este assumed and fulfilled roles in the marquisate of Mantua due to her husband's extended absences on the battlefields of Italy which included persuading King Louis XII of France not to invade her city in 1500, taking control of military forces from 1509, and hosting the Congress of Mantua in 1512.

We know of these four women because of their extensive written records, but lower down the social scale artisanal households, and those of peasants, often required a unity of economic endeavour that meant standard household roles could be divided in ways that defied John Ball's ready categorization. The harvest scene for the month of June in the *Très Riches Heures* of the Duc de Berry, for example, shows women prominently in the foreground raking the grain that their male counterparts are scything in the background,

---

[5] Christine de Pizan, *A Medieval Woman's Mirror of Honor: The Treasure of the City of Ladies*, trans. C. Cannon Willard, ed. M. Pelner Cosman (New York, 1989), repr. in E. Amt (ed.), *Women's Lives in Medieval Europe: A Sourcebook* (New York, 1993), p. 164.

and the month of September has women alongside men gathering grapes from their vines. The stresses of harvest season clearly required all available hands to assist regardless of idealized or standardized gender roles within a household.

Similarly, whilst a male-headed household might have been both the norm and the ideal across Europe, the reality on the ground was often more complex. Whilst there are no complete censuses for Europe in this period, we do have isolated detailed sources which give a sense of the variation in household makeup. The ground-breaking work of David Herlihy and Chistiane Klapisch-Zuber on the Florentine census, or *catasto*, of 1427 has enabled a rich picture of individual households at every level of this city. Using this data, Samuel K. Cohn has demonstrated that in 1427, 18.43 per cent of Florentine households were headed by women, a figure which increased to 21.52 per cent in 1458. Although this proportion fell dramatically to 6.74 per cent in line with the economic crises of the 1470s and 1480s, households headed by a single female were clearly not unusual in the period. Ninety per cent of these female-headed households in 1427 were those of widows, a proportion which fell to 75 per cent in 1458, but which rose again to 96 per cent in later decades.[6] Nor were these households necessarily poorer than those of men, with average taxable assets in 1458 rivalling male households (610 florins for female-headed versus 606 for male-headed households). In the 1427 *catasto*, women were also visible in a variety of trades—carpenters, goldsmiths, butchers, grain dealers, cobblers, painters—and a notable list of singulars—an oil merchant, a linen manu-facturer, a furrier, a slipper-maker, a stationer, a dealer in brass, a grocer, and so on.[7]

This is not to say that life was easy for members of a female-headed household, or for women such as Isabella d'Este, who took on significant roles of leadership—nor even for women affiliated to powerful men. As Lorenzo de' Medici's sister Lucrezia (Nannina) complained to her mother at the summary action of her husband in dismissing their children's tutor: 'you do not want to be born female if you want to do things your own way.'[8] Women could not represent themselves in court, and were often

[6] S. K. Cohn, 'Women and Work in Renaissance Italy', in Brown and Davis, *Gender and Society in Renaissance Italy*, pp. 107–26, at pp. 118–19.
[7] Ibid. 115.
[8] Archivio di Stato, Florence, MAP, filza 80, 69: 'non si vole nascere femina chi vuole fare a suo modo.' Translated by L. Kaborycha in *A Corresponding Renaissance. Letters Written by Italian Women, 1375–1650* (Oxford, 2016), l. 21, pp. 136–7. Translation my own.

vulnerable economically, especially if widowed. Christine de Pizan, widowed at 25 after ten years of marriage, and finding herself responsible for a niece, an invalid mother, and three young children, writes ruefully that she could only take on such a task through the transformation of her gender. I was, she writes, transformed overnight 'from a woman to a male'[9] and again, 'a woman, became a man by a flick of Fortune's hand.'[10] Similarly, as Guarino da Verona wrote to the Veronese scholar Isotta Nogarola in a moment of the latter's crisis, for a woman to show leadership in learning, she had to become male; any doubts in the enterprise revealed instead her 'womanish' spirit:

> when I saw fit to give my attention to that outstanding intellect of yours, with its attendant embellishments of learning, I was accustomed besides to express strongly my opinion that you were manly of spirit, that nothing could happen which you would not bear with a courageous and indomitable spirit. Now, however, you show yourself so cast down, humiliated and truly womanish that I am able to perceive nothing which accords with my previous magnificent opinion of you.[11]

Nogarola attempted to circumvent the standard gender roles altogether, living as a celibate scholar in a household with her brother Ludovico. However, this untried way of life seems to have provoked some scandal, as she found herself the subject of a scurrilous attack in an anonymous pamphlet in 1438 accusing her of living incestuously with Ludovico. Though it is not clear that other scholars gave much credence to this attack, Nogarola was evidently mortified, and retreated for some years from participation in intellectual life, returning instead to the home of her other brother, Antonio, in which her mother also lived, where her chastity and probity would not be questioned.

---

[9] Christine de Pizan, *Livre de la Mutacion de Fortune* (1400–1403), 'From the Book of the Mutation of Fortune', in *The Writings of Christine de Pizan*, trans. and ed. C. Cannon Willard (New York, 1994), l. 28.

[10] Ibid. l. 19.

[11] 'Hoc vesperi tuas accepi litteras querimoniae plenas et accusationis, quibus incertum me reddidisti tibine magis condoleam an mihi ipsi gratuler. Nam eum tuum istud perspexisse viderer ingeniu adiunctis doctrinae ornamenti insigne, te adeo virili animo et opinari et praedicare solebam, ut nihil accidere posset quod non forti et invicto ferres pectore. Nunc autem sic demissam abiectam et vere mulierem tete ostentas, ut nihil magnifico de te sensui meo respondere te cernam.' Remigio Sabbadini, *Epistolario di Guarino Veronese*, II (Venice, 1916), pp. 306–7. Translation as in L. Jardine, '"O Decus Italiae Virgo", or the Myth of the Learned Lady in the Renaissance', *Historical Journal* 28 (1985), pp. 799–819, at p. 808.

Family, marriage, dowry, and inheritance

Underlying all of these roles of men and of women was a view of the family as the central organizing structure of society. At its broadest, family was the whole Christian community whose members considered themselves 'brothers and sisters in Christ', with Mary as mother and God as father. This Christian family was not coterminous with one's earthly life. Obligations to pray for brothers and sisters in Purgatory, and expectations that those of sanctified life who were now in heaven might assist their brethren toiling in this world, created a continuum of the Christian family independent of time and space, reinforced by ritual and spiritual life and practices. But how the Christian family in this world was structured in its particulars varied widely across Europe, and there was no word for 'family' in medieval Latin with a meaning that we would recognize in our modern usage.

At its most general, family indicated a domestic unit living together in a household. This included, but was not limited to, those tied together by blood or marriage (both on the maternal and paternal side), children (whether legitimate or natural), and also household servants and staff. A husband and a wife were core to a family unit, but rarely lived or conceived of themselves as self-contained. From their marital hearth radiated outward layers of kinship and familial connections with numerous people who claimed the right to eat at the household table, or what Joel Rosenthal has evocatively called 'an individualised geometry of kinship'.[12] By the late Middle Ages, the patrilineage, or agnatic kin, had come to dominate over cognatic kin in matters of inheritance, and genealogical trees rarely included the name of a mother after one or two generations unless she came from an exceptional family. The so-called Hundred Years War (in reality a series of battles from 1337 to 1453) between the crowns of England and of France had at its origins a putative claim by England to the crown of France through a female line of inheritance, which ran counter to the French insistence on Salic law which excluded women from inheritance of thrones, fiefs, and other landed property. The devastating consequences of the Hundred Years War point to the usefulness of the Hungarian and Polish legal fiction of two female 'kings' outlined earlier. Vertical patrilineal domination in the family tree, especially in noble and royal families, simplifies what was a much richer horizontal reality of familial connections with wider

[12] J. Rosenthal, 'Family', in M. C. Schaus (ed.), *Women and Gender in Medieval Europe: An Encyclopedia* (New York, 2006), pp. 275–80, at p. 279.

kin networks. Such kinship could also include spiritual ties such as godparents, sworn knightly brotherhoods, or confraternities who offered assistance in times of need and whose members often cared for widows and orphans of their deceased confrères.

If family was the core social structure, then marriage was its perpetuation and its support. Marriage extended a family; it provided opportunities for the capital growth of a family; it provided an instituted means of procreation, and protected the upbringing of a community's children. Marriage created not just a social unit, but also an economic and a spiritual one. The later Middle Ages was marked by a gradual encroachment of the church into the celebration of marriage, and by the formal insistence in declarations in 1184, and again in 1208, 1274, and 1439, that marriage is a sacrament. The church's articulation of the nature of marriage also involved an emphasis on accepted degrees of kinship within which marriage was permitted, and this had an important influence on perceptions of family and of kin more widely. The Fourth Lateran Council of 1215 re-emphasized that marriage should occur outside the fourth degree of consanguinity (i.e. up to and including first cousins). However, in reality, in small isolated communities, or in restricted royal and aristocratic circles, this was often difficult to achieve and dispensations could be, and often were, granted. Prohibited degrees of consanguinity could also be invoked in unexpected ways as a reason, for instance, for subsequent annulment of a marriage should it prove unsuitable for whatever reason. Perhaps the most infamous example of this dual use of prohibited levels of consanguinity is that provided by the first, second, and fifth marriages of Henry VIII of England. His first marriage, to Catherine of Aragon, the wife of his deceased brother, was against the rules of consanguinity but had proceeded nonetheless. When, after 24 years, the marriage failed to produce a male heir, this same prohibited degree of relationship was used by the Archbishop of Canterbury, Thomas Cranmer, on Henry's behalf, to persuade the pope to annul the marriage. When Pope Clement VII refused to do so, Henry assumed headship of the Church of England and declared the marriage null in 1533. Henry then used accusations of incest to condemn his second wife, Anne Boleyn, to death, whilst subsequently gaining a dispensation from prohibited degrees of consanguinity to marry Anne's first cousin, Catherine Howard, as his fifth wife. Henry's legal manoeuvrings, even to the point of assuming headship of a church, rather than demonstrating the ready flouting of prohibited degrees of marriage, show instead that even the most powerful were bothered by, and respectful of, these entrenched understandings of kinship and marriage.

Marriage was not simply a sacrament but also created a social and economic unit. The dowry, and other marital gifts, was the mechanism by which this unit was activated. Differences in the legal process of the dowry across Europe could, therefore, have profound social consequences. Much has been written about the shift from the earlier Germanic Lombard tradition of the 'male dowry' to the so-called Falcidian quarter, or the Roman dowry, which predominated by the late Middle Ages, especially in the Mediterranean areas of Europe. In both systems, a couple was given a nominal 'quarter' of the patrimony to assist in the establishment of a new social economic reality in their spousal unit—in the case of the 'male dowry', the quarter was gifted to the groom; in the latter practice, the quarter was gifted to the bride and was considered her legal quarter of the natal patrimony (although in reality it was rarely worth anything approximating that value). The Falcidian quarter in this period was increasingly given as cash or its equivalent, rather than as landed property. Whilst the dowry remained the legal right and property of the marriageable daughters of a household, in practice it was administered by her husband on her behalf for the duration of the marriage. In theory, a woman's husband only had the right to invest it, and use any profits accruing from that investment, but was not to touch the capital itself. Should the husband predecease her, then a wife had the legal right to claim back her dowry. But in practice this was often quite difficult to achieve, and could involve lengthy court petitions whose success often depended upon strong family backing. As Dana Lightfoot has demonstrated, in the case of labouring-status women in Valencia, the lack of natal family support for these often immigrant labouring women made for greater vulnerability and hence often a lower success rate in the restitution of their dowries in the courts. Even once the dowry had been regained, a widow's natal family would often pressure her to allow them to renegotiate it to form another socioeconomic alliance with a new family. Women, therefore, always had an ambiguous relationship with their dowries— although it was theirs by legal right, it was often hard for them to access their dowries directly. The dowry became the signifier of a woman's worth, but often did little to empower her.

Paradoxically, the dowry was both a potent mechanism of social stability and also one with the potential for social disruption. Its stabilizing force lay in its protection of claims against family patrimony, and the contractual situation it created between two families in ensuring financial security for a new union between them. A husband could not simply use the dowry for his own ends, but had in effect to curate it on behalf of two family units.

However, the very power of the dowry, as the mechanism of the marriage contract, led to an inevitable escalation in the worth of dowries over the fourteenth and fifteenth centuries as families jockeyed to increase their social, economic, and political positions. In Italy, a series of laws attempting to cap dowries and marriage gifts, together with various investment funds to assist parents in the burden of accumulating the necessary capital, such as the *Monte delle doti* (literally the Dowry Mountain), did little to stop this escalation. Dowries in such a situation became social disruptors, causing a stalemate in the progress of a betrothal to its conclusion. Families simply could not afford the dowries and lavish trousseau expected of them, and nor could grooms provide the reciprocal marriage gifts whose anticipated value rose in tandem. Such stalemates were viewed with concern at all levels, not just by the families involved, with city statute books regularly bemoaning decreasing population levels that resulted from the low rate of marriages. Their anxieties were not unfounded. The Black Death which arrived in Italy in 1347, and which swept across all Europe in a circle from the Crimea to Italy, across to Spain and up to France and thence to England, to Iceland, Scandinavia, and back to Russia, caused a catastrophic decline in the population of Europe with an estimated 50 million deaths (or 60 per cent of the population) over the course of the fourteenth century. This was only exacerbated by the succession of smaller outbreaks of plague, which lasted until a final occurrence in Marseille in 1720. Few cities in Europe managed to recuperate their pre-plague populations until the eighteenth century. In such circumstances, impediments to marriage and fertility became not just general social problems, but pressing matters confronting a community's very survival.

The escalation in dowry prices had further consequences for family marriage strategies and subsequent fertility rates. Families with several daughters often decided to marry off only one or two, and placed remaining daughters in convents. Whilst a dowry also had to be paid to a convent, such institutions were obviously outside the competitive marriage market. Most notorious in this respect was the city of Venice, with a scandalous number of young girls subjected to enforced monachization, and where marriage for elite girls was the exception not the norm. Whilst this might bring some relief to a family's dowry pressures, it did little to increase the availability of nubile women able to replenish the city's population. Convent life at least preserved women from the threat of early death in childbirth, and often gave some women the opportunity for more education and agency than was available in the outside community. But the majority of women enclosed within conventual walls lived lives without agency, choice, or real vocation. We know little about their lived daily experiences except through isolated sources such as the fiery polemic of Elena Cassandra Tarabotti who, as suor Arcangela, in her *La tirannia paterna* (Fatherly Tyranny) and *L'inferno monacale* (Nun's Hell), is excoriating in her condemnation of enforced monachization and the patrician fathers of Venice who allowed it to happen.

Such stresses applied particularly in countries under Roman law such as Italy and Spain, which often still practised partible inheritance. But similar consequences were also seen in countries which practised non-partible inheritance and male primogeniture, such as England and France. Even in these countries, remaining members of the family, male as well as female, were given a share of the estate, often in the form of land. After the death of Thomas Collin of Halesowen near Birmingham in 1312, for instance, his seven daughters shared what remained of his landholding between them after the eldest daughter and her husband received the house. But even when women inherited in the absence of a male, such as in this example, laws of wardship and of marriage meant that they rarely had direct control over any land. Furthermore, if only the first-born male son had the right to inherit, then subsequent sons were usually encouraged to enter military or holy orders and seek their support elsewhere, and daughters too were encouraged to enter the convent. Neither scenario encouraged widespread fertility.

Neither men nor women had much choice in their marital destinies. For women especially, the choices—if they could be regarded as 'choices'—were unenviable. Their agency was almost always tied to the men with whom they were associated, whether their fathers, their husbands, or their sons. Women were regarded as the literal embodiment of the family's honour. Marriage, therefore, preferably at a young age, was the accepted ideal lest dishonour be brought upon the family through sexual indiscretion. If that were not possible, then monachization, often enforced, ensured that a family's honour might not be endangered. Widowhood posed further challenges. Whilst a widow had the right to eat at her natal family table, as she had now tasted the pleasures of the flesh, she was subject to suspicion and regulation, and many took tertiary vows and entered some form of conventual life. Christine de Pizan, herself a young widow, felt that widows were amongst the most vulnerable in society. And women who chose not to follow either of these conventional paths, of marriage or the convent, were often subjected to suspicion, derision, and scrutiny. As noted above, the decision of the learned Isotta Nogarola to live unmarried, dedicated to scholarship, led to scurrilous accusations of promiscuity and incest. And Joan of Arc's decision not to marry, nor to stay in the confines of the natal home, but to live amongst men in an army was the subject of a series of interrogations in her trial which focused particularly on her studied use of male clothing and her relations with men. Joan's decision to revert to men's clothing after promising not to do so spelt her doom as a recalcitrant heretic. Women could subvert the gendered norm, but often at great cost.

Masculinity, femininity, norms of gender and of sexual practice

The dominant culture of sexuality in late medieval Europe was one of sex within marriage (for women in elite families) or at betrothal (for women lower down the social scale), both with the goal of childbirth. The age of sexual consent was 12 for girls and 14 for boys. Men of course were subject to the same prohibitions, but in practice were able to flout them: pre- and extramarital sex was normative for men. According to Catholic dogma, the sole and 'natural' purpose of the sexual act was simply the procreation of children. Any sexual act contrary to this purpose—whether alone, between two men, two women, or between a man and a woman—that did not allow for the procreation of children was condemned as sinful and characterized as sodomitical. Such practices between two men in particular were regarded as a sin so abominable that, according to Pope Gregory XI, one dared not even mention its name. Sodomy could be punished by castration, dismemberment, imprisonment, or death by burning, though in practice the latter was rarely enforced, or only in extenuating circumstances in which other factors such as damage to a family's honour was seen to have occurred. That such sexual practices were widespread, at least in the republics of Florence and Venice, is indicated by the legislation and magistracies instituted in an attempt to regulate and/or extirpate them. In 1418 in Venice, the Council of Ten established a *Collegio Sodomitarum* (Sodomy Tribunal). In 1432 the Officers of the Night were established in Florence and tasked specifically with 'rooting out' and prosecuting sodomy. Whilst there was increasing hostility towards sodomy throughout Europe in the period, these two magistracies inaugurated the first large-scale persecution of sodomitical behaviour in Europe. Whilst magistracies elsewhere investigated sodomy as part of a range of crimes, the *Collegio Sodomitarum* and the Officers of the Night had sodomy as a specific crime under their remit. However, as Michael Rocke and Guido Ruggiero have established in their studies of sexual crime prosecutions in Florence and in Venice respectively, once sodomy became subject to special magistracies, its prosecution became more varied and subtle, indicating a reality on the ground that was more complex than the simple Catholic condemnations by theologians and preachers might suggest.[13]

It is also important to note Rocke's salient reminder that late medieval Europe did not have clearly delineated and separate categories of sexual identity such as 'homosexual', 'heterosexual', or 'bisexual'. These were all late nineteenth-century denominations and categorizations. The act of sodomy itself was not seen as tied to a particular gender or to a sexual orientation. What was important in the late medieval view was the age of the respective partners involved in such practices, and their perceived roles in sexual acts as 'active' or 'passive'. The standard model of sodomy was a sexual act between an older male partner who was designated as 'active' with a younger boy designated as 'passive'. Such categorizations fed into broader conceptions about the sexual development of men from childhood, through adolescence into adulthood—rites of passage in which sexuality was perceived as still in flux. The passive, younger male partner in a sodomitical act was also often labelled 'feminine', revealing the fluidities of the categories of masculine and feminine, and the longer tradition of women as passive recipients of the male sexual act.

David Herlihy and Christiane Klapisch-Zuber's research into age at first marriage for men and women in Tuscany highlights some of the crucial impacts marriage patterns had on sexual behaviours and perceptions of normative practice.[14] For instance, in his analysis of cause papers and poll tax records in York, Goldberg found an average age at first marriage for both men and women in their mid-20s.[15] Heath Dillard's research on legal records in Castile reveals that consummation often occurred once a couple was betrothed.[16] In such situations and societies, men and women had the opportunity for heterosexual sexual relations in relative synchrony and without lengthy delay. In republics such as Florence and Venice, however,

[13] M. Rocke, *Forbidden Friendships: Homosexuality and Male Culture in Renaissance Florence* (New York, 1996), and G. Ruggiero, *The Boundaries of Eros: Sex Crime and Sexuality in Renaissance Venice* (New York, 1985).
[14] D. Herlihy and C. Klapisch-Zuber, *Tuscans and their Families* (New Haven, CT, 1985), esp. pp. 202–11.
[15] P. J. P. Goldberg, *Women, Work, and Lifecycle in a Medieval Economy: Women in York and Yorkshire c.1300–1520* (Oxford, 1992).
[16] H. Dillard, *Daughters of the Reconquest: Women in Castilian Town Society 1100–1300* (Cambridge, 1989).

where women tended to be very young at first marriage (between 13 and 15), and where men delayed first marriage until they had reached political maturity in their late 20s, young men found themselves in situations of extended male companionship. Passive sodomitical acts in such circumstances were usually viewed more leniently, and the fifteenth-century Florence sources indicate that most of these young men eventually married. Repeated active sodomitical acts committed by men who were of marriageable age were regarded far more severely. Of the 243 young Florentine boys who confessed to sodomitical acts under interrogation by the Officers of the Night in the year of 1496, for instance, not one was executed, but all instead received minor fines. In Venice, instead, in 1474 Paduano d'Otranto and Marino Alegreti were deemed the active aggressors in sexual acts which took place in a group of six men, and were consequently beheaded and then burned, whilst the 18-year-old Simeone, deemed a passive participant in the same event, was sentenced to 25 lashes, banishment from the city of Venice for five years, and the cutting off of his nose, and an even younger participant, Aloysio Maronetti, was given only ten lashings 'due to his tender age'.[17]

North of the Alps, sodomy trials were far more infrequent, but a few showcase executions demonstrated the ways in which accusations of sodomy could be used as a potent political tool. Its status as an 'unnatural' sin could be paired with religious heresy and general depravity to bring down influential aristocrats and even a religious knightly order as powerful as the Knights Templar. The 60 Knights Templar executed in 1310 at the instigation of the French king Philip IV had a range of charges brought against them, articles 30–33 of which accused them of kissing each other in illicit places, while article 40 referred to their act of uniting 'carnally with one another'. The burning at the stake of the knight Richard Puller von Hohenburg with his squire Anton Mätzler in Zürich in 1482 was graphically portrayed in a woodcut in the *Chronik der Burgunderkriege* as a salutary reminder of the fate that could befall even a man of von Hohenburg's influence and status.

Though sodomy was condemned based on selective interpretations of the biblical fate of Sodom and Gomorrah, and was an act often associated with heretics, or used to condemn them as such (as in the case of the Knights Templar), for city governments, one of the primary concerns with such acts

---

[17] Ruggiero, *The Boundaries of Eros*, p. 122.

was simply that they were sterile and could never result in children to replenish their cities. This recurrent theme helps to explain why prostitution was often tolerated and even legalized whilst sodomy was universally condemned, even though both fornication and sodomy were viewed as sins.

The necessity of a dowry to activate a marriage, simple poverty, late age at first marriage for men, tightly controlled honour of unmarried women, increasing concentrations of people in towns—all of these factors and many more might contribute to situations in which women became prostitutes and in which men utilized their services. Though fornication was officially condemned, and the prostitute viewed as the embodiment of Eve as temptress, nonetheless prostitution was usually tolerated both by ecclesiastical and by municipal authorities throughout late medieval Europe, and indeed was often regulated and legalized. Such regulation was rarely for the protection of the prostitute, but was instead to help maintain social order and to proscribe the boundaries of illicit and licit activities within a town. Prostitution was seen as a means to encourage heterosexual sex that, even if sinful, might at least result in children, unlike sodomitical practices. The Franciscan theologian Francesc Eiximenis supported the legalization of brothels in Catalonia on the grounds that punishing fornication would lead men to the worse sins of adultery or sodomy. City authorities from Southwark to Florence, Seville to Dijon, Augsburg to Montpellier all passed a series of laws in this period to regulate prostitution and the location of brothels. Usually these laws restricted the practice of prostitution to a particular zone, and also required that prostitutes should live as well as work there. In 1285, for example, King Jaume I of Mallorca restricted the practice of prostitution in the university town of Montpellier to one street, known as 'Hot Street' (*Carreria calida*). Prostitutes had to live in this district and could not solicit elsewhere. In London in 1310 all brothels in the city were shut down by royal command, but by 1393 they were tolerated in Cock's Lane, and were otherwise confined to the bathhouses (or stews) under the jurisdiction of the bishop of Winchester in Southwark on the other side of the Thames and away from the city itself. Their legalization in Southwark was ambiguous, however, as men who frequented them could still be prosecuted by ecclesiastical courts. (The social disruption associated with these stews resulted in selective closure in 1506 and a final order of closure in 1546 under Henry VIII.) Prostitutes in Valencia under King Jaume II were confined to several streets in 1325, which was later reinforced by a high boundary wall—a practice later followed in Aragon and Castile. The Catholic monarchs, Isabella and Ferdinand, not only institutionalized

prostitution but, after 1494, rewarded vassals for loyal service by the granting of privileges to own or exploit the earnings of brothels (privileges which
were often hereditary).

Society and space

Clandestine prostitution was, of course, not eliminated by such regulations;
but what such efforts also indicate was the desire to regulate public space
and to demarcate and contain areas of purity and of danger. Designated
areas for brothels behind high walls cordoned off the possibilities for sinful
pollution of the rest of the city and kept men of sinful intention within their
borders, just as enclosure of celibate women behind similarly high walls in
convents protected them from the watchful gaze of the same men. Religion
was central to the shaping of the use of space, and found one of its clearest
expressions in the establishment of Europe's first ghetto for Jews in Venice
in March 1516. Jews were viewed as essential for the exchange and lending
of money, for the practice of medicine, and the selling and purchase of
secondhand goods, and the Venetians had no desire to expel them, as other
parts of Europe had done in successive waves. But their potential for
destabilizing the religious uniformity of the city meant that Jews had to be
contained in a readily identified and designated area with a nightly curfew
policed by two Christian boatmen who circled the perimeter of the ghetto.

The designated use of public and private spaces in Europe was affected
not just by notions of sexual purity and sexual sin, Christian practice,
and the idea of the 'perfidious Jew', but also by gender and other social
and political roles. Overwhelmingly, the public spaces of Europe were
dominated by men. Women, especially those of elite status, were officially
relegated to the private sphere. But one should not dismiss the permeability
of these spaces by women of different social classes—not just prostitutes, but
also serving girls, peasants with produce to sell at market, artisans, midwives,
and so on. Moreover, in a society in which men were often absent for long
periods, women maintained shop fronts for their merchant husbands and
negotiated with a range of traders and middlemen. Generally speaking,
however, the higher a woman's status the less visible her public agency,
and the more necessity for her to exercise in private what networks might be
available to her.

Space was also regulated by time and by status, as well as by gender and
religion. The bells of a city could be used to accentuate aurally the permitted

spaces and times for certain activities. Vestimentary codes were also used to demarcate social roles and spaces. Prostitutes had to be clearly distinguishable from women of honour, Jews had to be readily distinguished from Christians, nobles from their social inferiors, servants from their masters, and so on. A series of sumptuary laws passed across Europe specified, often in minute detail, the permitted fabrics, cuts, and styles of clothing to be worn by every social and professional category. Purity and danger, status and wealth—all had to be clearly visible and assessable at a glance.

The *Querelle des femmes*

Though women might find themselves increasingly contained and constrained in the later Middle Ages, behind doors they increasingly found a voice in the written canon. This does not necessarily mean that all of these women were literate—several of the most prominent were not—but it does indicate an increasing awareness by women of the power of text and of their voice. The fact that the majority of these texts were composed in their authors' respective vernaculars is indicative of the audibility that the increasing status of the vernacular gave to those who were otherwise excluded from a learned Latin culture. Some of these texts were, as one would perhaps expect, written by women living chastely and recording their religious devotion. Julian of Norwich's mystic visions of Christ, which she gathered together in her *Revelations of Divine Love* sometime after 1373, is the earliest extant book in English written by a woman. By 1438, the illiterate Margery Kempe, mother of at least 14 children and sometime visitor of Julian of Norwich, completed the dictation of her highly personal religious experiences in what is considered to be the first autobiography in the English language. Catherine Benincasa, known simply as Catherine of Siena, the 22nd of her parents' 25 children, daughter of a dyer, and never formally educated, miraculously learned to write late in life, and from 1375 began dictating some of the finest examples of letters in the Italian vernacular of the fourteenth century—some 400 in total. She wrote with uncompromising directness to the pope, addressing him as *babbo* 'daddy', as well as to Queen Joanna of Naples, and wrote with an authority which she believed derived from her mystical marriage to Jesus himself. Catherine of Siena was not constrained by convent walls nor by marriage to a layman, and was able to lead a remarkably unfettered life, travelling widely within Italy and even as an ambassador of the republic of Florence to the papacy in Avignon. The prominence and fame of all three of these women indicates the means by which intense devotion and notions of sanctity—in all three cases these women claimed to have visions, and direct access to the Divine—allowed for an agency and societal prominence normally denied to women. Reputed access to the Divine also accounts for the brief period of Joan of Arc's leadership over men on the battlefield, just as those same claims of divine visions were later used to accuse her of heresy and witchcraft.

These women did not question society's structures, even as their lives broke societal norms. Other women, however, began to question the structures which constrained them, and the classical and Christian arguments which were used to justify such constraints. One of the earliest to do so was Christine de Pizan. The great Francesco Petrarca might write of his life in scholarship as 'living through his pen', but Christine de Pizan was the first woman that we know of to make a literal living from her pen, with an extraordinary literary production which included 300 ballades, many shorter poems, and more than 20 books on topics as various as warfare, education, religion, philosophy, and good governance. Christine emphasized her personal experience, not just her learning, as giving her authority against which her detractors could not argue. De Pizan had been appalled in particular by the representation of women in one of the most popular chivalric romances of the day, *Le roman de la Rose*, or *The Romance of the Rose* begun by Guillaume de Lorris and completed by Jean de Meun. In her 'Letter to Cupid' of 1399, de Pizan wrote of the complaints that had come to her ears from women of all levels of society:

> The ladies mentioned here above complain
> Of damage done, of blame and blemished name,
> And of betrayals, very grievous wrongs,
> Of falsehoods uttered, many other griefs,
> Endured each day from those disloyal men
> Who blame and shame, defame and deceive them
>
> (11.8–22)

De Pizan founded her own chivalric order, the Order of the Rose—a knightly society dedicated to true love and the defence of women. Whilst reprimanded by Gontier Col, secretary to King Charles VI, and told to 'correct and amend your manifest error, folly, and excessive wilfulness which has risen in you, a woman impassioned in this matter, out of presumption or arrogance', de Pizan would not be silenced. Her *Book of the City of Ladies*, completed in 1405 in order to correct the widespread errors concerning women, and her *Treasury of the City of Ladies* full of advice for the women needed to populate her City, established the long-running argument in favour of the position of women, the so-called *Querelle des femmes* 'No matter which way I looked at it,' she wrote, 'and no matter how much I turned the matter over in my mind, I could find no evidence from my own experience to bear out such a negative view of female nature and habits.' De Pizan was, however, philosophical about the societal constraints around her. Her advice to women included simple words of support for wives of wandering husbands: 'Even if every suspicion is true, there is nothing she can do about it.'

De Pizan's eloquent words on behalf of women were joined by those of others, especially in fifteenth-century Italy, such as those of Nicolosa Sanuti of Bologna, Laura Cereta of Brescia, and Cassandra Fedele of Venice. In a speech before the doge and the Venetian Senate, Fedele reflected on the roles of men and women as articulated by John Ball that we heard earlier, and, whilst accepting that there was little women could do with their education, argued that it still had immense value in women's lives:

> When I meditate on the idea of marching forth in life with the lowly and execrable weapons of the little woman—the needle and the distaff—even if the study of literature offers women no rewards or honours, I believe woman must nonetheless pursue and embrace such studies alone for the pleasure and enjoyment they contain.[18]

Men as well as women entered into the *Querelle*, with several male scholars continuing to defend the existing status of women, as confirmed by classical and Christian authorities through the centuries. Other prominent male scholars, however, such as Guarino of Verona, educated women as well as men in his academy, and wrote of his great respect for women's worth: 'since I was born of a woman, and she most virtuous [...] I should seem ungrateful if to the best of my poor wit I should suffer the cause of women to be neglected and them to be condemned with their case unheard [...].'[19]

These contemporary interrogations of the social, familial, patriarchal, and gendered structures of late medieval Europe occurred just as those same

---

[18] Cassandra Fedele, *Letters and Orations*, trans. D. Robin (Chicago, 2000), p. 162.
[19] R. Sabbadini (ed.), *Epistolario di Guarino Veronese*, in *Miscellanea di storia veneta*, ser. 3, 14 (1919), letter 982, ll. 105–13, 529.

structures were becoming more rigidly expressed and defined. They point, however, to the vigour with which people responded to their circumstances, and the intellectual and cultural vibrancy which animated this period, and which fed into the western tradition in fascinating and often unpredictable ways. We might look to this period and place for evidence of the structures that underpin modern western society. And, indeed, they are there to be found. But just as intriguing, if not more so, are the ways in which very different practices and views animated people in late medieval Europe, and the divergent pathways along which western society might have been drawn. We need to be attentive to the wondrous and the strange, and the contingency of our current views and practices.

Plate 8. Abraham Cresques, *Atlas of Maritime Maps said the Catalan Atlas* (*c.*1375), West Africa

7

Global Middle Ages

The east

Catherine Holmes

This chapter considers societies and cultures outside western Europe from the early thirteenth to later fifteenth centuries. Rather than offering micro-surveys of a series of different contexts, some close to Europe and others further away, I want to think about the late medieval world in global terms. This is an approach which does not necessarily offer full planetary coverage, but instead prioritizes making comparisons and tracing connections (or fissures) between different societies. As I outline in the first two sections of this chapter, there are many ways to consider the late medieval world from a global perspective; many of those ways have the potential to bring late medieval evidence to bear on arguments about broader historical developments in early modern and modern global history. There are also potential late medieval global grand narratives to explore which connect environment, disease, economics, social change, and political formation. However, in order to offer a focused discussion, I will not be preoccupied with grand narrative trajectories on a variety of broad fronts, but instead with a somewhat more limited issue: the creation, projection, and realization of power by rulers during a period which has traditionally been associated with widespread turbulence and disintegration, and yet in which certain commonalities of political structures and culture can also be perceived. In these senses my global approach is comparative and largely political. However, integral to my argument are other striking dynamics which relate more to connectedness at social, economic, and cultural levels. These were dynamics which also often involved movement over scales of all sorts: local, regional, transregional, and even intercontinental.

The principal relationship I explore here is between those with aspirations to high, supra-local power, and those who peopled the more fluid, fractured, and sometimes very mobile formations that typify so much of the economic, social, religious, and cultural landscape of the late medieval centuries. The

The Later Middle Ages. Isabella Lazzarini, Oxford University Press (2021). © Isabella Lazzarini.
DOI: 10.1093/oso/9780198731641.003.0008

societies on which I focus with particular intensity were located in the eastern Mediterranean, a region where the growth of state power has recently been attributed to the astute management of religious and ethnic difference by rulers acting as brokers between different groups. I argue that a broker-centred approach has considerable potential for understanding late medieval politics not only in the eastern Mediterranean world but also further afield, in central, south, and east Asia. However, I also suggest that an exclusive focus on rulers as brokers risks overprivileging the roles of those who claimed power, and oversimplifying and underestimating the significance of the complex solidarities and loyalties of those they sought to govern. This was a period in which the tangible and intangible resources that rulers required were frequently held by other individuals and groups, many of whom conducted their day-to-day business with relatively little reference to clear-cut religious and ethnic identities and were involved in cross-cutting and overlapping social and economic networks. Rather than emphasizing the relationship between rulers and bounded groups, I argue that the late medieval period, when seen in global perspective, was one in which a plurality of regimes, many of them new, competed for the resources that were provided, and often controlled, by a variety of economic, social, and cultural networks, some local, others much more trans- or supraregional. This was not necessarily a period of chaos, but one in which the balance of power between those who claimed authoritative positions and those who provided the resources and political support on which those claims rested was delicate and constantly shifting.

Why study late medieval history globally?

To study any period which precedes the European voyages of discovery in the later fifteenth and sixteenth centuries in global terms is controversial; but, as far as the later medieval period is concerned, important groundwork is already in place with such landmark publications as Janet Abu Lughod's examination of an interconnected Eurasian commercial space during the Mongol hegemony and J. R. S. Phillips's investigation of the technological and imaginative developments which accompanied the medieval expansion of Europe.[1] More recently a wealth of scholarship has been published on a

---

[1] J. L. Abu-Lughod, *Before European Hegemony: The World System AD 1250–1350* (New York, 1989); J. R. S. Phillips, *The Medieval Expansion of Europe*, 2nd edn (Oxford, 1998).

wide variety of topics germane to a global late medieval history: the trans-continental impact of plague and climate change in the later Middle Ages; the connectivities discernible within the spaces which came under the direct control or indirect influence of the Mongols; contemporary cultures of travel; the background contexts to the voyages of Columbus; Ottoman interest in maritime expansion; and the sea-borne activities of Ming China, which by the early fifteenth century ranged as far as Sri Lanka, Madagascar, and east Africa.

This does not mean that doing late medieval global history is straightfor-ward. At a very basic level, different world regions do not offer equal densities of similar types of evidence (textual, material, and environmental) from which to generate universal explanatory models. Thus, a recent assess-ment of the impact of climate on socioeconomic changes in the late medieval world combines, somewhat asymmetrically, datasets related to climate change from across the entire late medieval natural world (e.g. tree rings, ice cores, coral growth) with the uniquely rich manorial records from one relatively remote corner of Eurasia, late medieval England.[2] Another prob-lem is that the long-established periodizations and conceptual frameworks fundamental to the traditional study of different world regions can be difficult to integrate into a single global narrative. Some scholars, for instance, find Europe-centred periodizations of the medieval awkward when applied to other world regions. Others distrust the eurocentricity of the term 'medieval' and its place in the systemization of knowledge that was part of nineteenth- and twentieth-century European nationalist and imperi-alist projects. Others regard 'global', in any period, as little more than passing academic fashion. These are all legitimate concerns, and in a book within the Short Oxford History of Europe series, there is certainly a risk that regions beyond western Europe can be treated merely as appendages to a European core.

But there are many reasons for considering late medieval global contexts even in a book that focuses primarily on Europe. There are, after all, important questions about European history in this period for which a more globalized perspective seems essential. To take a few examples: what was the impact of climate change and disease in the medieval world, and to what extent were experiences of natural and demographic crisis shared or regionally specific? In a period that witnessed the ongoing consolidation and

---

[2] B. M. S. Campbell, *The Great Transition: Climate, Disease and Society in the Late-Medieval World* (Cambridge, 2016), esp. pp. 26–7.

expansion of the beliefs, practices, and institutions of organized religion across large geographies, did the medieval world become more or less open to the transmission and reception of new experiences and systems of thought? How far, and in what ways, did the maritime enterprise sponsored by powers as various as Ming China, the Ottoman empire, and a variety of Atlantic-facing polities in the fifteenth century (e.g. Portugal, Castile, England) have common drivers, and to what extent did such activity build on or interact with other long-standing transregional and local systems of commerce and communications? Was this a period in which developments in commercial institutions and behaviours in western Europe began to lay the foundations for much later divergences in the economic performances of the west and the rest of the world? Full answers to this final controversial question require deep knowledge of trajectories and practices across the later medieval world and not purely those of western Europe.

The late medieval world: advantages and problems of a global grand narrative

One approach to the late medieval global is to operate at a macro-level of analysis, prioritizing the development of a transregional (or even a trans- or intercontinental) grand narrative. If we adopt this approach, it may be possible to identify three broad phases of development. The first, lasting from roughly the thirteenth century until the early (or in some accounts the mid-) fourteenth, is one of consolidation, as the already flourishing economies of many different world regions were brought into more regular contact with each other following the remarkable expansion and deepening of Mongol power between 1220 and *c*.1330, a integrative phenomenon which has been called a 'world system'. Within that system, it was not just commercial contacts which became stronger, but other forms of exchange and communication over long distances as well. This was the period of the pan-Eurasian travels of Franciscan envoys and missionaries such as John of Plano Carpini and William of Rubruck, and of Italian traders whose activities as far east as Iran, central Asia, and China are represented in the late thirteenth century by the career of Marco Polo, and to which *La pratica della mercatura*, an early fourteenth-century book of routes, weights, and measures by the Florentine banker Francesco di Balducci Pegolotti, also bears witness. Such travel, at least within areas that recognized the authority of the Mongol *qan*, was often facilitated by administrative devices associated with the *yam* (the Mongol communication system), including *paizas*, inscribed tablets akin to passports. Mechanisms of this sort did not just enable movement from west to east, they also allowed travel in the opposite direction, from Mongol-controlled areas into Europe, most famously from a western European perspective by Rabban bar Sauma, the Nestorian Christian who came as an envoy from the Mongols to a variety of European courts in the later years of the thirteenth century. But travel was not restricted to regions under the sway of Mongol power alone. Perhaps the most famous traveller of the entire later medieval period was Ibn Battuta, whose journeys as a scholar-pilgrim over three decades took him from his home in Tangier in the Maghreb (north-west Africa) to as far east as Aceh in northern Sumatra and Hangzhou in China. Later he crossed the Sahara into west Africa and the wealthy empire of Mali.

Powerful evidence of the exceptionally integrated nature of this first phase of the late medieval world seems to be provided by the speed with which plague in the mid-fourteenth century passed from central Asia to other regions within Asia, Europe, and (as new research now suggests) into sub-Saharan Africa as well. But, in grand narrative terms, plague was both witness to the interconnectedness of the late medieval world and its agent of disintegration. According to this narrative, plague, together with the onset of global cooling and the roughly contemporaneous collapse of Mongol authority across Asia, brought significant transregionalism to an end during the second half of the fourteenth century. The precocious proto-globalization of the Mongol world order would only re-emerge with the expansion of Iberian maritime power in Asia, the Atlantic world, and the Americas in the mid- to late fifteenth century.

For historians interested in grand narrative, this tripartite late medieval economic cycle of expansion and consolidation followed by collapse and only slow reconstitution may appear to replicate at a political level as well. Thus, the thirteenth century can be seen as a period of expansion and consolidation of state power. In some cases, and particularly in the early thirteenth century, those polities which had started to coalesce at different points between the tenth and twelfth centuries, such as Song China, Angkor (in the Khmer lands), Pagan (in Upper Burma), and Dai Viet (in northern Vietnam), reached even greater levels of organizational and ideological sophistication in their efforts to marshal loyalties and extract resources. In other cases, new polities emerged and expanded, most obviously the Mongols, whose conquests during the course of the thirteenth century reconfigured long-standing patterns of power in central Asia, Russia, the

Islamic world, and east Asia (including the takeover of the Song empire), and whose authority continued to embed and develop even after 1260 and the splintering of Mongol dominion into four separate khanates controlled by the Ilkhanids, the Golden Horde, the Chaghadayids, and the Yuan. Outside the Mongol sphere, extensive territorial expansion during the thirteenth century is also associated with the empire of Mali in west Africa, the power and transregional reputation of which was built upon control of the trans-Saharan gold trade. Various contemporary Muslim historians, including Ibn Khaldun, bear witness to the growth of Mali. That its wealth resonated within late medieval Europe as well within the Muslim zone of influence is indicated by the inclusion of Mansa Musa, the early fourteenth-century king of Mali, in the Catalan Cresques Atlas (*c*.1375), where he is depicted holding a large gold coin.[3]

It was not only at such macro-levels that new forms of political authority emerged in the thirteenth and early fourteenth centuries. In the eastern Mediterranean, for instance, while the unitary Byzantine empire of the early Middle Ages was fatally splintered in 1204 following the sack of Constantinople by the armies of the Fourth Crusade, the erstwhile Byzantine space in the Balkans, the Aegean coasts and islands, and western Anatolia was soon populated by relatively small but very aggressive political formations: a Bulgarian empire from *c*.1185, a Serbian equivalent from 1346, a Latin empire of Constantinople (1204–61), the crusader kingdom of Cyprus (from 1191), the presence of Venetian and Genoese power on the coasts and islands of the Aegean, and a series of political formations which grew up in Nikaia, Epiros, and Trebizond. The latter were governed by Orthodox Christian, Greek-speaking rulers claiming descent from the twelfth-century emperors of Byzantium. By 1261 one of those formations, the Palaiologoi of Nikaia, had seized Constantinople, claiming to restore Byzantine power of old. And somewhere between the transcontinental dominion of the Mongols and emperors of Mali and the somewhat micro-scale reach of the many Byzantine successor states of the early thirteenth century stood the meso-level authority of other polities. One such mid-range political society was that governed by the Mamluks, who had come to power in Egypt in 1250, and who thwarted the apparently inevitable westwards momentum of the Mongols at the battle of Ain Jalut in 1260.

---

[3] Cresques Atlas: http://www.cresquesproject.net/ (last accessed 2 July 2019).

Just as the economic growth of the thirteenth century gave way to disintegration by the mid-fourteenth, so too, according to a grand narrative approach, there was collapse and acute turbulence in the political sphere. It has been suggested that the states of Angkor, Pagan, and Dai Viet began to collapse during the fourteenth century in south-east Asia—an erosion of formal power caused in part by climate change. Elsewhere in Asia, Mongol state power is usually held to have diminished significantly between the 1330s and 1360s: in Ilkhanid Iran, in Yuan China, and, to a somewhat lesser extent, among the Golden Horde. Meanwhile in west Africa, the empire of Mali began to disintegrate after the 1360s amid civil war. Here the climate became drier, leading to the abandonment of the key trading city of Awdaghust on the southern reaches of the Sahara; by 1433 the kings of Mali had lost control of Timbuktu. In the Balkans and the Aegean world, civil and regional wars, as well as occasional urban insurrection (e.g. in Thessalonica in 1342), are said to have diminished the power bases of the Byzantine, Bulgarian, and Serb emperors—conflicts which were increasingly ruthlessly exploited by another regional competitor, the Ottoman Turks. From their bases in north-western Anatolia, they had reduced many of their Christian neighbours in the Balkans to vassal status by the 1390s, but the Ottomans were themselves crushed, for at least the short term, by Tamerlane, following the battle of Ankara in 1402. Indeed, for much of the fourteenth century, Anatolia had been a patchwork of competing Turkish emirates, with the Ottomans being only one of many such groupings. A similarly fragmented political world can be identified in fourteenth-century Russia, where power was distributed among a series of city-based princes, each in some sort of tribute relationship with the Golden Horde, each seeking to command a diverse set of communities within their own city-based polity.

As in the sphere of economics so in the field of politics, where a grand narrative approach to the later medieval world might argue for a slow recovery and reconstitution of state-like power, especially in the latter stages of the fifteenth century. Thus after the civil wars of the early fifteenth century, the Ottomans began to construct an increasingly imperial polity, based from 1453 in the old epicentre of Byzantine power, Constantinople; by 1517 Mamluk Egypt had been absorbed within this expanded Ottoman state, together with the holy sites of Mecca and Medina. In China, the Ming, the successors to the Mongol Yuan, turned away from maritime expansion in the second half of the fifteenth century, but at a domestic level their authority was assured. By the sixteenth century, we appear, in grand narrative terms, to be on our way to an age of early modern Eurasian empires: Ottoman, Safavid, Mughal, Ming, and Habsburg. Meanwhile, in the peripheries of Eurasia a series of territorially compact but increasingly bureaucratically sophisticated states were in formation by 1500, including France in the west, Muscovy in the north, Burma, Siam, and Vietnam in the south-east, and Japan in east Asia. Victor Liebermann has stressed the degree to which post-1500 states in the Eurasian periphery to east and west rebuilt, and found their sources of legitimacy in, the more temporally remote 'charter polities' which occupied roughly similar territorial regions in the high (pre-1300 C.E.) medieval period; a narrative trajectory which leaves the political and social fragmentation of the more chronologically proximate later Middle Ages as a temporary, if quite long, hiccough in the process of medieval state-building.

The advantages of a grand narrative approach to the later medieval period can appear self-evident: on the one hand, this allows us to connect together phenomena which have all too often been considered separately in more specialist regional studies, especially the socioeconomic impact of plague and climate change and the fortunes of large-scale polities. It can stimulate serious comparative work, particularly at the level of state formation across Eurasia—an approach which has the potential to be extended into Africa and with care into the Americas (which was not affected by the Black Death). It promotes the study of transmission and communication, particularly of peoples, goods, ideas, and microbes. And yet, despite the positives of such an outlook, an important question remains: does the grand narrative trajectory of integration, collapse, and eventual recovery actually hold up when subjected to close scrutiny, or are there worrying inconsistencies?

In a short chapter, a full answer to this question may not be possible, but we can at least point to some problems with an overly schematic grand narrative approach to the global later Middle Ages. There is evidence, for instance, to suggest that the expansion and integration of the economies of Eurasia and north and west Africa may have been overstated for the thirteenth century, while the fourteenth century may not be a simple story of commercial disintegration and collapse. Bruce Campbell has suggested that the significant climate changes which were fundamental to fourteenth-century demographic, economic, social, and political turmoil were in fact already under way in the later stages of the thirteenth century—a period which is often regarded by others (and perhaps by Campbell himself) as the heyday of the consolidation of communications and commerce inspired by

Mongol expansion.[4] But perhaps that heyday itself also requires nuancing: Janet Abu-Lughod stressed the relative superficiality, even fragility, of commerce within the Mongol world system of c.1250–1350. Much of what was traded consisted of low-volume, high-value goods such as silks and spices, rather than commerce involving the large-scale movement of raw and manufactured products and the mass migrations associated with modern empires.[5] Meanwhile, detailed study of the Mediterranean has cautioned against models which overemphasize international trade in any premodern epoch, including the later medieval period, and which ignore material and written evidence for much greater local and regional commerce in bulk, everyday materials, and products.[6]

In a similar way, while it would be rash to overstate the extent of thirteenth-century integration, it is clear that we should not overemphasize collapse in the second half of the fourteenth and early fifteenth centuries. Long-distance private commerce, of the sort to which the Polo family's experiences and Pegolotti's book bear witness, may have dwindled after the mid-fourteenth century, as the Mongol-controlled system of communication and protection that had promoted such trade broke down, but in the Black Sea region the evaporation of the Mongol presence offered new opportunities for the Venetians and Genoese to expand and deepen their political and commercial presence. Meanwhile, changes which are often interpreted as political turbulence could themselves act as the quickeners of commerce and communication. Amid the demise of a centralized Byzantine empire, the expansion of Italian maritime power, the Frankish settlements in Greece, and the impact of Mongol conquests, the regional economy of the late medieval fragmented eastern Mediterranean zone appears to have been fundamentally reorientated to service the Italian and Frankish presence, as well as to meet the increasing demands of the Anatolian emirates, the Ottomans included. And, as current research demonstrates, from the outset the early Ottomans were themselves sympathetic to commerce, and by the end of the fifteenth century they sought to command maritime spaces beyond the eastern Mediterranean, especially in the Red Sea and Persian Gulf. Finally, beyond the eastern Mediterranean and Middle Eastern worlds there are hints that routes initially opened up to

---

[4] Campbell, *The Great Transition*, pp. 3–10, 134–266.
[5] Abu Lughod, *Before European Hegemony*, 8–38, 353.
[6] P. Horden and N. Purcell, *The Corrupting Sea: A Study of Mediterranean History* (Oxford, 2000).

long-distance private traders in the wake of Mongol expansion continued to be active long after the subsidence of Mongol rule. The Venetian Niccolò de' Conti journeyed as far east as Sumatra and Java in the third and fourth decades of the fifteenth century. This occurred at the same time as the Portuguese were navigating their way down the west coast of Africa seeking to engage with the trans-Saharan trade routes which continued to operate despite the waning of the empire of Mali.

None of the scepticism implicit in such revisionist thinking seeks to overturn the evidence for climate change and demographic collapse in the fourteenth and early fifteenth centuries, but it does suggest that we need to be cautious about a very linear model of economic expansion, then decline, and only finally slow recovery. Much the same could also be said about macropolitics. That is to say, for some historians it now seems axiomatic that during the fourteenth century, amid the pressure of plague and climate change, erstwhile consolidation, especially by Eurasian polities, gave way, at least temporarily, to extreme political turbulence, and that any recovery in the fifteenth century was, for the most part, slow. But that narrative trajectory can also be questioned. Not all commonly accepted examples of aggressive state-building in the thirteenth and early fourteenth centuries are convincing. For instance, it can be argued that some state-like qualities, including a meritocratic bureaucracy and an abstract idealization of political order, only crystallized in Egypt as late as the fifteenth century, nearly two centuries after the initial seizure of power by the Mamluks.

In contrast, in India, a rather different trajectory can be discerned for a polity which, like the Mamluks, came into being in the thirteenth century. The Delhi sultanate was first established in 1210 in northern India following the invasion of the Ghurids from Afghanistan; but here the fourteenth century does not appear to have been a time of collapse as much as of increasing political consolidation under the Tughluqids, characterized by the transition from a tribal polity to one based around a hereditary kingship, together with an administration based on the distribution of iqtas (transferable assignments of fiscal revenues) to the regime's supporters. The pan-south Asian reach of the Delhi sultans may have diminished somewhat after 1350 during the reign of Firuz Shah (1351–88), but this hegemony continued to invest extensively during the second half of the fourteenth century in the religious and economic built environment, patronizing not just mosques but also hospitals, canals, and travellers' way-stations. However, in contrast to the Ottomans, Mamluk Egypt and some other regions of Eurasia, where consolidation and the growth of state-like institutions have been identified in the fifteenth century, during the post-1400 period the Delhi sultanate declined.

Brokerage in fragmented political landscapes

The evidence outlined above militates against a simple progression–retraction–rebuilding model of state- or polity-centred power during the later medieval period at a global level; it also suggests that we may struggle to find direct and causal connections between economic, demographic, and commercial change on the one hand and political formation and disaggregation on the other. This suggestion should not perhaps surprise us, especially given the state of research about Europe in the same period. In recent years, political historians of late medieval Europe have increasingly argued against narratives of state-level political consolidation and retraction determined by economic cycles, and focused instead on the very plural and fragmented political landscapes within which relationships between rulers and ruled were negotiated across the thirteenth to fifteenth centuries. In territorial monarchies, localized lordship continued to matter—a fact made clear by the continued incidence of private warfare in France, despite royal claims to a monopoly on violence. Strikingly, such conflicts often occurred with the tacit agreement of the French kings both in the thirteenth century, when royal power is often held to have expanded, and in the fourteenth, when it is regarded as having failed. In a similar way, violence and social protest in late medieval urban contexts are now less likely to be indexed by historians to episodes of plague and processes of economic retraction, but interpreted instead as the logical outgrowth of increasingly complex town environments, which were characterized by competition between different and overlapping jurisdictions and by increasingly high expectations of government. Whether dealing with towns or countryside, royal courts or consultative assemblies, the study of late medieval European politics is now focused on the day-to-day social relationships through which power was constructed and exercised. This is a process-centred reading of political life, in which the creation of power required alignment between the aspirations of those in governing circles and the multiple identities, loyalties, assumptions, and activities of the governed. It is a reading in which increasing amounts of attention has been paid to the activities of those political agents who acted as mediators between rulers and ruled: to those who can be identified as brokers.

To some extent similar shifts in historiographical approach can be detected in the study of late medieval regions of the world outside western Europe, particularly in zones which in common with western Europe can be typified as fragmented. One zone of this sort was the late medieval eastern Mediterranean world, a large area encompassing the Balkans, Anatolia, the Aegean, and the Levant which, as we have already seen, was radically reordered in this period, first by the capture of Constantinople during the Fourth Crusade (1204) and later by the intrusion of Mongol power into western Asia and the roughly contemporaneous rise of the Mamluks of Egypt. Fragmentation in this region took multiple forms. There were many competing polities: miniature empires and kingdoms ruled by different eastern Orthodox Christians; a constellation of Anatolian emirates, including the Ottomans; Frankish kingdoms and principalities such as those in the Peloponnese and Cyprus; Venetian and Genoese settlements. There were many regional languages, written and spoken: Greek, Latin, Arabic, Hebrew, Turkish, Persian, Armenian, Syriac, Slavonic, French, Italian, Catalan, Aragonese. Religious loyalties were diverse: western and eastern Christians of many sorts, including not only those under the jurisdiction of Rome and Constantinople but also members of the Armenian, Syrian, and Maronite Churches; Sunni and Shia Muslims, and in Lebanon, the Druze. There were many more local identities, regional and urban, as well as other forms of affiliation, including membership of guilds and brotherhoods of different sorts, and networks associated with the veneration of holy men (and occasionally women), who were often seen as figures of authority in their own right. Those dedicated to a life of devotion lived in a variety of contexts, including sufi lodges in Syria and Anatolia, and monasteries on holy mountains such as Mount Athos and the Meteora in Greece, the Black Mountain in northern Syria, and Mount Sinai (the location of the monastery of St Catherine)—sites which were also the destination of international and local pilgrims. This was a world in flux: long-standing local communities met invaders, incomers, and those who were travelling for all sorts of reasons—trade, conquest, settlement, pilgrimage, diplomacy, and curiosity. Individuals and communities from a kaleidoscope of different ethnic and religious backgrounds competed for recognition and resources. In the regions once dominated by Byzantine Constantinople, new political and commercial centres became prominent: Thessalonica, Arta, Edirne, Veliko Tarnovo, Candia, Famagusta, Bursa, Konya, Trebizond. Further south, in Mamluk-governed regions, some old centres boomed, above all Cairo; others, such as Damietta and Tinnis, both erstwhile important trading centres on the Nile Delta, waned; for others the picture is more mixed. General urban decay has been attributed to Alexandria, and yet it remained an important and exceptionally cosmopolitan port in which traders from across the Christian, Muslim, and Jewish Mediterranean met to exchange goods. Mujir al-Din al-Ulaymi, a late fifteenth-century local Muslim historian, portrays Jerusalem, the third great city of Islam, as an up-country backwater; but the accounts of contemporary pilgrims, present a very different impression, as Christian, Muslim, and Jewish devotees still flocked to a city and a region electric with charismatic charge.[7]

In recent years, this plural and fractured landscape of peoples and communities has become integral to the ways in which historians of this region understand political life. Particularly among historians dealing with the new regimes founded by Latin Christians and Anatolian Turks, there has been an emphasis on the strategies rulers employed to manage and exploit regional heterogeneity in the creation and legitimizing of power, with special attention being paid to the significance of ethnic and religious identity in relations between rulers and ruled. Some studies have focused primarily on the efforts used by would-be hegemons to create, reinforce, and police ethnic and religious difference, and on the importance of identities in patterns of indigenous resistance. Others have demonstrated how newcomers sought to overcome their alien status and strive for legitimacy by emulating or appropriating symbols associated with the indigenous regimes that they displaced, or by attempting to use written and visual culture to fuse preexisting singular identities into a more pliable and controllable regional loyalty. Thus, the Latin emperors of Constantinople in the early thirteenth century adopted the ceremonial and vestments of their Byzantine predecessors at the time of their inauguration; the fourteenth-century rulers of the Morea (Peloponnese) sought to retell the story of the thirteenth-century encounter of Franks and local Greeks in terms that were designed to promote a ruler-centred Moreote identity.

In the Anatolian sphere of competing emirates, meanwhile, many recent analyses have been preoccupied with explaining the emergence of the Ottomans in the fourteenth century. While debate continues among Ottomanists about the precise role that religiously inspired violence played in conflicts between rival Christian and Muslim regional hegemons in the

---

[7] Cited in R. Irwin, 'Palestine in Late Medieval Islamic Spirituality', in J. Harris, C. Holmes, and E. Russell (eds), *Byzantines, Latins, and Turks in the Eastern Mediterranean World after 1150* (Oxford, 2012), pp. 313–26, at p. 322.

fourteenth and early fifteenth centuries, most scholars would now agree that
the Ottomans demonstrated a remarkable willingness to work with the grain
of plurality and fragmented power that typified the contemporary Aegean,
Balkan, and Anatolian worlds. They made alliances with Christians. They
worked creatively with the plural forms of religious authority present in late
medieval Anatolia, including the *ulema* (religious scholars) and sufi mystics.
In legitimizing their authority they made use of a wide portfolio of ceremonial, motifs, and symbols appropriated from the spectrum of political
cultures they inherited, encountered, conquered, or reduced to vassal status.
Their own representations and performances of rulership, shaped by the
political traditions of steppe nomad tribes of central Asia, were fused with
those of Byzantium and a variety of Islamic imperial forebears and neighbours. Of course the Ottomans were not the only regime governing plural
populations; nor were they alone in mobilizing a variety of traditions in the
representation and projection of their authority. How and why they were the
regional 'winners' in a game that many others, including fellow Anatolian
emirs, also played is an important question, to which historical sociologist
Karen Barkey has given a powerful answer. Barkey's thesis, indeed, is one
that aligns in striking ways with recent historiographical developments in
the study of late medieval western European political history. Her suggestion
is that one of the critical strategies that the Ottomans employed was to act as
brokers between different groups and networks with different identities and
interests; it was the Ottomans' success in this brokering role which provided
the platform on which their regional power was based.[8]

Beyond brokerage

In invoking brokerage, Barkey elaborates a social formation that global
historians of many different time periods and geographical contexts have
found useful, particularly during periods of conquest and regime change
within fragmented and plural landscapes of power. For instance, brokerage
is a prominent theme in the study of extra-European history in more
recent periods, such as eighteenth- and nineteenth-century India, where
indigenous urban merchant communities have been seen as the enablers
of the expansion of British rule. It is a theme invoked in the histories of

[8] K. Barkey, *Empire of Difference: The Ottomans in Comparative Perspective* (Cambridge,
2008), pp. 28–66.

zones typified by commercial exchange between groups who spoke many different languages and belonged to different religious groups, but who nonetheless found ways to communicate across those barriers. The early modern Indian Ocean world is a case in point. In medieval contexts, attention has been paid above all to the role of cross-cultural brokers at royal courts including, in a late medieval Eurasian context, the cosmopolitan courts of the Mongol *qans*. It is an approach which is likely to be exploited more by medieval historians with global history interests in the future, in part, because its focus on the forging of social connections lends itself to methodologies and approaches that foreground connectivity; in part, because it can enable the making of comparisons across space and time. Nonetheless, it is an approach that we should handle with care, particularly when thinking about brokerage as a means to the creation of hegemony in the later medieval world. For there are two important interrelated dangers. The first is that we regard the fragments and pluralities that are said to typify late medieval societies as more atomized and in need of brokerage than they actually were; and the second is that we attribute too much agency to rulers who set themselves up as brokers, and too little to those groups and networks with whom the would-be ruler-brokers worked. Both of these dangers can be seen in case of the eastern Mediterranean political environment within which the Ottomans came to prominence; both caution against indiscriminate use of a brokerage model in other world regions of the late medieval world.

Let us start with atomization. Here, one important assumption of the brokerage model of the sort used to explain the rise of the Ottomans is that societies characterized by multiple languages and religious loyalties produce the kinds of social networks which only successful brokers can bring together to work to a common purpose. In the Ottoman case, those networks in the fourteenth century are said to have included urban *akhi* brotherhood organizations often associated with particular trades; urban and rural groups whose loyalty was focused on charismatic dervish mystics; and formations that were structured around religious difference. Thus, for Barkey, the early Ottomans and their associates were successful because they offered bridges between what were essentially separate communities: 'The foundation of Ottoman power then was the result of brokerage across boundaries, especially religious ones.'[9] And yet, there is evidence from across the late medieval eastern Mediterranean, Anatolian, and Balkan worlds, including in the regions dominated by the Ottomans and those close by,

[9] Ibid. 55.

which suggests that the groups and communities in question were far less bounded than this brokerage approach suggests, and that individuals and communities in these areas were often able to organize their own boundary-crossing without the intervention of those who claimed higher forms of authority. Thus, while it may be true that those representing organized religious life may have sought to demarcate boundaries to identify the orthodox and condemn the heretical or heathen, behind the carapace of the rhetoric of gatekeeper clerics and legal scholars, there was in fact far more plurality, overlap, and sharing in the pursuits of daily life, including devotional activities, than aggressive and exclusive singularity. For example, striking contrasts can be drawn between the invective thrown by late medieval eastern Orthodox Christian clerics at the erroneous doctrines and polluted praxis of the Latins and the degree to which Orthodox Christians in the same period appear to have adopted many beliefs and practices of their supposed Latin adversaries. In the late medieval Peloponnese, icons, often considered the holiest of sacred capital, were populated by clean-shaven saints—a style of grooming usually associated with Latins and in marked contrast to the usual Orthodox condemnation of the shaving of beards. Similarly in Mamluk-dominated territories, hyper-orthodox jurists and scholars such as Ibn Taimiyya might condemn the practice of pilgrimage (*ziyara*) to anywhere but Mecca, but late medieval Syria, Palestine, and Jerusalem still abounded in pilgrimage sites that were shared between Muslims, Christians, and Jews. Indeed one of the reasons why critics like Ibn Taimiyya were so hostile to pilgrimage to such locations was because of the potential contamination that good Muslims might pick up from Christian or Jewish practices they observed or in which they participated. And yet it is clear that many of the faithful took very little notice of such admonition. As Joseph Meri has noted, at such shrines:

> Jews, Muslims, and Christians interacted, commented on each other's piety, employed similar rituals to venerate their holy dead, and possessed similar frames of mind and expectations from the encounter. In performing pilgrimage and venerating saints, devotees traversed social boundaries and understood each other's objectives, such as receiving blessings and cures for themselves, their families, and their animals, rain and plentiful harvests, and seeking protection from evil.[10]

[10] J. W. Meri, *The Cult of Saints among Muslims and Jews in Medieval Syria* (Oxford, 2002), p. 124.

Other examples of shared practice across the eastern Mediterranean world were religious processions and festivals. In Cyprus, processions led by Latin clerics might also include other Christians (Armenians, Nestorians, Maronites, Georgians, and Ethiopians), as well as Muslim Turks and Arabs and Jews. Shared processions were often 'regular' in the sense that they were associated with annual feast days of saints, but they could also be a shared mechanism by which all those within a community responded to a common threat. During the outbreak of plague in 1348 a procession set out from the Great Mosque in Damascus to the mosque of the footprint of Moses. Joining local Muslims were Jews and Christians, female as well as male, with religious leaders carrying holy scriptures aloft. Similar shared practices—especially pilgrimage and mutual celebration of annual saints' days—have also been documented for the Ottoman-governed areas of late medieval north-west Anatolia.

Particularly interesting with regard to processes involving negotiation and brokerage is the fact that shared devotional cultures were often intimately connected with transactional arrangements of a more commercial sort. Pilgrimage and festivals did not just provide the space and opportunity for the performance of pious ritual; they were also moments and places of economic exchange. Trust-making mechanisms which were vital to the practice of trade across religious boundaries may also have involved the use of godly symbols shared by different faith groups, or involved a willingness on the part of traders within one tradition to articulate commercial relationships in terms that demonstrated a basic awareness of the sacred traditions of another. This is important because it suggests that apparently plural and fragmented societies such as those within which the Ottomans assumed power did not necessarily require a higher power to act as broker; instead more horizontal brokering mechanisms may have been available that allowed for operative and ordered societies.

Networks, cultural capital, and power in the eastern Mediterranean

One important implication of this argument about the mutually supportive brokerage systems that existed in the eastern Mediterranean is that we may need to reconsider the relationship between rulers and networks if we are to understand how those who claimed high power operated in plural and fragmented social, religious, and cultural contexts. Rather than assuming that high power emerged from rulers building bridges across essentially atomized groups, we need to think more about how the thick, web-like quality of criss-crossing networks typical of the late medieval world could itself generate power; about how those who wanted to build high power needed to work hard to channel and focus those networks on themselves; and about how success in this enterprise was not guaranteed. In short, about how the networks typical of the late medieval world were themselves the carriers of the peoples, ideas, and products of the authority that rulers needed in the creation of legitimacy. These were the ideas and products which could quite easily be moved elsewhere; these were the people who could shift loyalties, if rulers failed to offer adequate recompense or protection. To return to the points I made at the start of this chapter, if we are interested in the comparative global history topic of regime creation, we need to engage closely with the emphasis in global history on connectivities and movement. Networks which were vital to the provision of the tangible material resources and manpower were needed by local rulers. Such networks also enabled the transfer and mobilization of cultural capital, including intangible ideas about power, as well as the more concrete artistic and literary forms of representing power.

Macedonia in the fourteenth century, a region within the wider eastern Mediterranean zone, provides a useful example of this principle in action. This was an area where late medieval politics has usually been interpreted in terms of military competition between states such as Serbia and Palaiologan Byzantium, the creation of high-power alliances, and the movement of territorial frontiers. However, this state-like approach fails to take account of the exceptional volatility and fluidity of quotidian political life. It overlooks the frequency with which important regional urban centres such as Thessalonica, Serres, and Melnik changed hands; it understates the huge number of lesser political agents and groups with whom would-be rulers needed to negotiate power; and above all it makes little reference to the immensely lively social, cultural, and religious networks that operated both within and beyond the region, which rulers needed to employ and channel to project their power, including in the built environment. Thus, this was a time of immense investment in the building, rebuilding, and decoration of a series of Macedonian churches and monasteries. In the very early fourteenth century, for instance, the Serb king Stefan Milutin (1282–1321) was active as a patron across the region: at the Chilandar monastery on Mount Athos, at the church of the Virgin in Prizren, at St Niketas at Cucer (a church subsequently granted to Chilandar), at St George at Nagoricino near

Skopje, and at Gracanica near Pristina. However, in addition to Milutin there were other prominent founders, including Progonos Sgouros at St Clement's at Ochrid in the mid-1290s, a Byzantine commander who was married to a cousin of the Byzantine emperor Andronikos II Palaiologos and held the title of *megas hetaireiarches*. A host of churches were also founded or redecorated in Thessalonica, including the Church of the Holy Apostles, which was established *c.*1310 by Niphon, the Constantinopolitan patriarch, as well as others such as St Nicholas Orphanotrophos and St Catherine, whose founders are less clearly identifiable but may, at least in the case of St Nicholas, have been Milutin himself.

Particularly pertinent in a networks sense are the multiple connections that seem to link many of these foundations together. One connection, for at least some of these churches, is a common founder: Stefan Milutin. Another connection in several cases is the Chilandar monastery on Mount Athos, which was itself a hub of connections with other Orthodox monasteries and for pilgrims from across the Orthodox world and beyond. A rather similar link is the concentration of so many churches in the city of Thessalonica itself, another place which was a regional hub, in this case for commercial and artistic connections as well as devotional ones. Indeed, many churches within Thessalonica and beyond appear to have been decorated by the same group of artists, in particular a pair of painters called Michael Astrapas and Eutychios. What we can take from all these connections is that if we are interested in working out how royal power, Serbian in this case, consolidated and expanded in this zone of the eastern Mediterranean during the first few decades of the fourteenth century, then we need to pay attention not just to the sorts of high level diplomatic and military strategies on which historians usually concentrate (for instance, the marriage in 1299 of Milutin to Andronikos II's daughter Simonis) but also to the wider cultural, economic, and social networks of the region, including those whose business was the production of visual imagery, which the Serbian kings sought to channel to promote their own claims to authority.

Of course, this example is merely one taken from one small area within a complex eastern Mediterranean zone, which was itself only one region among many in a fragmented late medieval world typified by hegemons looking to build their power. However, there is certainly evidence to suggest that the Milutin instance was typical of a pattern across the wider eastern Mediterranean. Local rulers sought to employ networks of highly specialist, mobile technicians whose expertise was integral to the creation and sustenance of power and the representation and embedding of legitimacy. A group of late thirteenth-century stonemasons from the town of Ahlat was employed by both Muslim and Christian rulers across eastern Anatolia. Greek painters with connections outside the Islamic world worked at the thirteenth-century court of the Turkish Seljuk sultan of Rum at Konya in south-west Anatolia. Rulers in such fractured environments clearly drew on a wide heterogeneity of symbolic systems in the construction of their image, whether on coins, in literary presentation, or in court ceremonial—practices which presuppose networks of experts able to provide the knowledge and specialist 'craft' necessary to produce the required cultural capital. Scholarly attention has traditionally focused on the content and meanings of such cultural productions, but we could think more about the social and ultimately political significance of the networks of technicians who produced such works. An approach of this sort also requires integration of the relationship between rulers and other networks. Such additional and complementary networks might include international traders as well as religious experts, whether mystics or scholars, who could lend vital legitimacy to a ruler's aspirations to authority, especially as far as trans- or supraregional recognition was concerned, as well as more localized social networks, including urban brotherhoods, local militias, local landowners, or tribal leaders.

In some cases such networks were not only the suppliers of the cultural and social capital that was needed by rulers, but might also be its audience— that is, those who needed to be persuaded that the regime that they were supporting with their loyalty (and quite frequently their taxes) was in fact providing the protection that they had been promised and which the regime's self-presentation proclaimed. Certainly the testimony of Ibn Battuta provides invaluable evidence for the ways in which supraregional and local networks provided the social and cultural capital for the building and display of power at the many courts he visited; he also bears witness to the consumption of that display by the very same network members. Some of his encounters at the courts of local emirs in Anatolia are especially detailed, as in the case of his meetings with the sultan of Birgi at his ornate summer ceremonial tent (*kharqa*) and his permanent city palace. In such meetings, we can see first-hand how a religious expert from afar, valued for his associations with a wider world of Islamic scholars and his acquaintance with the courts of Muslim rulers, both neighbouring and distant, was courted by local rulers requiring legitimacy; at the same time, Ibn Battuta himself was also acutely aware of the other social connections that local hegemons forged in the construction of their power bases, and the other reservoirs of expert knowledge on whom such rulers visibly relied and to whom they broadcast their power. When attending a banquet hosted by the sultan of Birgi, Ibn Battuta references not only Muslim legal scholars like himself but Jewish doctors, Quran reciters, army officers and notable local citizens, some of whom were still Greek speakers and Christian in this period. In Ibn Battuta's testimony for Anatolia, it is possible to see how the power of local rulers was embedded in a plural and fragmented environment. In such environments, rulers could not afford simply to project power, but instead needed continuously to forge connections with the governed and with those beyond their immediate locality. These were processes in which those belonging to an array of social, cultural, and economic networks were integral.[11]

Networks and power beyond the eastern Mediterranean

While I have focused in this chapter principally on the eastern Mediterranean world, there are reasons for thinking that the reciprocal, network-based model of power which I have described above may also hold for other regions of the medieval world. The close and mutually beneficial relationship between the Mongols and networks of traders and technical specialists of all sorts has been noted by historians both in the initial expansionary phases of Mongol power during the thirteenth century and in its maintenance thereafter in regions such as Yuan China and Ilkhanid Iran. It has been argued that during the thirteenth century the balance of power between transregional networks and the Mongols was usually tilted in the direction of the *qans*, with the rulers able to move clusters of administrators and specialist craftsmen—particularly those involved in textile production—from one region of their empire to another at will. However, as Mongol power eventually regionalized, there is evidence to suggest that more economic and political leverage came to be exerted by these networks providing the resources which underpinned the status and prestige of the Mongol elite. This at least appears to have been the case in Yuan China if we look at the Mongols' relationship with groups of Muslim and Uighur *ortagh* merchants. These groups were state-protected trader-cum-money-lenders who received precious metal or paper money from the government and other members of the Mongol elite. They then invested

---

[11] H. A. R. Gibb, C. Defrémery, and B. R. Sanguinetti (trans.), *The Travels of Ibn Battuta, A. D. 1325–1354*, 2 vols (Cambridge, 1958–62), vol. 2, pp. 440–44.

these receipts into trans-Eurasian overland and maritime commerce, to the mutual financial benefit of both parties. The history of this trader–investor relationship is difficult to trace in extant records; and the status and precise ethnic identities of the merchants are hard to disentangle from the rather prejudiced rhetoric of Chinese imperial officials that colours many of the surviving records. Those caveats accepted, however, Elizabeth Endicott-West has suggested the following trajectory: that during the reign of Qubilai (d. 1294) state officials exercised a whip-hand over the activities of the *ortagh* merchants, but that this relationship began to shift during the fourteenth century, as members of the Mongol court racked up vast debts to those merchants in exchange for the precious commodities, particularly gems, which these groups could supply. If Endicott is right, then this alteration in *ortagh* practices suggests, at the very least, that the long-term maintenance and performance of high power in this part of the fourteenth-century Mongol world required the ruling elite to engage in complex ways with networks of providers. These networks were not as easily channelled and disciplined by the state as may once have been the case. Indeed, we may want to go further with this argument, and suggest that the frequency of attempts to regulate these merchants' activities during the reign of Qubilai itself indicates that the balance between these commercial networks, the Mongol elite, and other groupings associated with the Mongol government may always have been quite finely balanced, even during the heyday of Yuan power in the late thirteenth century.[12]

A similar picture of ruler–network relations emerges elsewhere, particularly in late medieval south Asia. For instance in north India, the demise of the Delhi sultanate at the end of the fourteenth century was followed by a century of so-called Afghan tribal rule. This period which prefigured the emergence of the Mughals has often been interpreted in terms of political anarchy. Yet it is now argued that many of the Afghan hegemons of northern India during the fifteenth and early sixteenth centuries were acutely conscious of a need for legitimacy that went beyond reliance on traditional intertribal relations and central Asian insignia of rule. Instead rulers built their power with an active awareness of the need to engage with local and supraregional networks which could provide social, economic, and cultural capital and which could enable them to tap into the long-standing local and more universal traditions that were the wellspring of political

---

[12] E. Endicott-West, 'Merchant Associations in Yuan China: The Ortogh', *Asia Major*, 3rd ser., 2 (1989), at pp. 127–9, 132–52.

legitimacy. As in the Anatolia visited by Ibn Battuta, such networks included traders, members of the ulema, and sufi saints. This too appears to have been an environment of power in which clearly bounded religious identities were of limited political importance.[13]

Similar conclusions have been reached with respect to the Deccan region further south, an area which during the post-Delhi sultanate era constituted a fractured frontier zone between different Muslim-ruled polities and the Hindu Vijaynagara empire. Here, in the Deccan, as late as the mid-sixteenth century, both Indic and Islamicate rulers sought to attract into their political orbit a corps of military specialists of high social status who moved easily and frequently between regimes. This high-ranking social group probably had its genesis during the southwards expansion of the Delhi sultanate in the fourteenth century, when immigrant Muslim warriors from the north encountered the indigenous Indic military elite. Repeated interaction, both hostile and peaceful, between these two martial groups led to a sharing of practices (mounted archery, systems of landholding, and forms of record-keeping) so that by the sixteenth century 'we can meaningfully speak of a single, trans-cultural military-political elite, multi-ethnic and multilingual in composition, but united through shared bodies of material culture and common social interests'.[14]

Of course, to argue that political power in regions such as China and India was created by exactly the same political formations, practices, and traditions as those in the late medieval eastern Mediterranean would be dangerously simplistic. The precise ways in which claims to authority, administrative apparatus, ethnic and religious identities, and social, economic, and cultural networks of different sorts interacted with each other in each region must always have been distinctive, especially given the very different scales at which different polities were operating and the local conditions within which rulership was created and exercised. The early fourteenth-century Yuan were able to harness far more tangible goods and manpower than the rulers of the petty statelets of the contemporary eastern Mediterranean; the Mamluks of Egypt were able to mobilize far greater resources than the Ottomans until the final decades of the fifteenth century. The territorial 'reach' of late medieval political regimes varied considerably.

[13] R. Aquil, *Sufism, Culture, and Politics: Afghans and Islam in Medieval North India* (New Delhi, 2007).
[14] P. Wagoner, 'Fortuitous Convergences and Essential Ambiguities: Transcultural Political Elites in the Medieval Deccan', *International Journal of Hindu Studies* 3 (1999), pp. 241–64.

However, what this chapter has tried to demonstrate is that in the later medieval period, despite differences of scale, there were common mechanisms at play in the practice of politics and the creation of power in a region stretching from the eastern Mediterranean to central, south, and east Asia. A crucial dimension of successful rulership in this period was the forging and maintenance of connections to social, economic, and cultural networks which operated on a variety of different scales: local, regional, trans-regional, even inter-continental. It is too reductive to argue that such connections were created principally by rulers acting as brokers between bounded groups which were themselves defined in terms of their ethnic and religious identities. The groups with which rulers had to deal were simply too unbounded, diverse, numerous, and capable of self-regulation for ruler-imposed brokerage to have been a realistic and sustainable strategy in many cases. Indeed, excessive attempts to broker on the part of rulers may have been counterproductive, and could lead to the alienation of those networks whose resources were most useful. Wise was the ruler who allowed for a degree of self-regulation. These conditions meant that the relationship between rulers and networks of different sorts was finely balanced and constantly shifting across the later medieval centuries. The forging of power through the active management of bounded and separate groups is likely to have been a phenomenon of later centuries, and perhaps even then, uneven in application and practice.

Plate 9. Raffaello Sanzio, *Portrait of Baldassarre Castiglione* (1514–1515)

Conclusion

Into the sixteenth century

Isabella Lazzarini

In 1516 the first edition of Thomas More's *Utopia, or the Island of Nowhere* was printed in Leuven: it would be followed by four more in More's lifetime, and countless more after his death. *Utopia*, the account of the invisible island of nowhere, is an extraordinary book, half a critique of the Europe of More's own time, half a 'bordering on the absurd' (as More defined his work in a letter to Erasmus) reflection on society through the medium of a fable. In such a tale, someone well aware that 'experience in our countries goes back a long way, and has led to a great number of innovations that have raised the standard of living, not to mention some fortuitous discoveries that no amount of intelligence could have devised', found themselves nevertheless in the position of imagining a society that, in the narrator's view, was 'not just the best, but actually the only "commonwealth" that can rightly claim that title'. If 'elsewhere people talk about the "common good" but it is only their private good they worry about', in Utopia 'there's nothing private, and they concentrate on what has to be done in the common interest'.[1]

Experience and knowledge, but also a clear aspiration to a whole new society whose location is nowhere to be found in the old world but may be hidden somewhere in the newly discovered one, and whose principles are based on a profound rethinking of ancient theories and a bold shaping of contemporary reality. Experience, knowledge, and aspirations: all expressed in an elegant language that, thanks to the polished Latin of humanism, was able to convey the restlessness, variety, theatrical quality, and contradictions of the early Renaissance. After all, as Michael Baxandall says, 'in 1300 a man

---

[1] T. Moore, *Utopia. The Island of Nowhere*, trans. R. Clarke (Richmond, 2017), at pp. 47 and 126.

The Later Middle Ages. Isabella Lazzarini, Oxford University Press (2021). © Isabella Lazzarini.
DOI: 10.1093/oso/9780198731641.003.0009

could not think as tightly in words as he could by 1500; the difference is measurable in categories and constructions lost and found.'[2]

In the early 1500s, a series of more or less related events—that seem momentous to us as they did to everyone back then—occurred. In 1517 Martin Luther wrote and discussed his Ninety-five Theses on indulgences and opened the gates to the breaking of the unity of the western Christian church. In 1519 Charles of Habsburg was elected Emperor Charles V, and in that same brief period the Spanish captain Hernán Cortés conquered the Aztec empire, and the Portuguese Fernão de Magalhães' fleet circumnavigated the globe under the flag of the crown of Spain (and the empire). Finally, in 1520, Charles V's Ottoman foe, Kanuni Suleiman (Suleiman the Lawgiver, or—as he is known in the west—the Magnificent), inaugurated his 46-year reign on the Sublime Porte. On the cultural side, in 1513 Machiavelli's *De principatibus* started to circulate in manuscript versions; 1516 saw not only the publication of More's *Utopia* and of Erasmus' translation of the New Testament but also the first printed edition of Ludovico Ariosto's *Orlando furioso*; between 1508 and its posthumous publication in 1528, Baldassarre Castiglione's *The Courtier* was written.

There are indeed many elements that can support the idea of the 1500s as a turning point in the history of Europe, and some clear fractures are visible in the fabric of the continent's history between the fifteenth and sixteenth centuries. However, one of the most important acquisitions in recent historiography is a lesson in prudence about identifying sharp turning points and clear-cut periodization. In this sense, the chapters of this volume, with a shared attention to complexity and a nuanced but constant reminder of the need to rewrite a story shaped for too long by one-way narratives, are more open to continuities than to fractures.

In political history (Watts, Chapter 1), the continental framework appears divided into at least three major regions in which many different polities were developing at different paces. Their discernible governmental growth seems not to result from a teleological progress towards a monarchical, bounded, and sovereign nation-state, but to emerge through many processes of intensification of political interactions from above and from below. The 'unusual' dynamic of the late medieval economy after the shock of the Black Death comes from specialization, substantial change in traditional activities such as the international financial markets, the role of technological

---

[2] M. Baxandall, *Giotto and the Orators: Humanist Observers of Painting in Italy, and the Discovery of Pictorial Composition, 1350–1450* (Oxford, 1971), p. 6.

progress, and a stronger, although differentiated, market integration. Against the traditionally grim landscape of setback and instability attributed to this period, the extent and complexity of trade undeniably increased. Its success was prompted by the substitution of the previous network of a few large gateways by a patchwork of increasingly integrated and functionally diverse economic regions (Epstein, Chapter 2).

Late medieval Europe identified itself as explicitly Christian and specifically catholic: it would be therefore anachronistic to deny the impact of the Reformation on the story of western Christianity. However, the whole picture reveals a more complex design, and deserves to be analysed without being overshadowed by the Reformation. The period between 1300 and 1500 saw a crossing of paths: preceding evolutions continued, but obscured tensions and ambiguities became more apparent, even though diversity had not yet produced adversity (Swanson, Chapter 3). The cultural landscape composed by literature, political and juristic thought, architecture, visual arts and music—the very field in which the Burckhardtian grand narrative of the Renaissance as a work of art was born—was actually characterized more by diversity than by a classical division between a traditional gothic north and an innovative humanistic south, and resembled a 'rich and discordant symphony of competing voices' in which crossings, connections, and borrowings were the norm (Lee, Chapter 4). Even in the domain of cultural concepts of time and space, in which traditional surveys had characterized the later Middle Ages as an age of discovery and of a crucial shift from 'religion' to 'science' and from 'medieval' to 'modern', such a process was far from straightforward. It involved a more complicated pattern of respective influences between 'high' and 'low' culture, Latin and vernacular, theoretical disciplines such as astronomy or geometry and practical arts such as navigation or metalwork, and the conventions underlying the representation of space and time. There was more than one way of seeing and understanding them, and the whole process was as much a reconnection to previous knowledge as an invention of new ideas and techniques (Kempshall, Chapter 5).

Society, family, and gender were in turn extremely variable across the geopolitical, legal, and social divide, and surprisingly fluid. Traditional and shared range of normative values—such as Christianity, a gendered vision of man and woman, or familiar and social structures based on patriarchy—regulated social relationships. However, confronted with extraordinary upheaval and great demographic and economic pressure on society, such values produced an extremely complex social life, characterized by intellectual and cultural vibrancy and divergences, and by a variety of unexpected views and practices across space, status, and time (Kovesi, Chapter 6). Finally, the broadening of the approach to European phenomena beyond the traditional continental boundaries has, on the one hand, revealed the persistency and diffusion of common demographic, economic, and political trends and of patterns of change inside and outside Europe. On the other, it has confirmed the crucial need for investigations more attentive to variety and multiplicity than in search of unifying models (Holmes, Chapter 7).

In the 1300s and 1400s, therefore, the polyphonic, vibrant, and sometimes contradictory fabric of politics, culture, and society takes centre stage. The legacy of such a complex period to the following centuries is represented by two parallel processes. The institutional and constitutional framework of power and authority showed a thickening and defining of its many forms, but despite the undeniable consolidation of its structures, politics remained a field open to many contrasting solutions. On the other hand, the emergence of a more defined written and spoken agency of individuals and groups that had previously been less visible or less audible created cultures and languages of power—humanism was the most effective among them—that rewrote tradition and enabled the many authors of such new languages to play on the ambiguities of their social and economic environment and to make themselves heard.

Further Reading

General

Although the following suggestions for further reading are mainly in English, it is worthy stressing that ground-breaking research—at once classic and recent—on the later Middle Ages has been produced in almost all the main European languages, and that an increasing and due attention to what we can call a 'larger Europe'—which includes previously less-known regions and increasingly porous borders—has produced a wealth of new research for these areas, some also in English. The detailed bibliography linked to the various chapters of the book will provide a significant overview on the many facets of the general picture, but some classic collective volumes will offer a very good starting point. First of all, the volumes of the New Cambridge Medieval History: vol. 6, *c.1300–c.1415*, ed. M. Jones, and vol. 7, *c.1415–c.1500*, ed. C. Allmand (Cambridge, 2000 and 1998); slightly outdated is the first volume of the New Cambridge Modern History: *The Renaissance: 1493–1520*, ed. G. R. Potter (Cambridge, 1951), although it includes some fine chapters (such as chapter 3 by H. Baron on the early Italian Renaissance and chapter 5 by R. Weiss on culture) and useful timelines on the major events. Some significant collective enterprises in the 1980s and 1990s have also been central in pioneering an innovative view on the later Middle Ages: among them, the series on the *Genèse de l'état moderne*, ed. J.-P. Genet (5 volumes between 1986 and 1990) and the collection of the European Science Foundation on *The Origin of the Modern State in Europe, 13th to 18th Centuries* (six volumes, published by Clarendon). Their focus on the genesis of the modern state has been partly reconsidered by recent research, such as the collection edited by Wim Blockmans, André Holenstein, and Jan Mathieu, *Empowering Interactions: Political Cultures and the Emergence of the State in Europe, 1300–1900* (Aldershot, 2009). Reference works such as C. Lansing and E. D. English (eds), *A Companion to the Medieval World* (Oxford, 2013), G. Ruggiero (ed.), *A Companion to the Worlds of the Renaissance* (Oxford, 2002 and 2007), W. Caferro (ed.), *Contesting the Renaissance* (Oxford, 2011), and R. E. Bjork (ed.), *The Oxford Dictionary of the Middle Ages* (Oxford, 2010) have useful articles and entries. For historical atlases that include the period, see A. Mackay and D. Ditchburn (eds), *Atlas of Medieval Europe* (London, 1997); R. McKitterick (ed.), *The Atlas of the Medieval World* (Oxford, 2004); and *The Times Atlas of European History* (London, 1998).

Sources

The primary sources available for the later Middle Ages display at once a typological and linguistic variety and a quantity that defies editions and surveys. These short notes provide only a very basic list of instruments to navigate through their sheer mass. For an introduction to the variety of the source material, see L. Genicot and R. Noel (eds, to 1993 and from 1994), *Typologie des sources du Moyen Âge occidental* (Turnhout, 1972–). For a first, detailed overview in English of the many series and collections of specific edited sources, a starting point is represented by the appendixes of vols 6 and 7 of the New Cambridge Medieval History where, chapter by chapter, the most relevant editions of narrative, historical, and documentary edited sources are listed. In particular, English editions of the main texts of the European literature are in vol. 6, pp. 945–6, while the main collection of public records for the European polities are organized in vols 6 and 7 according to the structure of each book (and therefore by themes and then by geopolitical areas). The public records issued by royal, princely, or republican chanceries have been published at a different pace and within different frameworks (national, regional, or urban), since the nineteenth century (famous examples are the *Ordonnances des rois de France* or the *Registres du Trésor des chartes* or the English various *Calendars of Rolls—Close, Fine, Patent, State*). Narrative and historical sources include the Italian *Rerum Italicarum Scriptores*, first edited by L. A. Muratori in the seventeenth century, and the 2nd and revised edition produced by the Istituto storico italiano per il Medioevo since the 1870s. Peace treaties and agreements are available in the still useful seventeenth- and early eighteenth-century editions (F. Léonard, *Recueil des traitez de paix [. . .] faits par les Rois de France*, Paris, 1693; G. Leibniz, *Codex juris gentium diplomaticus [. . .]*, Hanover, 1693; J. Bernard, *Recueil des traitéz de paix [. . .]*, Amsterdam, 1700; J. Dumont, *Corps universel diplomatique du droit de gens [. . .]*, Amsterdam, 1726–31). For the empire, and the many European regions that at one point or another were included in it, the Monumenta Germaniae Historica are still crucial (and have been entirely digitalized: www.mgh.de).

Only a small proportion of the records preserved in the European archives for this period have as yet been published in a systematic way, and even fewer have been translated into English: however, there are some notable exceptions. Because of the recent focus on literacy, information, and communication, massive attention has been devoted to letter-writing, in particular in the Italian case. Since the creation of the Ilardi collection of microfilms at Yale (http://www.library.yale.edu/Ilardi/il-home.htm), diplomatic correspondence between the Italian polities (and between some of them and the European kingdoms and principalities) have been edited (for references, see I. Lazzarini, *Communication and Conflict: Italian Diplomacy in the Early Renaissance, 1350–1520*, Oxford, 2015) and partly translated into English (M. Azzolini and I. Lazzarini (eds), *Italian Renaissance Diplomacy: A Sourcebook*, Toronto, 2017). Individual, familial, and dynastic correspondences have been edited and translated as well, with a distinctive attention to female letter-writing: see e.g. C. James (ed.), *Letters to Francesco Datini from Margherita Datini* (Toronto, 2015); J. Bryce (ed.), *Alessandra Macinghi Strozzi: Letters to her Sons, 1447–1470* (Toronto,

2016); D. Shemek (ed.), *Isabella d'Este: Selected Letters* (Toronto, 2017); a useful anthology is L. Kaborycha (ed.), *A Corresponding Renaissance: Letters Written by Italian Women, 1375–1630* (New York, 2015).

Introduction

Chris Wickham, *Medieval Europe. From the Breakup of the Western Roman empire to the Reformation* (New Haven, CT, 2016) and John Watts, *The Making of Polities: Europe 1300–1500* (Cambridge, 2009) provide an excellent introduction to the later Middle Ages (the first by including it in an innovative survey on the whole of European medieval history). Among the building blocks of some of the grand narratives on the period we still find the classics: J. C. L. S. de Sismondi, *Histoire des républiques italiennes au Moyen Âge* (Zurich, 1807–19); B. Constant, *De la liberté des Anciens comparée à celle des Modernes*, lecture given in 1819 at the Athénée Royale in Paris (for a contemporary edition, see *De la liberté des anciens comparée à celle des modernes*, ed. M. Gauchet, Paris, 1980); J. Burckhardt, *Die Kultur der Renaissance in Italien* (Basel, 1860); J. Huizinga, *The Autumn of the Middle Ages* (English trans., Chicago, 1996; ed. Harleem, 1919). On the discourse on decline, see G. Holmes, *Europe: Hierarchy and Revolt, 1320–1450* (London, 1975), and by comparison, R. Starn, 'The Early Modern Muddle', *Journal of Early Modern History* 6 (2003), pp. 296–307. On some of the more evident effects of the grand narrative of modernity, see J. Strayer, *On the Medieval Origins of the Modern State* (Princeton, NJ, 1970) or W. McNeill, *The Shape of European History* (New York, 1974): on the revision of the model, a good start is J. H. Elliott, 'A Europe of Composite Monarchies', *Past and Present* 137 (1992), pp. 48–71; important elements to the common debate in J. Kirshner (ed.), *The Origin of the State in Italy: 1300–1600* (Chicago, 1996).

On documentary evidence: J.-C. Maire Vigueur, 'Révolution documentaire et révolution scripturaire. Le cas de l'Italie médiévale', *Bibliothèque de l'École des Chartes* 153 (1995), pp. 177–85; M. Clanchy, *From Memory to Written Record: England 1066–1307* (Oxford, 1979); A. Petrucci, *Public Lettering: Script, Power, and Culture* (Chicago, 1993); R. H. Britnell (ed.), *Pragmatic Literacy. East and West, 1200–1300* (Woodbridge, 1997); G. M. Varanini, 'Public Written Records', in A. Gamberini and I. Lazzarini (eds), *The Italian Renaissance State* (Cambridge, 2012), pp. 385–405; O. Guyotjeannin (ed.), *L'art médiéval du registre. Chancelleries royales et princières* (Paris, 2018); for Renaissance and early modern developments, see now R. C. Head, *Making Archives in Early Modern Europe: Proof, Information, and Political Record Keeping* (Cambridge, 2019); on the cultural aspects of literacy, see P. Burke, *Languages and Communities in Early Modern Europe* (Cambridge, 2004).

On the events and the socioeconomic framework, see e.g. S. K. Cohen, *The Black Death Transformed* (London, 2002); C. Allmand, *The Hundred Years War* (Cambridge, 2001); J. Rollo-Koster and T. M. Izbicki (eds), *A Companion to the Great Western Schism (1378–1417)* (Leiden, 2009); S. Carocci, 'Social Mobility and the Middle Ages', *Continuity and Change* 26 (2011), pp. 367–404. On power, apart from what is listed above, and the bibliography provided by the chapter on political life, an interesting perspective is to be found in F. Titone (ed.), *Disciplined Dissent: Strategies of Non-Confrontational Protest in Europe from the Twelfth to the Early Sixteenth Century* (Rome, 2016), while the associative and multilayered nature of most polities has been recently emphasized by the analysis of the imperial case (D. Hardy, *Associative Political Culture in the Holy Roman Empire: Upper Germany, 1346–1521*, Oxford, 2018) and the Swiss confederation (H. Speich, *Burgrecht. Von der Einbürgerung zum politische Bündnis im Spätmittelalter*, Ostfildern, 2019).

Two recent major issues are gender studies and global history. On the first, an indispensable start is provided by M. E. Wiesner-Hanks, *Women and Gender in Early Modern Europe* (Cambridge, 2000), M. Schaus (ed.), *Women and Gender in Medieval Europe: An Encyclopedia* (New York, 2006), and R. Mazo Karras (ed.), *The Oxford Handbook of Women and Gender in Medieval Europe* (Oxford, 2013); on the second, useful introductions and insights are to be found in J. Belich, J. Darwin, and C. Wickham (eds), *The Prospect of Global History* (Oxford, 2016), and C. Holmes and N. Standen (eds), *The Global Middle Ages, Past and Present Supplement* 13 (2018).

Principalities, power, and political life (Chapter 1)

The main arguments of this chapter are developed at more length in J. Watts, *The Making of Polities: Europe, 1300–1500* (Cambridge, 2009). This book, which also has much to say about the thirteenth century, contains a substantial bibliography of English-language works on later medieval politics, including culture and ideas, which were published before 2008. Among other overview works, there are valuable essays on the politics of most countries in *New Cambridge Medieval History* vol. 6: *c.1300–c.1415*, ed. M. Jones (2000) and vol. 7: *1415–1500*, ed. C. Allmand (1999), and a number of helpful volumes in the European Science Foundation volumes on the Origins of the Modern State, edited by J.-P. Genet and W. Blockmans, notably *Economic Systems and State Finance*, ed. R. Bonney (Oxford, 1995), *Legislation and Justice*, ed. A. Padoa-Schioppa (Oxford, 1997), and *Power Elites and State Building*, ed. W. Reinhard (Oxford, 1996). More recently, the collection edited by W. Blockmans, A. Holenstein, and J. Mathieu, *Empowering Interactions: Political Cultures and the Emergence of the State in Europe, 1300–1900* (Aldershot, 2009), is very insightful on political culture and practice, while C. Briggs, *The Body Broken: Medieval Europe, 1300–1520*, 2nd edn (London, 2019) offers a good up-to-date treatment of politics and government set in a wider social and cultural context; D. Stasavage, *States of Credit: Size, Power and the Development of European Polities* (Princeton, NJ, 2011) takes a very different but also very interesting approach to explaining the fortunes of polities in the period. Analytical surveys of the historiography on politics can be found in Watts, *Making of Polities*, ch. 1, and see also H. Kaminsky, 'From Lateness to Waning to Crisis: the Burden of the Late Middle Ages', *Journal of Early Modern History* 4 (2000), pp. 85–125.

For overviews of the political background to our period, see the classic study of S. Reynolds, *Kingdoms and Communities in Western Europe, 900–1300*, 2nd edn (Oxford, 1997), the introductory essay by B. Weiler, 'Politics', in D. Power (ed.), *The Central Middle Ages* (Short Oxford History) (Oxford, 2006), pp. 91–121, and a new treatment by C. Wickham, *Medieval Europe: From the Breakup of the Western Roman Empire to the Reformation* (New Haven, CT, 2016), chs 8 and 9. For recent approaches to the period afterwards, see M. Greengrass, *Christendom Destroyed* (London, 2014), esp. ch. 9, and H. Scott (ed.), *The Oxford Handbook of Early Modern European History, 1350–1750*, 2 vols (Oxford, 2015), pt 6.

Some of the most interesting recent writing has dealt with themes. Popular politics has been one particularly vibrant area, on which see S. K. Cohn, *Lust for Liberty: the Politics of Social Revolt in Medieval Europe, 1200–1425* (Cambridge, MA, 2006), and his collection of documents, *Popular Protest in Late Medieval Europe* (Manchester, 2004); J. Firnhaber-Baker (ed.), *The Routledge History Handbook of Medieval Revolt* (London, 2017); and J. Dumolyn, J. Haemers, H. R. Oliva Herrer, and V. Challet (eds), *The Voices of the People in Late Medieval Europe* (Turnhout, 2014). F. Titone takes an interesting approach to rebellion in his collection of essays, *Disciplined Dissent* (Rome, 2016), while D. Nirenberg's *Communities of Violence: Persecution of Minorities in the Middle Ages* (Princeton, NJ, 1996) is an important study of relations between Jews and Christians. Most recent work on urban politics is found in essays or in national treatments, but note T. Scott's remarkable overview, *The City State in Europe, 1000–1600* (Oxford, 2012) and see also P. Lantschner, *The Logic of Political Conflict in Medieval Cities* (Oxford, 2015) for a stimulating comparative treatment of urban political life. On the political role of aristocrats, the work of H. Zmora is particularly useful, notably *Monarchy, Aristocracy and State in Europe* (London, 2001). On representative assemblies, the massive book by M. Hébert, *Parlementer* (Paris, 2014), is a rich treatment for those who can read French, while *Political Representation: Communities, Ideas and Institutions in Europe (c.1200–c.1690)*, ed. M. Damen, J. Haemers, and A. Mann (Leiden, 2018) and *Cultures of Voting in Pre-modern Europe*, ed. S. Ferente, L. Kunčević, and M. Pattenden (London, 2018), are two interesting collections surveying representative and consultative practice. J. Duindam, *Dynasties: A Global History of Power, 1300–1800* (Cambridge, 2015) has much to offer on the culture of kingship, queenship, and royal families, while M. Vale's *The Princely Court* (Oxford, 2001) is still unrivalled for its rich sense of courtly culture in fourteenth-century north-western Europe. For the rise of diplomacy, with its manifold causes and effects, see I. Lazzarini, *Communication and Conflict: Italian Diplomacy in the Early Renaissance, 1350–1520* (Oxford, 2015).

Since so much has been published on individual regions, this section will highlight material in English published in the last decade or so (older works are listed in the bibliographical section of *The Making of Polities*). On the British Isles, M. Brown, *Disunited Kingdoms* (Harlow, 2013) provides an excellent overview of the period 1280–1460, while P. Crooks, D. Green, and M. Ormrod (eds), *The Plantagenet Empire* (Donington, 2016) offers a collection of essays looking at the wider area affected by the adventurism of the English crown. On France, there is an excellent recent textbook by G. Small, *Late Medieval France* (Basingstoke, 2009) and a collection of comparative essays on *Government and Political Life in England and France, c.1300–c.1500*, ed. C. Fletcher, J.-P. Genet, and J. Watts (Cambridge, 2015). On the Iberian kingdoms, little has been published in English in the last decade or so that really gets under the skin of the political system, but T. F. Ruiz, *Spain's Centuries of Crisis: 1300–1474* (Oxford, 2007) is a helpful introduction, and A. R. Disney's two-volume *History of Portugal and the Portuguese Empire* (Cambridge, 2009) goes deeper into the politics of that small kingdom. On Italy, perhaps the most useful recent publication is *The Italian Renaissance State*, ed. A. Gamberini and I. Lazzarini (Cambridge, 2012), which contains both regional and thematic essays by today's leading Italian historians. On the empire, see L. Scales's masterly treatment of nationalism and collective sensibility, 1245–1414, *The Shaping of German Identity* (Cambridge, 2012); P. Wilson's overview, *The Holy Roman Empire* (London, 2016), ch. 8; and, for a new approach, D. Hardy, *Associative Political Culture in the Holy Roman Empire: Upper Germany, 1346–1521* (Oxford, 2018). Much of the newer work on the politics of the Low Countries takes the form of articles, notably (on the south) by J. Dumolyn, J. Haemers, and F. Buylaert; but see (more on the north) R. Stein, *Magnanimous Dukes and Rising States: the Unification of the Burgundian Netherlands, 1380–1480* (Oxford, 2017). D. Nicholas, *The Northern Lands: Germanic Europe, c.1270–c.1500* (Oxford, 2009) provides some useful material on the Baltic and North Sea world from German and Scandinavian literature, and contains a good chapter on commercial integration; there is also a lively introductory overview on medieval Scandinavia by S. Bagge, *Cross and Scepter* (Princeton, NJ, 2014). Otherwise, the best way of tackling the northern kingdoms may be through article literature, notably in the Anglophone *Scandinavian Journal of History*, which contains some pieces on the Middle Ages. On Poland-Lithuania, there is a rich treatment by R. Frost, *The Oxford History of Poland-Lithuania* (Oxford, 2015), of which vol. 1 covers 1385–1569; and for Poland specifically, see N. Nowakowska, *Church, State and Dynasty in Renaissance Poland* (Aldershot, 2007). A recent and helpful book on Hussite Bohemia is T. A. Fudge, *Jan Hus: Religious Reform and Social Revolution in Bohemia* (London, 2010). Bohemia, Hungary, and Poland are given a rounded treatment in N. Berend, P. Urbańczyk, and P. Wiszewski, *Central Europe in the High Middle Ages* (Cambridge, 2013), but the volume does not go beyond 1300.

The economy (Chapter 2)*

Some short overviews provide perspectives on the whole period with guides to further reading: Stephen Epstein (not Stephan, the author of this chapter), *The Economic and Social History of Later Medieval Europe* (Cambridge, 2009) covers the period 1000–1500, whereas K. G. Persson, *An Economic History of Europe* (Cambridge, 2010) surveys the whole of history with special insights on the later

* Stephan Epstein's chapter was left by his untimely death without a 'Further Reading' section: Christopher Dyer has provided this, and has added more titles to his final paragraph.

Middle Ages. The Cambridge Economic History of Europe includes the whole of the continent in some detail but is not up to date: vol. 1, *The Agrarian Life of the Middle Ages* (2nd edn, 1966); vol. 2, *Trade and Industry in the Middle Ages* (2nd edn, 1987); vol. 3, *Economic Organization and Policies in the Middle Ages* (1965). There are more recent surveys and bibliographies in the chapters on economic and social history in the *New Cambridge Medieval History*, vol. 6 on the fourteenth century, ed. M. Jones (2000), and vol. 7 on the fifteenth, ed. C. Allmand (1999). More recent works, full of new ideas, are J. L. van Zanden, *The Long Road to the Industrial Revolution: The European Economy in a Global Perspective, 1000–1800* (Leiden, 2009) and G. Clark, *Farewell to Alms: A Brief History of the World* (Princeton, NJ, 2007). Some authors seek to explain why parts of Asia, once in advance of Europe, were then outstripped: K. Pomeranz, *The Great Divergence: Europe, China and the Making of the World Economy* (Princeton, NJ, 2000), M. Mitterauer, *Why Europe? The Medieval Origins of its Special Path* (Chicago, 2010). The 'world system' approach shows how different regions interacted: J. L. Abu-Lughod, *Before European Hegemony: The World System AD 1250–1350* (Oxford, 1989).

How do we know about the medieval economy? Documents and writings contain economic evidence, but they also throw light on the uses of literacy as an aid to commerce: the illuminating capacity of documents is celebrated in I. Origo, *The Merchant of Prato* (Harmondsworth, 1963); a more functional approach is in R. H. Britnell (ed.), *Pragmatic Literacy, East and West 1200–1330* (Woodbridge, 1997). This was an age when numeracy increased, as shown in A. W. Crosby, *The Measure of Reality: Quantification and Western Society, 1250–1600* (Cambridge, 1997).

'Crisis' is a concept much used to interpret the period. Two catastrophes, the Great Famine and the Black Death, are described and discussed in W. C. Jordan, *The Great Famine: Northern Europe in the early Fourteenth Century* (Princeton, NJ, 1996) and J. Benedictow, *The Black Death 1346–1353: The Complete History* (Woodbridge, 2004). These two disasters were the consequences of climatic upheavals, according to B. Campbell, *The Great Transition. Climate, Disease and Society in the Late-Medieval World* (Cambridge, 2016). The theory advocated in the late twentieth century by M. M. Postan and G. Duby that ecological damage linked to population growth led to the crisis has been challenged by contributors to M. Bourin, F. Menant, and L. To Figuera (eds), *Dynamique du monde rural dans la conjoncture de 1300* (Rome, 2014); H. Kitsikopoulos (ed.), *Agrarian Change and Crisis in Europe, 1200–1500* (London, 2012); J. Drendel (ed.), *Crisis in the Later Middle Ages: Beyond the Postan–Duby Paradigm* (Turnhout, 2015). Indeed some of the authors doubt the severity of the crisis. The most thorough studies of the demographic background to the period are D. Herlihy and C. Klapisch-Zuber, *Tuscans and their Families: A Study of the Florentine Catasto of 1427* (London, 1985) and Z. Razi, *Life, Marriage and Death in a Medieval Parish: Economy, Society and Demography in Halesowen, 1270–1400* (Cambridge, 1980). Warfare contributed to the effects of crisis, and G. Bois, *Crisis of Feudalism: Economy and Society in Eastern Normandy c.1300–1550* (Cambridge, 1984) examines a province blighted by occupation by English armies. The crises also increased the frequency and intensity of popular rebellions: see S. Cohn, *Lust for Liberty: The Politics of Social Revolt in Medieval Europe, 1200–1425* (Cambridge, MA, 2006).

Throughout the period commerce was developing in new ways, especially with markets for labour, which differed greatly in town and country: in towns, craft guilds had an important influence in training and managing the workforce, as presented convincingly in S. R. Epstein and M. Prak (eds), *Guilds, Innovation and the European Economy, 1400–1800* (Cambridge, 2008). In the countryside the move to proto-industrialization, once regarded as an early modern development, is now seen as an important trend in the fourteenth and fifteenth centuries, as set out in S. R. Epstein, *Freedom and Growth: The Rise of States and Markets in Europe, 1300–1750* (London, 2000). Rural industry, in cloth-making and metal-working particularly, was important in England, but the term 'proto-industrialization' is not applied by historians. Rural industries tended not discriminate by gender or age in their employment of workers, and a growing number of women were hired in both town and country: T. de Moor and J. L. van Zanden, 'Girl Power: the European Marriage Pattern and Labour Market in the North Sea Region', *Economic History Review* 63 (2010), pp. 1–33.

A traditional view of the period after the Black Death (1347–50), and in particular between about 1400 and 1470, has emphasized the elements of recession and stagnation. This has been questioned in general terms, and 'the economic depression of the Renaissance' is no longer seen as a valid generalization about Italy's economic history (P. Malanima, 'Italy in the Renaissance: A Leading Economy in the European Context, 1350–1550', *Economic History Review* 71 (2018), pp. 3–30). A striking trend which contradicts negative assessments comes from technical innovations, such as R. W. Unger, *The Ship in the Medieval Economy 600–1600* (London, 1980); and the same author's *A History of Brewing in Holland 900–1900* (London, 2001). The period's reputation for economic depression has been applied to urban life, but although many towns diminished in size, it does not mean that they became poor and unimportant. The countryside lost people also, so the proportion of townspeople did not diminish, as argued in D. Nicholas, *The Later Medieval City, 1300–1500* (London, 1997). Great cities catered for the luxury tastes of very rich consumers, as argued in P. Spufford, *Power and Profit: The Merchant in Medieval Europe* (Cambridge, 2003). At the lower end of the urban hierarchy the smaller market towns maintained their relationship with country people, and sometimes expanded, as shown in regional examples in S. R. Epstein (ed.), *Town and Country in Europe, 1300–1800* (Cambridge, 2001). The town–country connection could be so close and so dynamic that we should study regions and see the urban and rural economies as functioning together, which could result in new growth: S. R. Epstein, *An Island for Itself: Economic Development and Social Change in Late Medieval Sicily* (Cambridge, 1992); T. Scott, *Regional Identity and Economic Change: The Upper Rhine, 1450–1600* (Oxford, 1997); B. van Bavel, *Manors and Markets: Economy and Society in the Low Countries, 500–1600* (Oxford, 2010).

Features of the period were new commercial methods, the introduction of commodities not previously traded and the forging of trading relationships. For example, gold replaced silver as the principal means of exchange: see P. Spufford, *Money and its Use in Medieval Europe* (Cambridge, 1988). Paper money could be employed instead of coins, as shown in M. Allen and N. Mayhew (eds), *Money and its Use in Medieval Europe: Three Decades On* (London, 2017). The supply of money has sometimes been portrayed as an independent variable, a fluctuating flow of precious metals acting as a stimulus or constraint on trade, but its production was an act of policy, as is outlined in C. Desan, *Making Money: Coins, Currency and the Coming of Capitalism* (Oxford, 2015). Trade could be conducted on the basis of trust and verbal promises, backed up by juries of merchants, as happened in the Baltic according to M. Kallioinen, 'Intercommunal Institutions in Medieval Trade', *Economic History Review* 70 (2017), pp. 1131–52. Old trading patterns changed, as discussed in E. Ashtor, *Levant Trade in the Later Middle Ages* (Princeton, NJ, 1983), and new ventures included the import and weaving of cotton: M. Mazzaoui, *The Italian Cotton Industry in the Later Middle Ages* (Cambridge, 1981). Did these changes lead to the rise of capitalism? The old question is given a gender dimension in M. Howell, *Commerce before Capitalism in Europe, 1300–1600* (Cambridge, 2010). Many books deal with aspects of economic thought, or the morality of commerce. The most straightforward introduction is D. Wood, *Medieval Economic Thought* (Cambridge, 2002).

   To the final considerations by Christopher Dyer the following titles must be added as reference: B. van Bavel, *The Invisible Hand? How Market Economies Have Emerged and Declined since AD 500* (Oxford, 2016); S. Ogilvie, *Institutions and European Trade: Merchant Guilds, 1000–1800* (Cambridge, 2011); A. B. Leonard, *Marine Insurance: Origins and Institutions, 1300–1850* (Basingstoke, 2016); T. de Moor, *The Dilemma of the Commoners: Understanding the Use of Common Pool Resources in Long-Term Perspective* (Cambridge, 2015); S. Broadberry et al., *British Economic Growth, 1270–1870* (Cambridge, 2015); G. Alfani and F. Ammannati, 'Long-Term Trends in Economic Inequality: The Case of the Florentine State, *c.*1300–1800', *Economic History Review* 70 (2017), pp. 1072–1102 ; B. Van Bavel and A. Rijpma, 'How Important were Formalized Charity and Social Spending before the Rise of the Welfare State? A Long Run Analysis of Selected Western European Cases, 1400–1850', *Economic History Review* 69 (2016), pp. 159–87; P. Freedman, *Out of the East: Spices and the European Imagination* (New Haven, CT, 2008); L. To Figueras, 'Wedding Trousseaus and Cloth Consumption in Catalonia around 1300', *Economic History Review* 69 (2016), pp. 522–47; T. Lange, *Excommunication for Debt in Late Medieval France: The Business of Salvation* (Cambridge, 2016); R. Hoffman, *An Environmental History of Medieval Europe* (Cambridge, 2014); E. Thoen and T. Soens (eds), *Struggling with the Environment: Land Use and Productivity* (Turnhout, 2015).

The church and religious life (Chapter 3)

The constant torrent of relevant books and articles means that a short list of further reading cannot address all aspects of the development of the church and religious life across the period. That is especially the case if the list is confined to material in English, which is often surprisingly patchy, with significant gaps in both general surveys and in more specialized treatments—including now among the latter articles often hidden in thematic volumes of essays labelled as *Companion*, *Handbook*, or

Introduction to their topic. F. Oakley, *The Western Church in the Later Middle Ages* (Ithaca, NY, 1979) offers an overview of most of the major points, and can be supplemented by several articles in the relevant volumes of the New Cambridge Medieval History. Vol. 6 (on the fourteenth century, ed. M. Jones, 2000) contains J. Catto, 'Currents of Religious Thought and Expression'; P. N. R. Zutshi, 'The Avignon Papacy'; and H. Kaminsky, 'The Great Schism'. Vol. 7 (on the fifteenth century, ed. C. Allmand, 1999) contains A. Black, 'Popes and Councils'; F. Rapp, 'Religious Belief and Practice'; J. Klassen, 'Hus, the Hussites and Bohemia'; and A. Ryder, 'The Papal States and the Kingdom of Naples'. A major examination of the fifteenth century is provided in J. van Engen, 'Multiple Options: The World of the Fifteenth-Century Church', *Church History* 77 (2008), pp. 257–84.

The history of the fourteenth-century papacy is relatively well covered, but the fifteenth has attracted little attention. G. Mollat, *The Popes at Avignon, 1305–1378* (Edinburgh, 1963), provides a serviceable discussion of the Avignon period, while useful biographies in English are available for two of the popes: S. Menache, *Clement V* (Cambridge, 1998) and D. Wood, *Clement VI: The Pontificate and Ideas of an Avignon Pope* (Cambridge, 1989). The challenge of a full analysis of the pontificate of John XXII, arguably the century's most important pope, remains unaddressed; his administrative reforms are treated in J. E. Weakland, 'Administrative and Fiscal Centralisation under Pope John XXII, 1316–1334', *Catholic History Review* 54 (1968), pp. 285–310.

For the years after 1378, coverage is less effective, with the Schism still lacking a full outline in English. The gap is partially filled by J. Rollo-Koster and T. M. Izbicki (eds), *A Companion to the Great Western Schism (1378–1417)* (Leiden, 2009). More broadly, C. M. D. Crowder (ed.), *Unity, Heresy and Reform 1378–1460: The Conciliar Response to the Great Schism* (London, 1977) offers a general outline, supported by translations of key documents. Constance is tackled in P. H. Stump, *The Reforms of the Council of Constance (1414–1418)* (Leiden, 1994); for Basle, a valuable perspective is provided in J. W. Steiber, *Pope Eugenius IV, the Council of Basel, and the Secular and Ecclesiastical Authorities in the Empire: The Conflict over Supreme Authority and Power in the Church* (Leiden, 1978); while A. Black gives a general discussion of late conciliarism in *Monarchy and Community: Political Ideas in the Late Conciliar Controversy, 1430–1450* (Cambridge, 1970). For the council which reunited the eastern and western churches in 1439, see J. Gill, *The Council of Florence* (Cambridge, 1959).

Key aspects of the relationship between the papacy and secular rulers are examined in J. A. F. Thomson, *Popes and Princes: Politics and Polity in the Late Medieval Church* (London, 1980); how those tensions evolved in England, over a longer period and in a broader context, is chronicled in P. Heath, *Church and Realm 1272–1461* (London, 1988). More exclusively focused on relations between England and the papacy are W. E. Lunt, *Financial Relations of the Papacy with England, 1327–1534* (Cambridge, MA, 1962); M. Harvey, *England, Rome, and the Papacy, 1417–1464: The Study of a Relationship* (Manchester, 1993); and now B. Bombi, *Anglo-Papal Relations in the Early Fourteenth Century: A Study in Medieval Diplomacy* (Oxford, 2019). The evolution of the papal principality in Italy is covered in the relevant sections of P. Partner, *The Lands of St Peter: The Papal State in the Middle Ages and the Early Renaissance* (London, 1972); he offers a more detailed examination of the immediate aftermath of the Great Schism in *The Papal State under Martin V* (London, 1958).

For generations, the main introduction to the late medieval world and its spirituality was Johann Huizinga, *The Waning of the Middle Ages* (first published in English 1924, numerous editions). A new translation, as *The Autumn of the Middle Ages* (Chicago, 1996), received mixed reviews. Recent expanding interest in late medieval spirituality has challenged Huizinga's approach, but his book remains readable. As a general survey, see R. N. Swanson, *Religion and Devotion in Europe, c.1215–c.1515* (Cambridge, 1995). Jill Raitt (ed.), *Christian Spirituality, II: High Middle Ages and Reformation* (London, 1987) contains a useful collection of essays. The first half of E. Duffy, *The Stripping of the Altars: Traditional Religion in England, 1400–1580*, 2nd edn (New Haven, CT, 2005) is a magisterial survey of how religion was experienced and performed among English catholics in the late pre-Reformation century. An increasing range of works cover other facets of the period's religion and spirituality, making selection problematic. On sainthood, R. Bartlett, *Why Can the Dead Do Such Great Things? Saints and Worshippers from the Martyrs to the Reformation* (Princeton, NJ, 2013) includes the period within its wider coverage. More detailed, and period-specific, is A. Vauchez, *Sainthood in the Later Middle Ages* (Cambridge, 1997), with A. M. Kleinberg giving a useful complement in *Prophets in Their Own Country: Living Saints and the Making of Sainthood in the Later Middle Ages* (Chicago, 1992). Preaching tends to generate regional surveys, with differing concerns, as in C. L. Polecritti, *Preaching Peace in Renaissance Italy: Bernardino of Siena and his Audience* (Washington, DC, 2000); L. Taylor, *Soldiers of Christ: Preaching in Late Medieval and Reformation France* (Oxford, 1992); and H. Leith Spencer, *English Preaching in the Late Middle Ages* (Oxford, 1993). For excellent illustrated discussions of devotional art, see J. H. Marrow, *Passion Iconography in Northern European Art of the Late Middle Ages and Early Renaissance: A Study of the Transformation of Sacred Metaphor into Descriptive Narrative* (Kortrijk, 1979), and H. van Os, *The Art of Devotion in the Late Middle Ages in Europe, 1300–1500* (Princeton, NJ, 1994). An intriguing analysis of the visual character of spirituality in a specific context is offered in J. F. Hamburger, *Nuns as Artists: The Visual Culture of a Medieval Convent* (London, 1997). For a wide-ranging discussion of pilgrimage, see J. Sumption, *Pilgrimage: An Image of Mediaeval Religion* (London, 1975); D. Webb, *Pilgrims and Pilgrimage in the Medieval West* (London, 1991) is shorter, with translated documents. Also worth mentioning here are P. Binski, *Medieval Death: Ritual and Representation* (London, 1996); M. Rubin, *Corpus Christi: The Eucharist in Late Medieval Culture* (Cambridge, 1991); S. K. Cohn, Jr, *The Cult of Remembrance and the Black Death: Six Renaissance Cities in Central Italy* (Baltimore, MD, 1992); P. Szarmach (ed.), *An Introduction to the Medieval Mystics of Europe* (Albany, NY, 1984); T. Verdon and J. Henderson (eds), *Christianity and the Renaissance: Image and Religious Inspiration in the Quattrocento* (Syracuse, NY, 1990); and C. Walker Bynum, *Christian Materiality: an Essay on Religion in Late Medieval Europe* (New York, 2011). Anticlericalism receives attention (but not full dissection) in

236   FURTHER READING

P. A. Dykema and H. A. Oberman (eds), *Anticlericalism in Late Medieval and Early Modern Europe* (Leiden, 1993).

Work on the religious orders is often specialist or specific, or lacks a 'period' focus (see e.g. E. Jamroziak, *The Cistercian Order in Medieval Europe, 1090–1500*, London, 2013), without generating a general overview for the late Middle Ages. The Franciscans and their turmoils attract considerable attention, their history outlined in J. R. H. Moorman, *A History of the Franciscan Order from its Origins to the Year 1517* (Oxford, 1968), or D. Nimmo, *Reform and Division in the Medieval Franciscan Order: From St Francis to the Foundation of the Capuchins* (Rome, 1987). The Spiritual Franciscans continue to torment historians, being usefully examined in D. Burr, *The Spiritual Franciscans: From Protest to Persecution in the Century after St Francis* (University Park, PA, 2001). Hostility to the friars is examined in G. Geltner, *The Making of Medieval Antifraternalism: Polemic, Violence, Deviance, and Remembrance* (Oxford, 2012). The hitherto understudied Observant tradition has begun to attract attention, with a useful collection of essays in J. D. Mixson and B. Roest (eds), *A Companion to Observant Reform in the Late Middle Ages and Beyond* (Leiden, 2015). Among lay spiritual movements, the *devotio moderna* receives detailed consideration in J. van Engen, *Sisters and Brothers of the Common Life: the* Devotio Moderna *and the World of the Later Middle Ages* (Philadelphia, PA, 2008); his earlier Devotio Moderna: *Basic Writings* (New York, 1998) offers a compact introduction and translated texts. See also W. Scheepsma, *Medieval Religious Women in the Low Countries: The Modern Devotion, the Canonesses of Windesheim, and Their Writings* (Woodbridge, 2004).

Intellectual history has been approached from varied angles. Theological developments, and the weakening of the intellectual consensus, are considered in two volumes of J. Pelikan, *The Christian Tradition: A History of the Development of Doctrine*: vol. 3, *The Growth of Medieval Theology (600–1300)* (Chicago, 1978), and vol. 4, *The Reformation of Church and Dogma (1300–1700)* (Chicago, 1984); and from a different perspective in A. McGrath, *The Intellectual Origins of the European Reformation*, 2nd edn (Oxford, 2008). Political ideas are usefully covered in essays in J. H. Burns (ed.), *The Cambridge History of Medieval Political Thought, c.350–c.1450* (Cambridge, 1988), and surveyed in A. Black, *Political Thought in Europe, 1250–1450* (Cambridge, 1992). For the universities, the articles in H. de Ridder-Symoens (ed.), *A History of the University in Europe*, vol. 1: *Universities in the Middle Ages* (Cambridge, 1992) are a valuable springboard. A good readable view of the general intellectual milieu is provided in J. Verger, *Men of Learning in Europe at the End of the Middle Ages* (Notre Dame, IN, 2000). While rather heavy going, the two volumes of C. Trinkaus, *'In Our Image and Likeness': Humanity and Divinity in Italian Humanist Thought* (London, 1970), provide an important analysis of the Christian elements in humanism.

The turbulence in recent work on earlier heresy and dissent has not significantly disrupted scholarship on this period, where the boundaries between heresy and orthodoxy have always appeared less rigid. M. Lambert, *Medieval Heresy: Popular Movements from the Gregorian Reform to the Reformation*, 3rd edn (Oxford, 2002) offers a good foundational survey, now outdated in places. Being even older, G. Leff,

Medieval Heresy (2 vols, Manchester, 1968) must be used with caution, but is more detailed and has greater emphasis on individuals (including William of Ockham). The classic treatment of heresy in its social setting is E. Le Roy Ladurie, *Montaillou: Cathars and Catholics in a French village, 1294–1324* (Harmondsworth, 1980). Work on specific heresies varies. The last years of Catharism are considered in J. B. Given, *Inquisition and Medieval Society: Power, Discipline and Resistance in Languedoc* (Ithaca, NY, 1997). For Hussitism, the key work in English—although chronologically limited—is H. Kaminsky, *A History of the Hussite Revolution* (Berkeley, CA, 1967). A lively discussion of the movement's popular side is offered in T. A. Fudge, *The Magnificent Ride: The First Reformation in Hussite Bohemia* (Aldershot, 1998).

Lollardy in England attracts attention and provokes debate in equal measure. Despite its age, K. B. McFarlane, *Wycliffe and English Nonconformity* (Harmondsworth, 1972) remains a useful introduction to the early years, and to Wyclif and his ideas. Current approaches to Wyclif are revealed in S. E. Kahey, *John Wyclif* (Oxford, 2009), and I. C. Levy (ed.), *A Companion to John Wyclif: Late Medieval Theologian* (Leiden, 2006). The main survey of later events and persecution remains J. A. F. Thomson, *The Later Lollards, 1414–1520* (Oxford, 1965). Lollard writings and ideas are covered exhaustively and expertly in A. Hudson, *The Premature Reformation: Wycliffite Texts and Lollard History* (Oxford, 1988), although some aspects of the analysis are not universally accepted. A robust challenge to Hudson's approach (also not universally accepted) appears in R. Rex, *The Lollards* (Basingstoke, 2002). More recent evolutions in the scholarship are covered in J. Patrick Hornbeck II (with M. Bose and F. Somerset), *A Companion to Lollardy* (Leiden, 2016).

Other strands in the history of late medieval heresy are considered in R. Kieckhefer, *The Repression of Heresy in Medieval Germany* (Liverpool, 1979) and R. E. Lerner, *The Heresy of the Free Spirit in the Later Middle Ages* (Berkeley, CA, 1972). Waldensianism is surveyed in E. Cameron, *Waldenses: Rejections of Holy Church in Medieval Europe* (Oxford, 2001). For the growing concern with witchcraft, see R. Kieckhefer, *European Witch Trials: Their Foundations in Popular and Learned Culture, 1300–1500* (London, 1976); also M. D. Bailey, *Battling Demons: Witchcraft, Heresy, and Reform in the Late Middle Ages* (University Park, PA, 2003). The history and experiences of the Jews in Christian Europe are dealt with exhaustively in vols 9–13 of S. W. Baron, *A Social and Religious History of the Jews*, 2nd edn (New York, 1966). M. Rubin, *Gentile Tales: The Narrative Assault on Late Medieval Jews* (New Haven, CT, 1999) offers a valuable and powerful analysis of anti-Jewish activity in the period; also valuable, despite its close focus, is R. Po-Chia Hsia, *Trent 1475: Stories of a Ritual Murder Trial* (New Haven, CT, 1992). The specific Spanish situation is covered in vol. 2 of Y. Baer, *History of the Jews in Christian Spain* (Philadelphia, PA, 1961), and in B. Netanyahu's massive *The Origins of the Inquisition in Fifteenth-Century Spain*, 2nd edn (New York, 2001). Newer scholarship has begun a seismic shift in approach: see J. Elukin, *Living Together, Living Apart: Rethinking Jewish–Christian Relations in the Middle Ages* (Princeton, NJ, 2007); R. Chazan, *Reassessing Jewish Life in Medieval Europe* (Cambridge, 2010).

The church's attitude to the world beyond catholic Europe is analysed in J. Muldoon, *Popes, Lawyers, and Infidels: The Church and the Non-Christian*

World, 1250–1550 (Phildelphia, PA, 1979). For crusading, the main survey is
N. Housley, *The Later Crusades: From Lyons to Alcazar, 1274–1580* (Oxford,
1992). The use of military violence to resolve Europe's internal religious tensions is
also addressed in his *Religious Warfare in Europe 1400–1536* (Oxford, 2002).

Culture and the arts (Chapter 4)

Historical conceptions of fourteenth- and fifteenth-century European culture have
long been overshadowed by J. Burckhardt, *The Civilization of the Renaissance in
Italy*, trans. S. G. C. Middlemore (London, 1995). Burckhardt's distinction between
Italy and the rest of Europe is developed further in J. Huizinga, *Autumn of the Middle
Ages*, trans. R. J. Payton and U. Mammitzsch (Chicago, 1995) and E. Panofsky,
Renaissance and Renascences in Western Art (Stockholm, 1960). For later challenges
to this paradigm, see e.g. P. Burke, *The European Renaissance* (Oxford, 1998).

For the development of literacy, the best places to begin are the four articles on
'Education in the Renaissance and Reformation' in *Renaissance Quarterly* 43 (1990);
for its antecedents, see the pioneering book by M. Clanchy, *From Memory to Written
Record: England 1066–1307* (Oxford, 1979). On education in Italy, see P. F. Grendler,
Schooling in Renaissance Italy: Literacy and Learning, 1300–1600 (Baltimore, MD,
1989) and, for Tuscany, R. Black, *Education and Society in Florentine Tuscany:
Teachers, Pupils, and Schools, c.1250–1500* (Leiden, 2007); on rural literacy,
D. Balestracci, *The Renaissance in the Fields: Family Memoirs of a Fifteenth-
Century Tuscan Peasant* (University Park, PA, 1999). On education in England, see
N. Orme, *Medieval Schools: From Roman Britain to Renaissance England*, rev. edn
(New Haven, CT, 2006). On the German lands, a good introduction is provided by
D. L. Sheffler, *Schools and Schooling in Late Medieval Germany: Regensburg,
1250–1500* (Leiden, 2008). The greatest among the literary 'crowns' of the fourteenth
century—from Dante to Chaucer—are far too big a subject to be approached here:
nonetheless, useful introductions could be found in the *Cambridge Companions*
devoted to Dante (ed. R. Jacoff, 2007) and to Boccaccio (ed. G. Armstrong,
R. Daniels, and S. J. Milner, 2015), and D. Gray (ed.), *The Oxford Companion to
Chaucer* (Oxford, 2003). On Petrarch, see N. Mann, *Petrarch* (Oxford, 1984);
V. Kirkham and A. Maggi (eds), *Petrarch: A Critical Guide to the Complete Works*
(Chicago, 2009).

Any serious study of humanism should begin with R. G. Witt, *In the Footsteps of
the Ancients: The Origins of Humanism from Lovato to Bruni* (Leiden, 2000), which
argues convincingly that the new learning arose out of grammar and not—as had
previously been assumed—out of rhetoric: see also Ronald Witt's last book on the
medieval origins of humanism, *The Two Latin Cultures and the Foundation of
Renaissance Humanism in Medieval Italy* (Cambridge, 2012). For the view that
humanism had two points of origin rather than one, see R. Weiss, *The Dawn of
Humanism in Italy* (London, 1947). A pioneering essay on the relationships between
humanism and the arts is M. Baxandall, *Giotto and the Orators: Humanist Observers
of Painting in Italy and the Discovery of Pictorial Composition* (Oxford, 1971); an

interesting point of view in C. Celenza, *The Lost Italian Renaissance: Humanists, Historians, and Latin Legacy* (Baltimore, MD, 2004). Important essays can be found in J. Kraye (ed.), *The Cambridge Companion to Renaissance Humanism* (Cambridge, 1996) and A. Rabil, Jr (ed.), *Renaissance Humanism: Foundations, Forms, and Legacy*, 3 vols (Philadelphia, 1988). H. Baron, *The Crisis of Early Italian Renaissance: Civic Humanism and Republican Liberty in an Age of Classicism and Tyranny* (Princeton, NJ, 1960) remains a pivotal text on humanism and republicanism; Baron's work, among others, paved the way for the now classical studies of Pocock and Skinner on the roots of liberalism in the West: J. G. A. Pocock, *The Machiavellian Moment: Florentine Political Thought and the Atlantic Republican Tradition* (Princeton, NJ, 1975); Q. Skinner, *The Foundations of Modern Political Thought*, vol. 1: *The Renaissance* (Cambridge, 1978). For a critical revision of Baron's theories, see J. Hankins (ed.), *Renaissance Civic Humanism: Reappraisals and Reflections* (Cambridge, 2000) and more recently N. S. Baker and B. J. Maxson (eds), *After Civic Humanism: Learning and Politics in Renaissance Italy* (Toronto, 2015); A. Lee, *Humanism and Empire: The Imperial Ideal in Fourteenth-Century Italy* (Oxford, 2018). On the political and juridical thought, a first introduction is provided by J. H. Burns (ed.), *The Cambridge History of Political Thought, c.350–1450* (Cambridge, 1988) and by A. Black, *Political Thought in Europe, 1250–1450* (Cambridge, 1992); valuable points of view can be found in M. Kempshall, *The Common Good in Late Medieval Political Thought* (Oxford, 1999) and J. P. Canning, *Ideas of Power in the Late Middle Ages, 1296–1417* (Cambridge, 2011); on Marsilius of Padua, see G. Garnett, *Marsilius of Padua and 'The Truth of History'* (Oxford, 2006); on Bartolus of Saxoferrato, D. Quaglioni, *Politica e diritto nel Trecento italiano. Il 'De Tyranno' di Bartolo da Sassoferrato (1314–1357)*, with the edition of the treatise (Florence, 1983).

On architecture, a valuable overview can be found in P. Frankl, *Gothic Architecture*, rev. P. Crossley (Yale, CT, 2001). The standard works on England are P. Binsky, *Westminster Abbey and the Plantagenets: Kingship and the Representation of Power 1200–1400* (New Haven, CT, 1995); *Gothic Wonder: Art, Artifice and the Decorated Style 1290–1350* (New Haven, CT, 2014); and J. H. Harvey, *The Perpendicular Style, 1330–1485* (London, 1978). On Germany, a useful overview is provided by N. Nussbaum, *German Gothic Church Architecture*, trans. S. Kleager (New Haven, CT, 2000). On Peter Parler and Charles IV's reconstruction of Prague, see K. Benešovská and I. Hlobil, *Peter Parler and St. Vitus's Cathedral, 1356–1399* (Prague, 1999) and B. Drake Boehm and J. Fajt (eds), *Prague: The Crown of Bohemia, 1347–1437* (New Haven, CT, 2005). On Italy, see e.g. J. A. Ackerman, '*Ars sine scientia nihil est*: Gothic Theory of Architecture at the Cathedral of Milan', *Art Bulletin* 31(2) (1949), pp. 84–111; R. Goldthwaite, *The Building of Renaissance Florence* (Baltimore, MD, 1980); M. Tafuri, *Interpreting the Renaissance: Princes, Cities, Architects* [1992] (New Haven, CT, 2006).

On the visual arts, valuable discussions of the impact of socioeconomic change in Italy can be found in M. Baxandall, *Painting and Experience in Fifteenth-Century Italy*, 2nd edn (Oxford, 1988); B. Klempers, *Painting, Power and Patronage: The Rise of the Professional Artist in Renaissance Italy*, trans. B. Jackson (London, 1987);

M. Hollingsworth, *Patronage in Renaissance Italy: From 1400 to the Early Sixteenth Century* (London, 1994). On Italian stylistic changes, see E. Welch, *Art and Society in Italy, 1350–1500* (Oxford, 1997) and J. Pope-Hennessy, *Italian Renaissance Sculpture* (London, 1971). M. Meiss, *Painting in Florence and Siena after the Black Death* (Princeton, NJ, 1971) controversially attributes a decisive impact to the plague; on the less-than-communal origins of the Buongoverno's frescoes in Siena, see R. M. Dessì, *Les spectres du Bon Gouvernement d'Ambrogio Lorenzetti. Artistes, cités communales et seigneurs angevins au* Trecento (Paris, 2017). E. Panofsky, *Early Netherlandish Painting*, 2 vols (Cambridge, MA, 1953) is still a classic; but J. Chipps Smith, *The Northern Renaissance* (London, 2004) presents an up-to-date overview of recent research.

Helpful introductions to the history of music in this period include R. Strohm, *The Rise of European Music, 1380–1500* (Cambridge, 1993) and I. Fenlon (ed.), *Music in Medieval and Early Modern Europe* (Cambridge, 1991). On the *ars nova*, see D. Leech-Wilkinson, 'The Emergence of *ars nova*', *Journal of Musicology* 13(3) (1995), pp. 285–317. A recent challenge to received views is provided by K. Desmond, *Music and the moderni, 1300–1350: The* ars nova *in Theory and Practice* (Cambridge, 2018). D. Fallows, 'The *contenance angloise*: English Influence on Continental Composers of the Fifteenth Century', *Renaissance Studies* 1 (1987), pp. 189–208, presents a good introduction to the impact of John Dunstaple and his circle. On printing, the best starting points are E. Eisenstein, *The Printing Press as an Agent of Change*, 2 vols (Cambridge, 1979); *The Printing Revolution in Early Modern Europe* (Cambridge, 1983); and H. Lebvre and H.-J. Martin, *The Coming of the Book: The Impact of Printing, 1450–1800*, trans. D. Gerard, ed. G. Nowell-Smith and D. Wooton (London, 1984). For more focused studies of leading printers, see M. Lowry, *The World of Aldus Manutius* (Oxford, 1979); *Nicholas Jenson and the Rise of Venetian Publishing in Renaissance Europe* (Oxford, 1991).

Space, time, and the world (Chapter 5)

This is a deliberately synthetic chapter on subjects which have been treated in a wide range of overviews and specialist studies, each with their own extensive bibliographies. What follow are therefore selective suggestions for further reading in English.

For the science underpinning conceptions of both space and time, see D. C. Lindberg (ed.), *Science in the Middle Ages* (Chicago, 1978); D. Lindberg and M. Shank (eds), *The Cambridge History of Science*, vol. 2: *Medieval Science* (Cambridge, 2013). An essential starting-point is the classical material on which this science was itself based, both integral individual works and late antique or early medieval digests. For surveys of such material, see E. Grant, *A Source Book in Medieval Science* (Cambridge, MA, 1974); J. E. Murdoch, *Album of Science: Antiquity and the Middle Ages* (New York, 1984). For individual sources, see J. Barnes (ed.), *The Complete Works of Aristotle: The Revised Oxford Translation*, 2 vols (Princeton, NJ, 1984); Ptolemy, *Almagest*, trans. G. J. Toomer (London, 1984); Ptolemy, *Geography*, trans. J. L. Berggren and A. Jones, in *Ptolemy's Geography: An*

Annotated Translation of the Theoretical Chapters (Princeton, NJ, 2000); Pliny, *Natural History*, trans. H. Rackham (Cambridge, MA, 1938); Macrobius, *Commentary on the Dream of Scipio*, trans. W. H. Stahl (New York, 1952); Martianus Capella, *The Marriage of Philology and Mercury*, trans.W. H. Stahl (New York, 1977); Isidore of Seville, *De Natura Rerum*, trans. C. B. Kendall and F. T. Wallis, *On the Nature of Things* (Liverpool, 2016); Bede, *De Temporum Ratione*, trans. F. T. Wallis, in *The Reckoning of Time* (Liverpool, 1999); Bede, *De Natura Rerum* and *De Temporibus*, trans. C. B. Kendall and F. T. Wallis, in *On the Nature of Things* and *On Times* (Liverpool, 2010). For an example of what this material could then produce, see *The Calendar and the Cloister: Oxford, St John's College MS 17*, digital.library.mcgill.ca/MS-17. For later medieval sources, see Albertus Magnus, *De Natura Locorum*, trans. J. P. Tillmann in *An Appraisal of the Geographical Works of Albertus Magnus* (Ann Arbor, MI, 1971); Albertus Magnus, *Speculum Astonomiae*, trans. P. Zambelli, in *The Speculum Astronomiae and its Enigma: Astrology, Theology and Science in Albertus Magnus and his Contemporaries* (Boston, MA, 1992); Campanus of Novara, *Theorica Planetarum*, ed. and trans. F. S. Benjamin and G. J. Toomer, *Campanus of Novara and Medieval Planetary Theory* (Wisconsin, MI, 1971); Robert Kilwardby, *On Time*, trans. A. Broadie (Oxford, 1993). For John of Sacrobosco (and Robertus Anglicus), see L. Thorndike, *The Sphere of Sacrobosco and its Commentators* (Chicago, 1949). For Bartolomeus Anglicus, see M. C. Seymour et al. (eds), *Bartolomeus Anglicus and his Encyclopaedia* (London, 1992) and, in French translation, *De Proprietatibus Rerum*, trans. B. Ribemont, *Le Livre des Propriétés des Choses* (Paris, 1999). Also in French, see Nicole Oresme, *Le Livre du ciel et du monde*, ed. and trans. A. D. Menut and A. J. Denomy (Wisconsin, MI, 1968); Pierre d'Ailly, *Ymago Mundi*, ed. and trans. E. Buron (Paris, 1930).

For surveys of medieval maps, see J. B. Harley and D. Woodward (eds), *Cartography in Prehistoric, Ancient and Medieval Europe and the Mediterranean* (Chicago, 1987); E. Edson, *Mapping Time and Space: How Medieval Mapmakers Viewed their World* (London, 1997); E. Edson and E. Savage-Smith, *Medieval Views of the Cosmos* (Oxford, 2004); R. Talbert and R. W. Unger (eds), *Cartography in Antiquity and the Middle Ages: Fresh Perspectives, New Methods* (Leiden, 2008). In French, see above all the work of P. Gautier Dalché, *La Géographie de Ptolémée en Occident (IVe–XVIe siècle)* (Turnhout, 2009); *L'espace géographique au Moyen Âge* (Florence, 2013); *La Terre. Connaissance, représentations, mesure au Moyen Âge* (Turnhout, 2013).

For individual maps, see hereford.digitalmappa.org, with N. R. Kline, *Maps of Medieval Thought: The Hereford Paradigm* (Woodbridge, 2001); www.landschaftsmuseum.de/Seiten/Museen/Ebstorf1.htm, with H. Kugler, *Die Ebstorf Weltkarte, Kommentierte Neuausgabe in 2 Bänden* (Berlin, 2007); www.bl.uk/medieval-literature/collection-items (Pietro Vesconte; Matthew Paris); www.goughmap.org; G. Grosjean (ed.), *Mappamundi: The Catalan Atlas for the Year 1375* (Zurich, 1978).

For geographical discoveries to which these maps were responding, see J. R. S. Phillips, *The Medieval Expansion of Europe*, 2nd edn (Oxford, 1998); S. Westrem (ed.), *Discovering New Worlds: Essays on Medieval Exploration and*

Imagination (New York, 1991); J. B. Friedman and K. Mossler Figg (eds), *Trade, Travel and Exploration in the Middle Ages: An Encyclopaedia* (Routledge, 2000). For their influence, see G. Ferro, *The Genoese Cartographic Tradition and Christopher Columbus* (Rome, 1996); V. Flint, *The Imaginative Landscape of Christopher Columbus* (Princeton, NJ, 1992).

For surveys of time, see A. Borst, *The Ordering of Time: From the Ancient Computus to the Modern Computer* (Cambridge, 1993); G. Dohrn-van Rossum, *History of the Hour: Clocks and Modern Temporal Orders* (Chicago, 1996); G. Jaritz and G. Moreno-Riaño (eds), *Time and Eternity: The Medieval Discourse* (Turnhout, 2003). In French, see B. Ribemont (ed.), *Le Temps, sa mesure et sa perception au Moyen Âge* (Caen, 1992). For the calendar, see E. G. Richards, *Mapping Time: The Calendar and its History* (Oxford, 1998), with T. Perez-Higuera, *Medieval Calendars* (London, 1998). For books of hours, see R. S. Wieck, *Time Sanctified: The Book of Hours in Medieval Art and Life* (New York, 1988), with *Les Tres Riches Heures du Duc de Berry*, ed. J. Longon and R. Cazelles (London, 1969).

For specific cultural and technical aspects of time, see C. Humphrey and W. M. Ormrod (eds), *Time in the Medieval World* (Woodbridge, 2001); J. Le Goff, 'Merchant's Time and Church's Time in the Middle Ages', in *Time Work and Culture in the Middle Ages* (Chicago, 1980); A. Gell, *The Anthropology of Time. Cultural Constructions of Temporal Maps and Images* (Berg, 1992); S. A. Bedini and F. R. Maddison, 'Mechanical Universe: The Astrarium of Giovanni de' Dondi', *Transactions of the American Philosophical Society* 56 (1966), pp. 1–69; J. D. North, *God's Clockmaker: Richard of Wallingford and the Invention of Time* (London, 2005). For scholastic conceptualization, see R. C. Dales, *Medieval Discussions of the Eternity of the World* (Leiden, 1999); P. Porro (ed.), *The Medieval Concept of Time: Studies on the Scholastic Debate and its Reception in Early Modern Philosophy* (Leiden, 2001). The propositions condemned in 1277 are translated by E. Fortin and P. O'Neill, 'Condemnation of 219 propositions', in R. Lerner and M. Mahdi (eds), *Medieval Political Philosophy: A Sourcebook* (Toronto, 1963); for their impact, see E. Grant, 'The Effect of the Condemnation of 1277', in N. Kretzmann, A. Kenny, and J. Pinborg (eds), *The Cambridge History of Later Medieval Philosophy* (Cambridge, 1982), pp. 537–9. For eschatology, see B. McGinn (ed.), *Visions of the End: Apocalyptic Traditions in the Middle Ages* (New York, 1979) and, for astrology, J. D. North, 'Medieval Concepts of Celestial Influence: A Survey', in P. Curry (ed.), *Astrology, Science and Society* (Woodbridge, 1987), pp. 5–19; L. A. Smoller, *History, Prophecy and the Stars: The Christian Astrology of Pierre d'Ailly* (Princeton, NJ, 1994).

For art-historical perspectives on both subjects, see J. B. Friedman, *The Monstrous Races in Medieval Art and Thought* (Cambridge, MA, 1981); M. Camille, 'New Visions of Time', in *Gothic Art: Visions and Revelations of the Medieval World* (London, 1996), pp. 71–102; L. Andrews, *Story and Space in Renaissance Art: The Rebirth of Continuous Narrative* (Cambridge, 1998); S. Cohen, *Transformations of Time and Temporality in Medieval Art* (Leiden, 2014).

Society, family, and gender (Chapter 6)

The study of gender in this period is a vibrant area of ongoing research, with a rich bibliography to match. For a foundational overview, the work of M. E. Wiesner-Hanks is indispensable. See e.g. her *Women and Gender in Early Modern Europe* (Cambridge, 2000), as well as the collection of essays in T. A. Meade and M. E. Wiesner-Hanks, *A Companion to Gender History* (Malden, MA, 2004). The latter is particularly useful as an overview of recent approaches in the field, as its chronological and geographical remit is global rather than eurocentric. Wiesner-Hanks also provided the introductory essay to the excellent collection of essays edited by M. Cassidy-Welch and P. Sherlock, *Practices of Gender in Late Medieval and Early Modern Europe* (Turnhout, 2011), in which the enactment of gender is the focus. Two seminal edited collections are those edited by J. Bennett and R. Mazo Karras, *The Oxford Handbook of Women and Gender in Medieval Europe* (Oxford, 2013, 2016), and by M. Schaus, *Women and Gender in Medieval Europe: An Encyclopedia* (New York, 2006), which has more than 560 articles by almost 360 authors. For the rearticulation of gender as social personhood, T. Kuehn's 'Understanding Gender Inequality in Renaissance Florence: Personhood and Gifts of Maternal Inheritance by Women', *Journal of Women's History* 8 (1996), pp. 58–80, is very useful, as is the broader collection of essays edited by J. C. Brown and R. C. Davis, *Gender and Society in Renaissance Italy* (London, 1998, 2014). Another excellent collection of essays is that edited by M. G. Muravyeva and R. M. Toivo, *Gender in Late Medieval and Early Modern Europe* (New York, 2013). The essay by A. Dialeti in this collection, 'From Women's Oppression to Male Anxiety: The Concept of "Patriarchy" in the Historiography of Early Modern Europe', also highlights the newer field of masculinity studies. A useful collection of essays in this area is that edited by C. A. Lees, T. S. Fenster, and J. A. McNamara, *Medieval Masculinities: Regarding Men in the Middle Ages* (Minneapolis, 1994). More recent is the work of G. L. Mosse, *The Image of Man: The Creation of Modern Masculinity* (New York, 2010).

Few discussions of the family and of marriage can overlook the work of David Herlihy and Christiane Klapisch-Zuber which was based on detailed quantitative analysis of the Florentine census, or *catasto*, of 1427–30 covering 260,000 individuals in roughly 60,000 households. After initial articles in the early 1970s, their broader study was published in French as *Les Toscans et leurs familles. Une étude du catasto florentin de 1427* (Paris, 1978), and then translated as *Tuscans and their Families* (New Haven, CT, 1985, 2008). Both authors continued to produce a range of studies utilizing this invaluable material including a collection of essays by Klapisch-Zuber, *Women, Family, and Ritual in Renaissance Italy*, trans. L. G. Cochrane (Chicago, 1987) and Herlihy's *Medieval Households* (Cambridge, MA, 1985). The availability of this same data online has furnished rich material for many other studies on the Florentine and Tuscan family.

For the implications of marriage on women, see V. Cox, 'The Single Self: Feminist Thought and the Marriage Market in Early Modern Venice', *Renaissance Quarterly* 48 (1995), pp. 513–81. And for a useful comparative insight into the situation in Valencia, see D. Wessell Lightfoot, *Women, Dowries and Agency: Marriage in Fifteenth Century Valencia* (Manchester, 2013).

An excellent collection of primary source material for the lived reality of women's lives in the period can be found in E. Amt (ed.), *Women's Lives in Medieval Europe: A Sourcebook* (New York, 1993). P. J. P Goldberg's *Women, Work, and Lifecycle in a Medieval Economy: Women in York and Yorkshire c.1300–1520* (Oxford, 1992) provides a detailed examination of a particular area of England over a two-century span, whilst Heath Dillard provides a similar study for Castile in the period 1100–1300: *Daughters of the Reconquest: Women in Castilian Town Society 1100–1300* (Cambridge, 1989).

Central to any study of the legal situation regarding sex in this period is the work of James Brundage, whose *Law, Sex, and Christian Society in Medieval Europe* (Chicago, 1987) was revised as *Sex, Law, and Marriage in the Middle Ages* (Aldershot, 1993). Now in its 3rd edn, Roth Mazo Karras's *Sexuality in Medieval Europe: Doing Unto Others* (Abingdon, 2017) is another essential text. The legal understandings of sex in the period as they were articulated in the tribunals of Venice have been unravelled in fascinating detail by Guido Ruggiero in *The Boundaries of Eros: Sex Crime and Sexuality in Renaissance Venice* (New York, 1985). Similar use of the criminal record in the city of Florence has been made by Michael Rocke, whose *Forbidden Friendships: Homosexuality and Male Culture in Renaissance Florence* (New York, 1996) is a seminal text for the subtleties of understandings of what we would now call 'homosexual' culture. M. Goodlich's *The Unmentionable Vice: Homosexuality in the Later Medieval Period* (Santa Barbara, CA, 1979) is an early contribution to the field, whilst a broader collection of essays on the topic can be found in the book edited by K. Gerard and G. Hekma, *The Pursuit of Sodomy: Male Homosexuality in Renaissance and Enlightenment Europe* (New York, 1989, 2013). Of particular note in this collection is the essay by G. Dall'Orto, '"Socratic Love" as a Disguise for Same-Sex Love in the Italian Renaissance'. Robert Mills's *Seeing Sodomy in the Middle Ages* (Chicago, 2015) is a fascinating cross-disciplinary study of the visibility of those who crossed accepted gender norms in medieval society, and extends the study to the applicability of categories such as 'transgender', 'butch', and 'femme' to this period. J. M. Saslow's 'Homosexuality in the Renaissance: Behavior, Identity, and Artistic Expression', in M. B. Duberman, M. Vicinus, and G. Chancey Jr (eds), *Hidden from History: Reclaiming the Gay and Lesbian Past* (New York, 1990), pp. 90–105, is a similarly important study of the ways in which those of differing sexual orientations identified themselves. And Judith Brown's monograph, *Immodest Acts: The Life of a Lesbian Nun in Renaissance Italy* (New York: Oxford University Press, 1986), is an important reminder that such culture was not restricted to male enclaves. Comparative studies for Germany and Switzerland can be found in the work of H. Puff, *Sodomy in Reformation Germany and Switzerland, 1400–1600* (Chicago, 2003), as well as of W. Monter, 'Sodomy and Heresy in Early Modern Switzerland', in S. J. Licata and R. P. Petersen (eds), *Historical Perspectives on Homosexuality* (New York, 1981), pp. 41–55; and for England in the work of A. Bray, *Homosexuality in Renaissance England* (New York, 1996). The study of prostitution for this period has resulted in several detailed case studies, mainly based on legal records and criminal prosecutions. The range of studies, from medieval England to France, Seville, and Augsburg, allows for excellent comparative work.

Some of the key researchers in this respect are Ruth Mazo Karras, whose 1989 article 'The Regulation of Brothels in Later Medieval England', *Signs* 14, *Working Together in the Middle Ages: Perspectives on Women's Communities* (1989), pp. 399–433 was expanded into her monograph *Common Women: Prostitution and Sexuality in Medieval England* (New York, 1996); M. E. Perry, 'Deviant Insiders: Legalized Prostitutes and a Consciousness of Women in Early Modern Seville', *Comparative Studies in Society and History* 27 (1985), pp. 138–58; L. Roper, 'Discipline and Respectability: Prostitution and the Reformation in Augsburg', *History Workshop* 19 (1985), pp. 3–28; J. Rossiaud, 'Prostitution, Sex and Society in French Towns in the Fifteenth Century', in P. Aries and A. Béjin (eds), *Western Sexuality: Practice and Precept in Past and Present Times* (Oxford, 1985), pp. 76–94; E. Lacarra Lanz, 'Legal and Clandestine Prostitution in Medieval Spain', *Bulletin of Hispanic Studies* 79 (2002), pp. 265–85; and L. L. Otis, *Prostitution in Medieval Society: The History of an Urban Institution in Languedoc* (Chicago, 1985).

Finally, the conceptualization of medieval urban spaces—aural as well as physical—and their creation by understandings of gender as well as their impact upon its enactment, have been the focus of many studies. One of the most recent is the collection of essays in Merry Wiesner Hanks's edited collection, *Mapping Gendered Routes and Spaces in the Early Modern* World (Aldershot, 2015), but also pertinent is Marc Boone and Martha Howell's edited collection *The Power of Space in Late Medieval and Early Modern Europe: The Cities of Italy, Northern France and the Low Countries* (Turnhout, 2013). Will Coster and Andrew Spicer's edited collection of essays *Sacred Space in Early Modern Europe* (Cambridge, 2005) broadens the study of space out from gender to the impact of the paradigms of sacrality. Neil Atkinson's *The Noisy Renaissance: Sound, Architecture, and Florentine Urban Life* (Pennsylvania, 2016) is one of the more imaginative and evocative studies in the field, recreating an aural landscape and its multiple meanings and implications.

Global Middle Ages: the east (Chapter 7)

The subject of medieval global history is still very new, despite the existence of well-known seminal studies such as J. L. Abu-Lughod, *Before European Hegemony: The World System AD 1250–1350* (New York, 1989) and J. R. S. Phillips, *The Medieval Expansion of Europe*, 2nd edn (Oxford, 1998). The practice, terminology, parameters and legitimate content of this new field are contested, as is its relationship to the global history of other chronological periods. J. Belich, J. Darwin, and C. Wickham (eds), *The Prospect of Global History* (Oxford, 2016) provides a basic introduction to the themes and problems of global history. The issue of scale in global history is considered in 'AHR Conversation. How Size Matters: A Question of Scale in History', *American Historical Review* 118 (2013), pp. 1431–72. Some introductory thoughts about the relationship of medieval global history to the wider field of global history are provided by K. Davis and M. Puett, 'Periodization and "The Medieval Globe": A Conversation', *Medieval Globe* 2 (2015), pp. 1–14, and C. Holmes and N. Standen, 'Introduction: Towards a Global Middle Ages', in Holmes and Standen

(eds), *The Global Middle Ages, Past and Present* Supplement vol. 13 (2018), pp. 1–44.
A. Greif, *Institutions and the Path to the Modern Economy: Lessons from Medieval Trade* (Cambridge, 2006) set up a vigorous debate about the degree to which late medieval institutions lay the foundations for global divergence in later centuries; G. Clark, *Journal of Economic Literature* 45 (2007), pp. 727–43, provides a thoughtful riposte. P. Boucheron, J. Loiseau, P. Monnet, and Y. Potin (eds), *Histoire du monde au XVe siècle* (Paris, 2009) provide a *tour d'horizon* of the world in the fifteenth century, albeit mainly focused on Europe and the Islamic world.

An integrated global history of the later medieval world needs to take account of recent studies of plague and climate change, including V. Lieberman, 'Charter State Collapse in Southeast Asia *c.*1250–1400, as a Problem in Regional and World History', *American Historical Review* 116 (2011), pp. 937–63; V. Lieberman and B. Buckley, 'The Impact of Climate on Southeast Asia, *c.*950–1820: New Findings', *Modern Asian Studies* 46 (2012), pp. 1049–96; B. M. S. Campbell, *The Great Transition: Climate, Disease and Society in the Late-Medieval World* (Cambridge, 2016); and above all, M. H. Green (ed.), *Pandemic Disease in the Medieval World: Rethinking the Black Death, Medieval Globe*, special issue 1 (2014). Exploring the connections that were forged and facilitated by the expansion of the Mongols is also good way of thinking globally, at least with regard to late medieval Eurasia. The literature available for considering the Mongols and the 'world system' they generated is gigantic. In addition to Abu Lughod and Phillips, D. Morgan, *The Mongols*, 2nd edn (Oxford, 2007) provides a good starting point. L. Komaroff and S. Carboni (eds), *The Legacy of Genghis Khan: Courtly Art and Culture in Western Asia, 1256–1353* (New York, 2002) includes illustrations of *paizas*. T. T. Allsen, *Commodity and Exchange in the Mongol Empire: A Cultural History of Islamic Textiles* (Cambridge, 1997) and *Culture and Conquest in Mongol Eurasia* (Cambridge, 2001), emphasizes that the Mongols did not just facilitate vast transregional connections forged by others but actively created such links themselves.

There is a very extensive literature on late medieval western European diplomatic, commercial, and religious exchange with the Mongols: Peter Jackson, *The Mongols and the West* (Harlow, 2005); C. Dawson, *The Mongol Missions; Narratives and Letters of the Franciscan Missionaries in Mongolia and China in the Thirteenth and Fourteenth Centuries* (London, 1955); J. Larner, *Marco Polo and the Discovery of the World* (Princeton, NJ, 1999). Western engagement with the Mongols may have influenced the thinking of long-distance travellers at the very end of the medieval period, including Columbus: V. I. J. Flint, *The Imaginative Landscape of Christopher Columbus* (Princeton, NJ, 1992) and D. Abulafia, *The Discovery of Mankind: Atlantic Encounters in the Age of Columbus* (New Haven, CT, 2008). Of course, the Mongols' interaction with and impact on China, the Islamic world, and eastern Europe was much more profound and long-lasting than their engagement with western Europe: P. Jackson, *The Mongols and the Islamic World: From Conquest to Conversion* (New Haven, CT, 2017); D. G. Ostrowski, *Muscovy and the Mongols: Cross-Cultural Influences on the Steppe Frontier, 1304–1589* (Cambridge, 1998). Thinking globally in the later medieval period encourages us to focus on individuals and communities other than western Europeans who were willing to travel long distances: see e.g. *The*

Monks of Ḳûblâi Khân Emperor of China or the History of the Life and Travels of Rabban Ṣâwmâ, Envoy and Plenipotentiary of the Mongol Khâns to the Kings of Europe, and Marḳôs who as Mâr Yahbhallâhâ III Became Patriarch of the Nestorian Church in Asia, trans. E. A. Wallis Budge (1928). G. Casale, *The Ottoman Age of Exploration* (Oxford, 2010) has opened up the maritime world of the Ottomans, and E. L. Dreyer, *Zheng He: China and the Oceans in the Early Ming Dynasty, 1405–1433* (London, 2007) that of Ming China. R. E. Dunn, *The Adventures of Ibn Battuta: A Muslim Traveler of the 14th Century*, updated edn (Berkeley, CA, 2012) provides a clear introduction to Ibn Battuta. The material discussed in this chapter is drawn from the first two volumes of the translation of his travels: H. A. R. Gibb, C. Defrémery, and B. R. Sanguinetti, *The Travels of Ibn Battuta, A.D. 1325–1354*, vols 1 and 2 (Cambridge, 1958, 1962).

A short bibliographical survey cannot do justice to the specialist literature on the economic, social, and political history of the many regions touched upon in this chapter; but some starting points for the different world regions discussed here are: for central and east Asia: J. W. Chaffee and D. Twitchett (eds), *The Cambridge History of China*, vol. 5, part 2: *Sung China, 960–1279* (Cambridge, 2015); N. Di Cosmo, A. J. Frank, and P. B. Golden, *The Cambridge History of Inner Asia: The Chinggisid Age* (Cambridge, 2009); T. Brook, *The Troubled Empire: China in the Yuan and Ming Dynasties* (Cambridge, MA, 2010). For south-east Asia: V. B. Lieberman, *Strange Parallels: Southeast Asia in Global Context, c.800–1830*, vol. 1: *Integration on the Mainland* (Cambridge, 2003), and 'Transcending East–West Dichotomies: State and Culture Formation in Six Ostensibly Disparate Areas', *Modern Asian Studies* 31 (1997), pp. 463–546. For west Africa: D. C. Conrad, 'Early Polities of the Western Sudan', in B. Z. Kedar and M. E. Wiesner-Hanks (eds), *The Cambridge World History*, vol. 5: *Expanding Webs of Exchange and Conflict, 500 CE–1500 CE* (Cambridge, 2015), pp. 597–602; T. Insoll, *The Archaeology of Islam in Sub-Saharan Africa* (Cambridge, 2003); T. Green, *The Rise of the Trans-Atlantic Slave Trade in Western Africa, 1300–1589* (Cambridge, 2012). For the late medieval Byzantine world: S. Reinert, 'Fragmentation (1204–1453)', in C. Mango (ed.), *The Oxford History of Byzantium* (Oxford, 2002), pp. 248–83; A. Laiou, 'Byzantium and the Neighbouring Powers: Small-State Policies and Complexities', in S. T. Brooks (ed.), *Byzantium: Faith and Power (1261–1557). Perspectives on Late Byzantine Art and Culture* (New Haven, CT, 2006), pp. 42–53. For Egypt and north Africa: R. Irwin, *The Middle East in the Middle Ages: The Early Mamluk Sultanate, 1250–1382* (Carbondale, IL, 1986); J. Van Steenbergen, P. Wing, and K. D'hulster, 'The Mamlukization of the Mamluk Sultanate? State Formation and the History of Fifteenth Century Egypt and Syria', *History Compass* 14 (2016), pp. 549–69. For the Ottomans: C. Kafadar, *Between Two Worlds: The Construction of the Ottoman State* (Berkeley, CA, 1995), pp. 118–50; K. Fleet, *European and Islamic Trade in the Early Ottoman State: The Merchants of Genoa and Turkey* (Cambridge, 1999); H. Lowry, *The Nature of the Early Ottoman State* (Albany, NY, 2003). For Russia and eastern Europe: D. Obolensky, *The Byzantine Commonwealth. Eastern Europe 500–1453* (London, 1971); J. Shepard, 'The Byzantine Commonwealth', in M. Angold (ed.), *The Cambridge History of Christianity*, vol. 5: *Eastern Christianity* (Cambridge,

2006), pp. 3–52; D. Ostrowski, *Muscovy and the Mongols*. For India: P. A. Jackson, *The Delhi Sultanate: A Political and Military History* (Cambridge, 1999); R. Aquil, *Sufism, Culture and Politics: Afghans and Islam in Medieval North India* (Oxford, 2007). For the Americas: E. M. Brumfiel, 'Aztec State Making: Ecology, Structure, and the Origin of the State', *American Anthropologist*, n.s. 85 (1983), pp. 261–84.

To suggest that there is historiographical consensus about economic, social, and political trajectories across the whole late medieval period would be wrong. However, an expansion–decline–slow recovery picture is the most frequently invoked: e.g. by Bruce Campbell in *The Great Transition*, and by Victor Lieberman, whose views are crystallized in 'Charter State Collapse in Southeast Asia *c.*1250–1400, as a Problem in Regional and World History', *American Historical Review* 116 (2011), pp. 937–63. Among the studies which have the potential to problematize that linear trajectory relate to the economy: N. Di Cosmo, 'Black Sea Emporia and the Mongol Empire: A Reassessment of the Pax Mongolica', *Journal of the Economic and Social History of the Orient* 53 (2010), pp. 83–108; G. Christ, 'Collapse and Continuity: Alexandria as a Declining City with a Thriving Port (Thirteenth to Sixteenth Centuries)', in W. Blockmans, M. Krom, and J. Wubs-Mrozewicz (eds), *The Routledge Handbook of Maritime Trade around Europe 1300–1600* (London, 2017), pp. 121–40; and with respect to politics: Van Steenbergen, Wing and D'hulster, 'The Mamlukization of the Mamluk Sultanate?'

Work by scholars of late medieval western Europe can be useful as points of comparison for political processes happening elsewhere in the late medieval world. I have found the following useful: J. Watts, *The Making of Polities: Europe, 1300–1500* (Cambridge, 2009), especially pp.13–26, 420–25; J. Firnhaber-Baker, 'Seigneurial War and Royal Power in Later Medieval Southern France', *Past and Present* 208 (2010), pp. 37–76; P. Lantschner, *The Logic of Political Conflict in Medieval Cities: Italy and the Southern Low Countries, 1370–1440* (Oxford, 2015), and his 'Fragmented Cities in the Later Middle Ages: Italy and the Near East Compared', *English Historical Review* 130 (2015), pp. 546–82, which compares Bologna and Damascus. H. De Weerdt, C. Holmes, and J. Watts, 'Politics, *c.*1000–1500: Mediation and Communication', in Holmes and Standen, *Global Middle Ages*, pp. 261–96, integrate the historiographies of brokerage and mediation in western and eastern Eurasia. This is a theme developed by K. Barkey, *Empire of Difference. The Ottomans in Comparative Perspective* (Cambridge, 2008), with reference to the Ottomans. It has also been explored recently by others working on the eastern Mediterranean (G. Christ, 'The Venetian Consul and the Cosmopolitan Mercantile Community of Alexandria at the Beginning of the Ninth/Fifteenth Century', *Al-Masaq* 26 (2014), pp. 62–77), and those like Thomas Allsen working on the Mongols. Thought-provoking studies of brokerage in contexts beyond the late medieval include: C. A. Bayly, *Rulers, Townsmen and Bazaars: North Indian Society in the Age of British Expansion 1770–1870*, 3rd edn (Oxford, 2012); M. Pearson, 'Connecting the Littorals: Cultural Brokers in the Early Modern Indian Ocean', in P. Gupta, I. Hofmeyr, and M. N. Pearson (eds), *Eyes across the Water: Navigating the Indian Ocean* (Pretoria, 2010), pp. 32–47. Note, however, that F. Trivellato, *The Familiarity of Strangers: The Sephardic Diaspora, Livorno, and Cross-Cultural Trade* *in the Early Modern Period* (New Haven, CT, 2009), pp. 1–20, provides some robust criticism of the overuse of the term 'broker' and of unfounded assumptions that communities inevitably require brokerage. As the chapter here suggests, there are alternative ways of thinking about how individuals and communities communicated with each other and established relations of trust. Some thinking in this direction is developed by J. Shepard, 'Networks', in Holmes and Standen, *Global Middle Ages*, pp. 126–34, and by A. Haour and I. Forrest, 'Trust in Long-Distance Relationships, 1000–1600 CE', pp. 191–213 in the same volume. Useful comparative thinking from the early modern world is provided by G. Sood, 'Circulation and Exchange in Islamicate Eurasia: A Regional Approach to the Early Modern World', *Past & Present* 212 (2011), pp. 145–7.

The literature on the late medieval eastern Mediterranean world as a zone of immense social and political fluidity and mobility is huge. The following are useful collections of essays: B. Arbel, B. Hamilton, and D. Jacoby (eds), *Latins and Greeks in the Eastern Mediterranean World after 1204* (London, 1989); M. Balard and A. Ducellier (eds), *Migrations et diasporas méditerranéennes. Xe–XVIe siècles* (Paris, 2002); J. Harris, C. Holmes, and E. Russell (eds), *Byzantines, Latins, and Turks in the Eastern Mediterranean World after 1150* (Oxford, 2012); G. Christ (ed.), *Union in Separation: Diasporic Groups and Identities in the Eastern Mediterranean (1100–1800)* (Rome, 2015); A. C. S. Peacock, B. De Nicola, and S. Yildiz (eds), *Islam and Christianity in Medieval Anatolia* (Burlington, VT, 2015).

There are several themes through which it is possible to trace the complexity of interactions between individuals and communities within the eastern Mediterranean region. Pilgrimage is one: J. W. Meri, *The Cult of Saints among Muslims and Jews in Medieval Syria* (Oxford, 2002); N. Ševčenko, 'The Monastery of Mount Sinai and the Cult of Saint Catherine', in Brooks, *Byzantium: Faith and Power*, pp. 118–37; C. Morris, *The Sepulchre of Christ and the Medieval West: From the Beginning to 1600* (Oxford, 2005); K. Beebe, *Pilgrim and Preacher: The Audiences and Observant Spirituality of Friar Felix Fabri (1437/8–1502)* (Oxford, 2014); V. Della Dora, *Landscape, Nature, and the Sacred in Byzantium* (Cambridge, 2016); G. Majeska, 'Russian Pilgrims in Constantinople', *Dumbarton Oaks Papers* 56 (2002), pp. 93–108. Some of this literature demonstrates widespread sharing of religious cult sites and rites: C. Schabel, 'Religion', in A. Nicolaou-Konnari and C. Schabel (eds), *Cyprus: Society and Culture 1191–1374* (Leiden, 2005).

Another powerful strand of recent research into the late medieval eastern Mediterranean focuses on the formation of religious and ethnic identities: S. McKee, *Uncommon Dominion: Venetian Crete and the Myth of Ethnic Purity* (Philadelphia, PA, 2000); T. M. Kolbaba, *The Byzantine Lists: Errors of the Latins* (Urbana, IL, 2000); G. Page, *Being Byzantine: Greek Identity Before the Ottomans* (Cambridge, 2008); T. Shawcross, *'The Chronicle of Morea': Historiography in Crusader Greece* (Oxford, 2009). The relationship of religion and military conquest remains a matter of debate in the Ottoman world, so long dominated by the influential Paul Wittek thesis of 1938, which saw the early Ottomans fighting as holy raiders (*gazis*) in the name of Islam: D. Kastritsis, 'Conquest and Political Legitimation in the Early Ottoman Empire', in Harris, Holmes, and Russell,

Byzantines, Latins and Turks, pp. 226–34, provides a good introduction to this debate.

Central to a great deal of recent work on the late medieval eastern Mediterranean have been processes of political legitimation in a landscape of fragmented power. This is examined in the case of the Ottomans (G. Necipoğlu, *Architecture, Ceremonial, and Power: The Topkapi Palace in the Fifteenth and Sixteenth Centuries* (New York, 1991); D. Kastritsis, 'Religious Affiliations and Political Alliances in the Ottoman Succession Wars of 1402–1413', *Medieval Encounters* 13 (2007), pp. 222–42; D. Kastritsis, 'Conquest and Political Legitimation', in Harris, Holmes, and Russell, *Byzantines, Latins, and Turks*, pp. 234–41; K. Moustakas, 'The Myth of the Byzantine Origins of the Osmanlis: An Essay in Interpretation', *Byzantine and Modern Greek Studies* 39 (2015), pp. 85–97); in the case of incoming Latin rulers (T. Shawcross, 'Conquest Legitimized: The Making of a Byzantine Emperor in Crusader Constantinople (1204–1261)', in Harris, Holmes, and Russell, *Byzantines, Latins, and Turks*, pp. 181–220)); and in the case of what remained of Byzantium (R. Macrides, J. A. Munitiz, and D. Angelov, *Pseudo-Kodinos and the Constantinopolitan Court: Offices and Ceremonies* (Farnham, 2013)). Numismatic evidence is a particularly rich resource with which to examine this phenomenon: E. Georganteli, 'Transposed Images: Currencies and Legitimacy in the Late Medieval Eastern Mediterranean', in Harris, Holmes, and Russell, *Byzantines, Latins and Turks*, pp.141–79. E. Dursteler, *Venetians in Constantinople: Nation, Identity and Coexistence in the Early Modern Mediterranean* (Baltimore, MD, 2006) and T. Papademetriou, *Render Unto the Sultan: Power, Authority, and the Greek Orthodox Church in the Early Ottoman Centuries* (Oxford, 2015) may be useful in helping us to decide whether the balance of power between governing authorities and other more fluid religious, social, and political formations in the eastern Mediterranean world shifted all that substantially in the early modern period.

A global history of the relationship between networks of specialist technicians and the wielders of local political power has yet to be written. However, I found the following useful for thinking about the Macedonian evidence: C. Mango, *Byzantine Architecture* (London, 1986); M. Živojinović, V. Kravari, and C. Giros, *Actes de Chilandar. Des origines à 1319* (Paris, 1998); P. Lethielleux. E. Kourtkoutidou-Nikolaidou, and A. Tourta, *Wandering in Byzantine Thessaloniki* (Athens, 1997); A. J. Wharton and G. Babić, 'Monuments of Ohrid', *Oxford Dictionary of Byzantium* (online version, last accessed 9 July 2019); A. Cutler, 'Michael (Astrapas) and Eutychios', *Oxford Dictionary of Byzantium* (online version, last accessed 9 July 2019; S. Kalopissi-Verti, 'Patronage and Artistic Production during the Palaiologan Period', in Brooks, *Byzantium: Faith and Power*, pp. 76–97. The relationship between rules and networks of craftsmen in Anatolia is examined by A. Eastmond, *Tamta's World: The Life and Encounters of a Medieval Noblewoman from the Middle East to Mongolia* (Cambridge, 2017) and by T. Uyar, 'Thirteenth-Century "Byzantine Art" in Cappadocia and the Question of Greek Painters at the Seljuq Court', in A. C. S. Peacock and B. de Nicola (eds), *Islam and Christianity in Medieval Anatolia* (London, 2015), pp. 215–32.

Merchant networks and political legitimacy in the Mongol world are discussed in the publications of Thomas Allsen and Komaroff & Carboni mentioned above, and especially by E. Endicott-West, 'Merchant Associations in Yuan China: The Ortogh', *Asia Major*, 3rd ser. 2 (1989), pp. 127–54. R. Aquil, *Sufism, Culture and Politics: Afghans and Islam in Medieval North India* (Oxford, 2007) and P. Wagoner, 'Fortuitous Convergences and Essential Ambiguities: Transcultural Political Elites in the Medieval Deccan', *International Journal of Hindu Studies* 3 (1999), pp. 241–64, include examples of the dependency of local hegemons in India on networks of those with religious, commercial, and martial expertise.

Chronology

The following chronology overlaps the one in the previous volume of The Short Oxford History of Europe (P. Power (ed.), *The Central Middle Ages*, Oxford, 2006) for the years 1300–1347, and the one in the following volume (E. Cameron (ed.), *The Sixteenth Century*, Oxford, 2006) for the years 1494–1520.

1300	Pope Boniface VIII (Benedetto Caetani) celebrates the first Jubilee in Rome.
	Václav II of Bohemia is elected king of Poland.
1301–9	Death of the last Arpád king of Hungary, Andrew III: after few years (1309), the crown is taken by Charles-Robert of Anjou (great-grandson of the Arpád king Stephen V and grandson of Robert king of Naples), who establishes the Angevin dynasty of Hungarian kings.
1302	Boniface VIII issues the papal bull *Unam sanctam*.
	Peace of Caltabellotta between Charles II of Anjou, king of Sicily (Naples and the continental south), and Frederick III of Aragon, king of Trinacria (Sicily); temporary end of the conflict for the control of Sicily after the island rebelled against the Angevin kings in 1282.
1303	Death of Boniface VIII.
	Albert of Habsburg becomes emperor.
	Ferdinand IV of Castile becomes king.
1305	Election of Pope Clement V (Bertrand de Got).
	William Wallace of Scotland is defeated and executed by Edward I of England.
	Giotto di Bondone (1266–1337) paints the Scrovegni Chapel at Padua.
1306	Robert I Wallace 'The Bruce' seizes the Scottish throne.
1308	The emperor Albert of Habsburg is murdered: Henry VII, of Luxembourg, becomes king of the Romans.
	Dante Alighieri (1265–1321) starts to write the *Divine Comedy*.
1309	The papal court is transferred to Avignon.
	Death of Charles II of Anjou, king of Naples: his son Robert becomes king and is crowned by the Pope Clemens V in Avignon.
	The Grand Master of the Teutonic Order, Siegfried von Feuchtwangen, establishes the capital of the order in the fortress monastery of Marienburg, in Prussia.

1311	Henry VII of Luxembourg recognizes as imperial vicars the Visconti in Milan, the della Scala in Verona, and some other lords of the Po plain. John of Luxembourg, Henry VII's son, is crowned king of Bohemia.
1311–2	Pope Clement V (Bertrand de Got) summons a council in Vienne in which the Order of Knights Templars is suppressed.
1312	Henry VII of Luxembourg crowned emperor in Avignon. Death of Ferdinand IV of Castile: his son Alfonso (XI) is only 11 years old, and factions and conflicts grow around him.
1312–3	Dante Alighieri writes the *De monarchia*
1313	Death of Emperor Henry VII.
1313–22	A series of famines hits the continent.
1314	Frederick (III) of Habsburg and Louis (IV) of Bavaria are simultaneously elected kings of the Romans. Death of the king of France, Philip the Fair: his son Louis X becomes king. Death of Pope Clement V. Battle of Bannockburn: Robert Bruce defeats Edward II. King Robert of Anjou becomes papal vicar for the whole of Italy.
1316	Louis X's death: Louis's uncle, Philip, earl of Poitiers, becomes regent of France.
1317	Philip V is crowned king of France
1320	Ladislas Piast becomes king of Poland. Declaration of Arbroath expounds Scottish claims to independence.
1321	Death of Dante Alighieri.
1322	Battle of Mühldorf: Louis the Bavarian defeats Frederick of Habsburg. Death of Philip V of France: succession of Charles IV, earl of La Marche.
1323–5	William Ockham (*c*.1285/7–*c*.1347) writes the *Summa logicae*.
1324	Pope John XXII (Jacques Duèze) excommunicates Louis IV of Bavaria, and supports Charles IV of France's claim to the imperial crown. Marsilius of Padua (*c*.1275–*c*.1342) writes the *Defensor pacis*.
1325	Agreement between Louis IV of Bavaria and Frederick of Habsburg. Cortes of Valladolid: Alfonso XI becomes king of Castile. Charles, duke of Calabria and heir to the Neapolitan throne, becomes lord of Florence.
1327	Louis IV of Bavaria is crowned in Milan. Edward II of England is deposed and replaced by his son Edward III. Death of James II of Aragon: his son Alfonso IV becomes king.
1328	Louis IV is acclaimed emperor in Rome by the Romans, and deposes Pope John XXII, nominating the antipope Nicholas V instead. Death without heirs of Charles IV of France: the crown goes to his cousin Philip of Valois; this is the end of the Capetian dynasty.

Edward III of England recognizes Scottish independence.

Michael of Cesena, the Franciscan minister general of the order, and William Ockham flee Avignon after a serious conflict with Pope John XXII, and find refuge with Emperor Louis IV of Bavaria.

1332 Treaty between Robert of Anjou, king of Naples, and his nephew Charles-Robert, king of Hungary: the treaty stipulates the marriage between Joan, Robert's granddaughter and heir, and Andrew, Charles-Robert's son.

1333 Ladislas of Poland is succeeded by his son Casimir the Great.

1336 Death of Alfonso IV of Aragon: his son Peter IV is crowned king.
Portuguese first exploration of the Canary Islands.

1337 The Hundred Years Wars is declared between France and England.
Death of Frederick III of Aragon, king of Sicily.

1338 Diet of Rhens: the German princes declare the independence of the German crown from the pope.

1338–9 Ambrogio Lorenzetti (c.1290–1348) depicts the frescoes of *The Allegory of Good and Bad Government* in the Hall of the Nine, in the public palace of Siena.

1340 Battle of Salado: Alfonso XI of Castile defeats the Muslims who in 1333 had conquered Gibraltar.

1341 Francesco Petrarca (1304–74) is proclaimed poet laureate in Rome.

1342 Walter of Brienne, duke of Athens, becomes lord of Florence.
Death of Robert of Anjou, king of Naples: his granddaughter Joan I becomes queen.
Death of Charles-Robert of Anjou, king of Hungary: his son Louis the Great becomes king.

1342–3 Bankruptcy hits the Bardi and Peruzzi companies in Florence.

1344–5 Bridgit of Sweden (1303–73) establishes the religious community of the Order of the Most Holy Saviour at Vadstena.

1346 Battle of Crécy, won by the English (death on the battlefield of John of Luxembourg, king of Bohemia).
The Serbian empire is created by Stefan Dusan.

1347 Edward III conquers Calais; the Order of the Garter is created.
Cola di Rienzo takes the power in Rome, but has to escape from the city.
Death of the Emperor Louis IV: Charles IV of Luxembourg, son of John, king of Bohemia, becomes king of Germany.

1348 The Black Death.
Giovanni Boccaccio (1313–75) conceives his *Decameron*, probably completed by 1353.

1350 Death of Philip VI of France: his son John II the Good becomes king.

Death by plague of King Alfonso XI of Castile during the siege of Gibraltar; while his legitimate son, Peter I (the Cruel), is crowned king, Alfonso's five natural sons (from Elisabeth of Guzman) do not accept it, and a long period of internecine conflicts begins.

Archbishop Giovanni Visconti, lord of Milan, conquers Bologna.

1352   Louis the Great of Anjou, king of Hungary, renounces his claims to the throne of Naples.

1353   Eight Swiss towns enter into the so-called Confederation of the Eight Cantons.

1354   Mallorca and Roussillon are annexed to the crown of Aragon.

Cola di Rienzo returns to Rome, but is killed by the crowd.

The German cities in the Rhein region stipulate a defensive league.

1355   Charles IV of Luxembourg is crowned king of Italy in Milan, and the emperor in Rome, Bartolus de Saxoferrato (1313–57), writes the treaty *De tyranno*.

Death of Stefan Dusan.

1356   Diet of Metz: the election of the emperor is regulated by the Golden Bull, issued by Charles IV, and seven German princes (four secular, and three ecclesiastical) are entrusted with the choice.

Battle of Poitiers: John II of France is imprisoned by the English.

In Genoa, a popular insurrection frees the city from the Milanese control and gives power to Doge Simon Boccanegra.

1357   Cardinal Egidius Albornoz, papal legate for Italy from 1353 and 1367, issues the so-called *Constitutiones aegidianae*.

1358   Rural revolts in France (*jacquerie*) and in Paris (the urban revolt is led by Etienne Marcel).

1360   Peace of Brétigny and treaty of Calais between England and France: John II is freed, and Edward III renounces his claim to the throne of France in exchange for control over Gascony and northern France.

1361   Bologna is acquired by the church.

1364   Death of John II of France: Charles V is crowned king.

1365   Giovanni de' Dondi (1330–88) builds an astronomical public clock in Padua.

1366   Henry of Trastamara, one of the illegitimate sons of Alfonso XI of Castile, defies King Peter I; their conflict also involves Henry, the Black Prince, of England (who supports Peter) and Charles V of France (who supports Henry).

1368   Creation of the Franciscan Observance.

1369   Hostilities resume in France.

Peter I of Castile is murdered in Montiel: Henry of Trastamara becomes king (Henry II), but because of the wedding of John of Gaunt, son of the

English king Edward III, with a daughter of King Peter, the duke of Lancaster takes on the title of king of Castile.

Jean Froissart, after the death of Queen Philippa of Hainaut, leaves England and starts composing his *Chronicles*.

1370 Treaty of Stralsund: the German Hansa controls the mercantile traffic in the Baltic.

At the death of Casimir the Great, king of Poland, his nephew Louis of Anjou, king of Hungary, becomes king.

1372 Naval battle of La Rochelle: the English fleet is destroyed by the Spanish.

Peace of Catania between Queen Joan I of Naples and Frederick IV of Sicily: the Angevins renounce their claims to the island in favour of the Aragonese.

1376 League of the Swabian cities against Earl Everard of Württemberg.

1377 Pope Gregory XI (Pierre Roger de Beaufort) returns the papal curia to Rome.

Death of both Edward III of England and his heir, the Black Prince: the throne goes to the king's grandson, Richard II.

Death of Frederick IV of Sicily: a period of internal struggle begins.

Charles V of France commissions Nicolas Oresme (1320–82) to write the *Livre du ciel et du monde*, a French translation of Aristotle's treatise.

Jogaila, grandson of Grand Duke Gediminas of Lithuania, becomes grand duke at the death of his father, Algirdas.

1377–8 Catherine of Siena (1347–80) composes *The Dialogue of Divine Providence*.

1378 Death of the emperor Charles IV; his son, Wenceslas, king of Bohemia, is crowned king of Germany.

Death of Pope Gregory XI: the double election of Urban VI (Bartolomeo Prignano) in Rome and Clement VII (Robert of Geneva) in Avignon opens up the so-called Great Schism.

The 'Ciompi' revolt hits Florence.

1379 Death of Henry II of Trastamara, king of Castile: his son John I becomes king.

1380 Death of Charles V of France: his son Charles VI is crowned king.

Battle of Kulikovo: the Grand Prince of Moscow, Dmitry Donskoy, defeats the Mongols.

1381 Revolt of the peasants in England, led by John Ball and Wat Tyler.

The league of south-western German cities is created by unifying the Swabian and the Rhenish leagues.

Charles of Anjou-Durazzo deposes Joan I, queen of Naples (murdered in 1382).

1382	John Wyclif (*c.*1320–84) translates part of the Bible into English in what becomes known as Wyclif's Bible; his ideas foster the movement of Lollardy.
	Death of Louis the Great of Anjou, king of Hungary and Poland: his daughter Mary is crowned king of Hungary.
1383	Death of Dom Fernando, king of Portugal, without a male heir.
1384	King Louis the Great of Hungary's second daughter, Jadwiga, is crowned king of Poland.
1385	Battle of Aljiubarrota: Dom João I of Avis, bastard son of King Pedro, becomes king of Portugal and founds the second Portuguese dynasty (1385–1580).
	Gian Galeazzo Visconti deposes and murders his uncle Bernabò, and becomes lord of Milan.
1386	Union of Krevo: Jogaila/Wladislaw, grand duke of Lithuania, by marrying Jadwiga of Anjou and by converting to Catholicism, becomes king of Poland and unifies Lithuania and Poland (Jagellonian dynasty); his brother Vytautas rules Lithuania on his behalf.
1387	Sigismund of Luxembourg, husband of Mary of Anjou, supported by his brother, Wenceslas IV of Bohemia, is recognized as king of Hungary.
	Treaty of Troncoso: John I of Castile organizes the wedding of his son Henry with the daughter of John of Gaunt; the two dynasties descended from Peter I are reunited.
	Death of Peter IV of Aragon; his son John I becomes king.
	Geoffrey Chaucer (1343–1400) starts writing the *Canterbury Tales*, completed by 1400.
1388	Death of John I of Castile: his son, Henry, is still minor, and internal conflicts erupt.
	Gian Galeazzo Visconti conquers Verona and Padua, taking the Milanese borders close to Venice.
1389	Peace of Eger: the German urban leagues are dissolved.
1391	By the virtue of the marriage between Grand Prince Vasilii I Dimitrievich of Moscow and Sofia, daughter of the Lithuanian Vytautas, the Jagellonians start exercing influence in Moscow.
1392	Charles VI shows signs of mental illness: the kingdom of France is divided into two factions, the Armagnacs, led by Louis, duke of Orléans, brother of the king, and the Burgundians, led by Duke Philip the Bold of Burgundy, uncle of the king.
	Peace between Gian Galeazzo Visconti and the anti-Viscontean league
	Martin, duke of Montblanc (later King Martin I of Aragon), puts his son Martin the Young, the husband of Queen Mary of Sicily, on the Sicilian throne.

1395	Death of John I of Aragon: his brother Martin (I) of Montblanc becomes king.
	Gian Galeazzo Visconti is nominated duke of Milan by Emperor Wenceslas.
1396	Battle of Nicopolis: an army of Hungarian, Croatian, French, English, Burgundian, and German crusaders (and a Venetian fleet) is defeated by the Ottomans.
1397	Union of Kalmar between Norway, Denmark, and Sweden under the rule of Queen Margaret, daughter of King Waldemar of Denmark and widow of King Magnus of Sweden and Norway
1399	Richard II of England abdicates in favour of his cousin, Henry IV, son of John of Gaunt.
1400	Diet of Obelhanstein: Emperor Wenceslas is deposed by the ecclesiastical electors, and replaced with Rupert of the Palatinate.
	Owen Glyndŵr starts 15 years of Welsh revolts against the English on the Welsh borders.
1401	Rupert of the Palatinate is crowned king of Italy.
1402	Death of Gian Galeazzo Visconti, duke of Milan; his regional domain breaks down.
	Battle of Ankara: Tamerlane crushes the Ottoman Turks.
1405	Venice conquers Verona and Padua.
	Christine de Pizan (1364–c.1430) completes *The Book of the City of Ladies*.
1406	Death of Henry III of Castile: his son John II is proclaimed king, but the regent of the realm is his uncle, Don Ferdinand de Antequera.
	Florence annexes Pisa and obtains direct access to the Mediterranean.
1407	Louis of Valois, duke of Orléans, is murdered.
1409	The Council of Pisa, held to end the Schism, deposes both popes (at the time, Benedict XIII, Pietro Orsini, and Gregory XII, Angelo Correr) and elects a third claimant, Alexander V (Pietro Filargo), who is succeeded after a few months by John XXIII (Baldassarre Cossa).
	Jean Gerson (1363–1429) writes several treaties during the council, among which are the *Trilogus in materia schismatis* and the *De unitate ecclesiae*.
1410	Death of Emperor Rupert III: Charles IV's son, Sigismund of Luxembourg, is elected king of Bohemia, but Jan Hus and his followers rebel against him.
	Death of Martin I of Aragon: his succession is disputed.
	Pierre d'Ailly (1351–1420) composes the treatise *Imago mundi*: Christopher Columbus, decades later, buys and annotates a copy of its first printed edition (1480–83).
	Battle of Tannenberg: the Lithuanian-Polish army defeats the Teutonic Order.

1412	Conference of Caspe: Ferdinand of Trastamara (Castile) becomes king of Aragon.
1412–6	The Limbourg brothers illuminate the manuscript of the *Très Riches Heures* for Duke John of Berry.
1413	Death of Henry IV of England: his son Henry V is crowned king.
1414	An ecumenical council is held in Constance to end the Schism (1414–18).
	Death of Ladislas of Anjou-Durazzo, king of Naples: his sister Joan II becomes queen.
1415	Battle of Agincourt.
	Jan Hus is executed after being condemned by the Council of Constance.
	João I of Portugal conquers Ceuta.
1416	Death of Ferdinand I of Aragon: his son Alfonso V (the Magnanimous) becomes king of Aragon, Catalonia, Mallorca, Valencia, and Sicily.
	Amedeus VII, count of Savoy, is nominated duke by Emperor Sigismund.
1417	The council of Constance elects Odo Colonna as pope (Martin V) and ends the Great Schism.
1419	John the Fearless, duke of Burgundy, is murdered.
	John II of Castile comes of age and is crowned king.
1420	Treaty of Troyes between France and England; Henry V marries Catherine of France, daughter of Charles VI.
1420s	The Portuguese prince Henry the Navigator promotes a wave of maritime journeys towards Madeira and the Azores, and Cape Verde.
1421	Joan II of Anjou, queen of Naples, seeks the alliance of Alfonso V of Aragon against Louis III of Anjou, count of Provence, and promises her throne to the Aragonese king.
	Filippo Maria Visconti, duke of Milan, annexes Genoa.
	Venice occupies the Friuli and Istria regions after a war against the empire.
1422	Death of both Henry V of England and Charles VI of France: Charles VII is recognized king by the Armagnacs, and reigns in the south of France, while the rest of the kingdom is under English rule; in England, Henry VI is crowned king; because of his young age, John duke of Bedford is regent.
1423	Joan II of Naples disinherits Alfonso V of Aragon, and recalls Louis III of Anjou.
1428	Venice takes Brescia and Bergamo from Milan.
1429	Joan of Arc retakes Orléans from the English.
1430s	Margery Kempe (*c.*1373–after 1438) starts dictating her *Book*.

1431   Charles VII is crowned king in Reims; Joan of Arc is executed in Rouen. Death of Pope Martin V: Pope Eugene IV (Gabriele Condulmer) is elected.

Council of Basle–Ferrara–Florence (1431–49) is summoned with the aim of ending the schism with the Byzantine church.

1434   Cosimo de' Medici (the Elder) becomes the leader of the Medicean *reggimento* in Florence.

Leon Battista Alberti (1404–1472) writes the *Libri della famiglia* in the Florentine vernacular.

Death of Wladislaw II Jagello, king of Poland-Lithuania: his son Wladislaw III, 10 years old, becomes king of Poland, while Wladislaw's younger brother, Casimir, is sent in Lithuania as royal lieutenant, and acclaimed grand duke by the Lithuanians

1435   Conference of Arras: Charles VII and Philip the Good of Burgundy reconcile.

Death of Joan II of Anjou, who has declared Louis III of Anjou's brother, René, her heir to the crown of Naples; Filippo Maria Visconti and Genoa support René, and defeat Alfonso V of Aragon at the naval battle of Ponza.

1436   Charles VII enters Paris.

Agreement of Basle: a section of the Hussites (the Utraquists) recognizes Sigismund of Luxembourg as king of Bohemia, while the Taborites do not.

Filippo Brunelleschi (1377–1446) completes the dome of the cathedral of Santa Maria del Fiore in Florence

1437   Death of Sigismund of Luxembourg, king of Bohemia and Hungary, and emperor.

1438   Albert (II) of Austria becomes king of Bohemia and Hungary, then of the Romans.

The Pragmatic Sanction is issued in Bourges.

1439   Death of Albert II of Habsburg: his cousin Frederick is regent on behalf of Albert's infant son, Ladislas the Posthumous; the Hungarian barons elect King Wladislaw III of Poland as Ladislas's heir.

1439–47   Lorenzo Valla (*c.*1406–57), at the court of Alfonso V of Aragon in Naples, among other works writes the *De falso credita et ementita Constantini donatione*.

1440   Frederick III of Habsburg is crowned king of the Romans.

1442   Alfonso V of Aragon conquers the kingdom of Naples; his wife, Queen Mary, remains in Aragon and rules the Iberian domains of the dynasty in his name.

1444   Battle of Varna: the king of Hungary and Poland, Wladislaw III, is killed by the Ottomans, and his brother Casimir (IV) becomes king, reuniting Poland and Lithuania under his personal rule.

1445–8   Charles VII reforms the French army.

1446   János Huniady is elected regent of Hungary on behalf of Ladislas Posthumous, son of Albert II of Habsburg.

1450   The *condottiere* Francesco Sforza, having married in 1441 Bianca Maria Visconti, the sole heir to the duchy of Milan, becomes duke: while supported by the Milanese, he would never receive the imperial investiture to the duchy.

1452   Frederick III of Habsburg is crowned emperor in Rome (this is the last imperial coronation in Rome).

1452–4   Last war between Milan and Venice.

1453   Fall of Byzantium at the hands of the Ottoman sultan Mehmed the Conqueror.

           Battle of Castillon and end of the Hundred Years War.

           Richard duke of York is nominated *Defensor regni* by Parliament, de facto replacing the increasingly unreliable Henry VI: the so-called War of the Roses between Lancaster and York for the crown of England begins.

           Ladislas V, the Posthumous, becomes king of Hungary and Bohemia.

1454   Death of John II of Castile: his son Henry IV becomes king.

           Peace of Lodi among Francesco Sforza, duke of Milan, and the republics of Venice and Florence.

1455   Italic League established among Milan, Venice, Florence, Rome, Naples, and all the minor Italian powers.

1457   Death of Ladislas V, the Posthumous, of Hungary and Bohemia: all his dynastic domains are inherited by the emperor Frederick III.

1458   Death of Alfonso V of Aragon: his son Ferdinand I (Ferrante) becomes king of Naples, while Alfonso's brother John II of Aragon rules the Iberian domains and Sicily.

           Matthias Hunyadi (Corvinus), son of János (who died while freeing Belgrade from the Ottomans in 1456), becomes king of Hungary.

           The pro-Hussite George Podebrady becomes king of Bohemia.

1458–64   The pro-Angevin Neapolitan barons rebel against King Ferrante.

1461   Death of Charles VII of France and succession of Louis XI.

           Death of Richard of York, presumptive heir of Henry VI: his son Edward (IV), earl of March, proclaims himself king.

1465–77   The 'League of the *Bien Public*' among the dukes of Burgundy, Bourbon, and Brittany defies Louis XI of France; this crisis inaugurates a period of ruthless struggle between the king and his princely opponents.

1466	The Polish–Lithuanian Union annexes Prussia at the cost of the Teutonic Order.
1467	Death of Philip the Good of Burgundy and succession of Charles the Bold.
1468	Rebellion of the Castilian nobility led by King Henry IV's siblings Alfonso and Isabella: Henry IV, who recovers his throne, is forced to nominate his sister Isabella as his heir.
1469	Edward IV is captured by the Lancaster Isabella of Castile marries Ferdinand, heir to the Aragonese crown. Matthias Corvinus becomes king of Hungary.
1470	Henry VI of England is back on the throne.
1471	Battle of Tewkesbury: the winner, Edward IV, enters in London as king. Diet of Ratisbon: Frederick III recognizes King Matthias Corvinus of Hungary and King George Podebrady of Bohemia.
1474	Death of Henry IV of Castile: before dying, he divests his sister Isabella from the crown in favour of his daughter Joan. Andrea Mantegna (1431–1506) finishes (presumably) the frescoes of the *Camera picta* in the castle of San Giorgio in Mantua.
1476	Matthias Corvinus, king of Hungary, marries Beatrice of Aragon, daughter of King Ferrante of Naples.
1477	Death of Charles the Bold of Burgundy in the battle of Nancy against the Swiss.
1478	Ivan III, Grand Prince of Moscow, annexes Novgorod. The Pazzi conspiracy threatens the Medici hegemony in Florence.
1479	Treaty of Truillo: at John II of Aragon's death, his son Ferdinand, Isabella's husband, becomes king. The Catholic kings Ferdinand and Isabella rule almost all of the Iberian kingdoms, apart from Portugal and Navarra (which is incorporated into Castile in 1512).
1480	An Ottoman expedition conquers Otranto, in the kingdom of Naples. Ivan III of Moscow defeats a Great Horde major campaign and 'throws off the Mongol yoke'.
1481	Death of the Ottoman sultan Mehmed the Conqueror.
1482	Peace of Arras between Louis XI of France and Maximilian of Habsburg, heir to the Burgundian dominions by the marriage with Mary, Duke Charles the Bold's only heir; the agreement stipulates the marriage of Charles, son of Louis, and Margaret, daughter of Maximilian.
1483	Death of Louis XI and succession of Charles VIII. Death of Edward IV; his brother Richard (III) of Gloucester eliminates Edward's two young sons and becomes king of England.

1485	Battle of Bosworth: Richard III is defeated by Henry Tudor, who becomes Henry VII of England.
	Matthias Corvinus enters Vienna, defeating Emperor Frederick III.
1485–6	The so-called 'Conspiracy of the Barons' threatens the rule of King Ferrante of Naples.
1486	Publication of the *Malleus maleficarum*, the classic handbook of witch detection.
*c.*1489	Philippe de Commynes (1447–1511) starts writing his *Mémoires*.
1490	Death of Matthias Corvinus, king of Hungary: he is succeeded not by his illegitimate son John, but by King Wladislaw of Bohemia, elected by the Hungarian diet.
1491	Charles VIII of France repudiates Margaret of Austria (daughter of Maximilian of Habsburg), and marries Anne of Brittany.
1492	Granada, the last Muslim outpost in Spain, is conquered by Ferdinand and Isabella; the Jews are expelled from all the kingdoms of the Catholic kings.
	Christoph Columbus (1451–1506) reaches the Americas in the name of the Spanish kings, and lands on Hispaniola.
	Death of Lorenzo 'the Magnificent' de' Medici in Florence
	Rodrigo Borja becomes Pope Alexander VI.
	Death of Casimir IV, king of Poland and grand duke of Lithuania
1493	Death of Emperor Frederick III; his son Maximilian becomes king of the Romans.
	Peace of Senlis: Charles VIII of France renounces to his claims to the Franche Comté and Artois, in favour of Maximilian of Habsburg.
	Peter Martyr of Angleria (1457–1526) describes Columbus' discoveries in a letter to Cardinal Ascanio Maria Sforza.
1494	Treaty of Tordesillas between Spain and Portugal.
	Death of Ferrante, king of Naples; Charles VIII invades Italy, opening the first phase of the Italian Wars.
	Piero, son of Lorenzo de' Medici, is expelled from Florence: a new republican government is set up under the spiritual leadership of Fra Girolamo Savonarola.
	Ludovico Sforza, 'Il Moro', is recognized as duke of Milan by Maximilian of Habsburg.
1495	Battle of Fornovo on the Taro between Charles VIII of France and the league set up by Venice, Milan, Rome, and many other minor Italian powers.
	Diet of Worms: a general and perpetual peace in the empire is stipulated.
1497–8	Vasco da Gama (*c.*1460s–1524) begins his expedition to India via the Cape of Good Hope and arrives in Calicut.

1498	Death of Charles VIII of France; his cousin Louis of Orléans becomes King Louis XII.
	Execution of Savonarola in Florence.
1499	The Swiss acquire de facto independence from the empire.
1500	The French army definitively occupies the duchy of Milan; Duke Ludovico is taken prisoner to France.
	Pedro Alvares Cabral (1467–1520) discovers what is now Brazil on behalf of the king of Portugal.
1501	Isma'il becomes the first Safawid shah of Persia.
1504	Death of Isabella of Castile.
1506	Pope Julius II (Giuliano della Rovere) commissions Donato Bramante (1444–1514) to begin the reconstruction of St Peter in Rome.
1508	Establishment of the League of Cambrai between the papacy, France, Spain, and the empire against Venice.
	Michelangelo Buonarroti (1475–1564) starts painting the Sistine Chapel.
1509	Death of Henry VII of England: his son Henry VIII becomes king.
	Battle of Agnadello: the army of the League of Cambrai defeats Venice.
1511	Pope Julius II dissolves the League of Cambrai and addresses his efforts, within the new Holy League, against Louis XII of France.
	Desiderius Erasmus of Rotterdam (1466–1536) publishes *In Praise of Folly*.
1512	Death of the Ottoman sultan Bayazed.
	Battle of Ravenna: the French army, led by Gaston de Foix, defeats the League, but the French captain dies on the field.
1513	Niccolò Machiavelli (1469–1527) writes *De principatibus* (first printed edition, 1532).
	League of the Swiss Thirteen Cantons.
	Death of Pope Julius II: Leo X (Giovanni de' Medici) becomes pope.
1514	Battle of Tchaldiran between the Ottoman sultan Selim I and the Safawid shah Isma'il: Selim controls a strong frontier province along the border with Persia.
1515	Death of Louis XII of France: Francis I becomes king.
	Battle of Marignano: the French and Venetian armies (allied after dissolution of the previous leagues) defeat the Swiss, who controlled the duchy of Milan.
1516	Death of Ferdinand of Spain; his grandchild Charles of Habsburg becomes king.
	Utopia, by Thomas More (1478–1535), is printed in Leuven.
	Erasmus of Rotterdam issues his *Novum instrumentum* (translation of the New Testament).
	The *Orlando furioso* by Ludovico Ariosto (1474–1533) is printed in Ferrara.

1517	Ninety-five Theses written by Martin Luther.
	Mamluk Syria and Egypt are conquered by the Ottoman sultan Selim I.
1519	Death of Maximilian I; his grandson Charles of Habsburg becomes Emperor Charles V.
	Hernán Cortés (1485–1547) lands in Mexico.
	Fernão de Magalhanes (1480–1521) leaves Spain for the journey that will circumnavigate the world.
1520	Suleiman the Magnificent becomes sultan of the Ottoman empire.

Maps

Map 1. Europe, *c.* 1320

Map 1b.

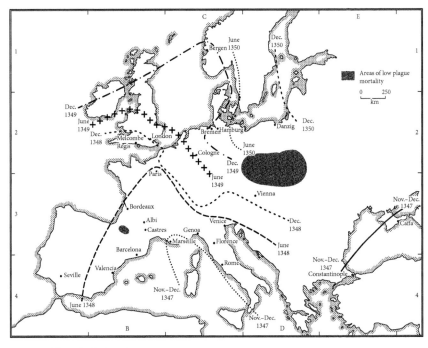

Map 2. The Black Death

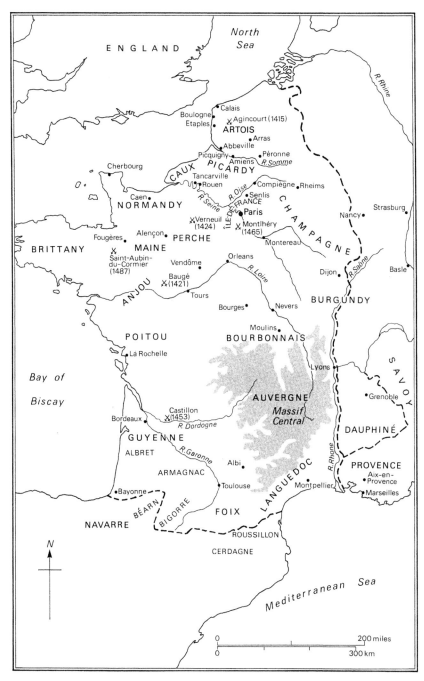

Map 3. France (fifteenth century)

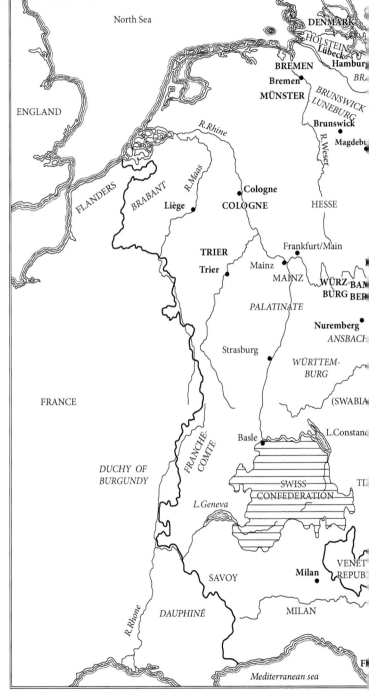

Map 4. Germany and the empire (fifteenth century)

Map 4b.

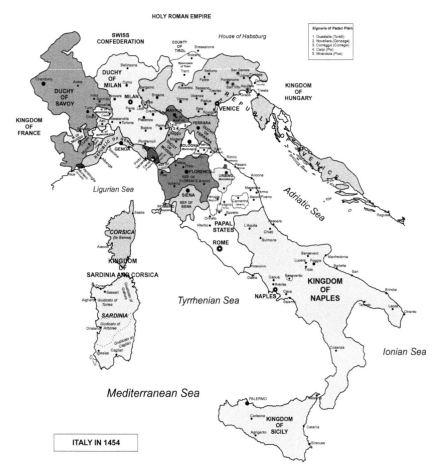

Map 5. Italy in 1454

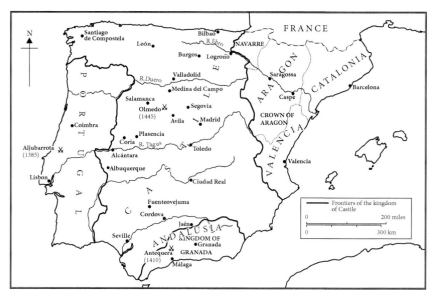

Map 6. The Iberian kingdoms (fifteenth century)

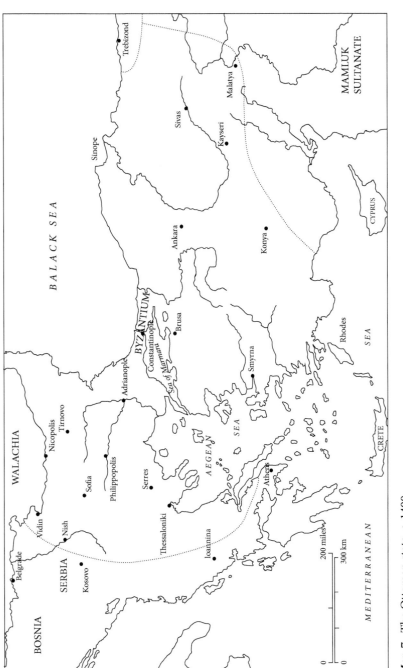

Map 7. The Ottoman state, c. 1400

Map 8. Baltic Europe (fourteenth century)

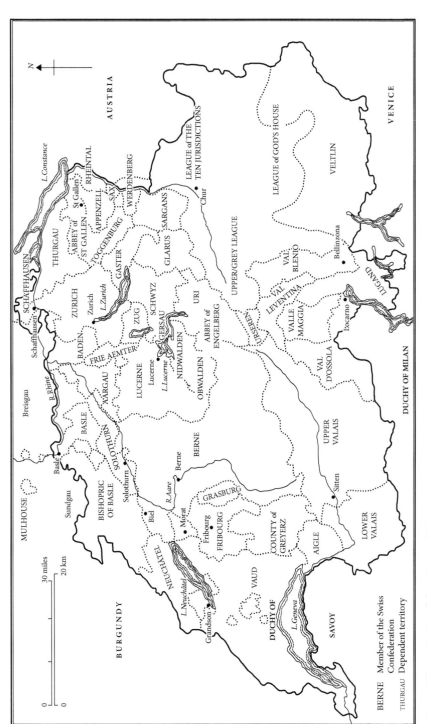

Map 9. The Swiss Confederation, c. 1500

BERNE   Member of the Swiss
             Confederation
THURGAU   Dependent territory

Index

For the benefit of digital users, indexed terms that span two pages (e.g., 52–53) may, on occasion, appear on only one of those pages.